ZOOM IN
ZOOM OUT

A **close-up** and **far-out** look at **our world**

**LONDON, NEW YORK,
MELBOURNE, MUNICH, AND DELHI**

Senior editor Jenny Finch
Senior art editor Stefan Podhorodecki
Editors Steven Carton, Jessamy Wood
Designers Mik Gates, Spencer Holbrook, Katie Knutton, Johnny Pau
US editor Rebecca G. Warren

Managing editor Linda Esposito
Managing art editor Jim Green

Category publisher Laura Buller

Creative retouching Steve Willis
Picture research Nic Dean
DK picture researchers Lucy Claxton, Emma Shepherd
Production editor Andy Hilliard
Senior production controller Angela Graef
Jacket design Hazel Martin
Jacket editor Matilda Gollon
Development designer Laura Brim
Senior development editor Jayne Miller
Design development manager Sophia M. Tampakopoulos Turner

Consultants Kim Bryan, Philip Parker, Richard Walker

First published in the United States in 2011 by DK Publishing
375 Hudson Street, New York, New York 10014

Copyright © 2011 Dorling Kindersley Limited

11 12 13 14 15 10 9 8 7 6 5 4 3 2 1
001 – 180930 – 07/11

DK books are available at special discounts when purchased in bulk for sales promotions, premiums, fundraising, or educational use. For details, contact: DK Publishing Special Markets, 375 Hudson Street, New York, New York 10014, SpecialSales@dk.com

A catalog record for this book
is available from the Library of Congress.

ISBN: 978-0-7566-8269-9

Color reproduction by MDP, UK
Printed and bound by Leo, China

Discover more at
www.dk.com

ZOOM IN
ZOOM OUT

A close-up and far-out look at our world

Written by Mike Goldsmith, Susan Kennedy, Steve Parker, Carole Stott, Isabel Thomas, and John Woodward

CONTENTS

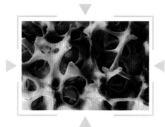
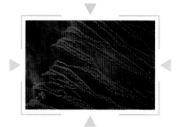

CONTENTS

CONTENTS

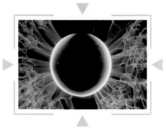

ZOOM THROUGH THIS BOOK

Each chapter in this book forms a sequence, zooming from one page to the next. You can explore a flower in minute detail on one page, before zooming out to see it in a garden on the next page. A background detail you can't quite make out might be the next zoom. Bring it closer simply by turning the page.

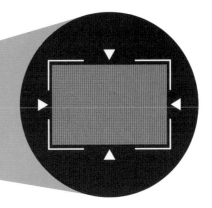

Zoom in
When you see this frame, you'll know that turning the page will show you this part of the scene in greater detail.

Frame indicates where the next spread takes you

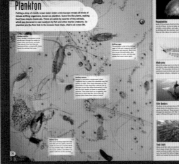

See in sequence
From a scene showing mollusks on the bottom of the Red Sea, you'll zoom right in to look at the tiny organisms drifting in the water. Turning the page zooms out so these organisms are in an entirely different place, and you're face to face with a tropical fish.

Frame shows how the previous spread fits into this image

Zoom out
This frame means you've zoomed out from the previous double-page spread to a new scene. Look out for it to show you how the previous pages fit into the image you're looking at. The whole of the last spread is now a small part of this one.

Zoom further
To travel further than the eye can see, follow a series of zooms in or out. This one takes you from city streets in China to a view of the whole country.

The eye of this parrotfish is set high on the side of the fish's head to give an extremely wide field of vision.

NATURE

From the simplicity of the tiniest microbe to the glorious complexity of a mammal or bird, nature is astonishing in its diversity. There are so many different types of insects alone that scientists have still not identified and named them all. Each living thing interacts with others to form an intricate web of life that flourishes all over the globe.

Ecosystems

A tropical coral reef is a spectacularly rich and colorful ecosystem—a web of life that makes the best of a particular environment. Other ecosystems range from small patches of wild landscape, such as swamps and heaths, to huge "biomes" that include deserts and rainforests. Thanks to a special relationship between corals and tiny algae, a coral reef is nearly completely self-supporting.

Reef visitor
The plant-eating adult green sea turtle finds plenty of food growing among the corals and in the shallow lagoons that separate the reefs from the shore. It also lays its eggs on the beaches of coral islands.

Stony corals
This coral is part of a chain of reefs extending along the coasts of the Red Sea for 1,240 miles (2,000 km). The reefs contain more than 400 different kinds of coral. Many form branching colonies like these, each made up of hundreds of interconnected animals resembling tiny sea anemones. They are supported by stony skeletons that build up over the centuries to form rocky reefs thousands of years old.

Thorny threat
Many tropical coral reefs are menaced by the crown-of-thorns starfish, a big sea star that bristles with long, venomous spines. It often multiplies into swarms that devour large patches of living coral, leaving just bare rock. The starfish has only one natural enemy—a predatory marine snail called the giant triton. This one has crept up on a crown-of-thorns and is about to launch an attack.

Raspers and cleaners
The reef teems with fish such as parrotfish, which use their beak-like teeth to rasp algae from the coral. This parrotfish is having parasites removed from its scaly skin by a small cleaner wrasse.

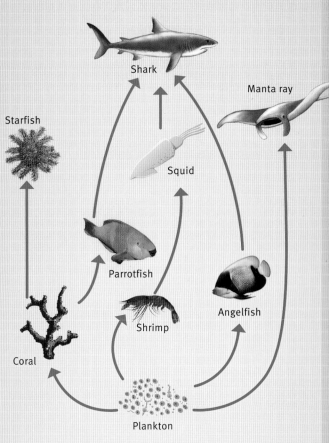

Shark

Starfish

Manta ray

Squid

Parrotfish

Angelfish

Coral

Shrimp

Plankton

Food web

All the living things in an ecosystem are linked by the way they feed. This is known as a food web. On a coral reef a lot of food is made by microscopic algae living in the corals, but other algae form part of the drifting plankton. This is eaten by animals that may be eaten in turn by other predators.

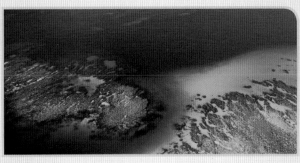

Giant reef

The Great Barrier Reef off northeastern Australia is the biggest coral reef complex in the world. Some 1,600 miles (2,600 km) long, it is a mosaic of at least 2,900 reefs, separated by shallow channels and dotted with low coral islands. It is home to more than 1,500 species of fish and 5,000 kinds of mollusk.

Reefs under threat

Like many ecosystems, coral reefs are under threat. Many suffer from sewage pollution, which promotes the growth of coral-choking seaweeds like these off Hawaii. But the worst threat is rising ocean temperatures, which make the corals eject their life-giving algae, turn white, and eventually die.

Hungry hunter
All the fish feeding on the reef attract big predators such as the blacktip reef shark. Despite its size, it swims into very shallow water, tracking its prey with its acute sense of smell.

The reef ecosystem
Reef corals live in clear tropical water where there is little food. They survive because microscopic algae living in their tissues use the energy of light to make sugar from water and dissolved carbon dioxide. The corals use some of this as food. Meanwhile they extend their feathery tentacles (below) into the water to trap plankton, containing vital nutrients, and pass some of these to the algae. This partnership is the basis of a complex ecosystem featuring a fantastic diversity of animals and seaweeds, each specialized for a particular way of life on the reef.

Protective shell
All kinds of crustaceans live on the reef, including an amazing variety of crabs, lobsters, and shrimp. Hermit crabs such as this use empty mollusk shells to protect their unusually soft bodies.

Dazzling displays

Cephalopods such as this broadclub cuttlefish are amazing creatures. They are surprisingly intelligent, with excellent vision. They have special color cells in their skin that expand or contract in response to nerve signals, so they can change color instantly and even generate rippling patterns. They use these patterns and colors for display, or to blend in with the background and hide from their enemies.

Monster bivalve

The magnificent giant clam is a bivalve, with two ridged shells connected by a hinge, but unlike most bivalve mollusks it cannot clamp its shells tightly shut. It lives on coral reefs, where it spends its life rooted in one place, growing up to 5 ft (1.5 m) across. It filters plankton from the water but, like corals, it also has tiny algae living under the skin of its soft tissues that use the energy of sunlight to make sugar.

Mollusks

Some of the oddest of all animals are mollusks—a group that includes snails, clams, mussels, octopuses, and squid. Most of the 100,000 species are aquatic, and some of the most spectacular live on tropical coral reefs like this. Although soft-bodied, many have beautiful shells. Some are highly intelligent while others, almost uniquely, have no heads at all.

Stealthy predator

The day octopus hunts crabs, fish, and other mollusks, seizing them in its long, suckered arms and biting them with its stout beak. Like other cephalopods it changes color constantly for camouflage.

Hidden beauty

The largest group of mollusks are the gastropods. They include land snails, whelks, limpets, conches, and others like this tiger cowrie—unusual for the way its soft mantle partly covers its beautiful shell.

Spanish dancer

The flamboyant Spanish dancer is a nudibranch, also called a sea slug. It gets its name from the way its red mantle swirls like a dancer's skirt when it swims, but here it is gliding over the coral like a snail.

Land snails

Only about a third of the known species of mollusks live on land. They are all slugs and snails, which are essentially the same except that snails have visible shells. They creep around on a lubricated "foot" extending the length of the body and, unlike most mollusks, they use simple lungs to breathe air.

Clamming up

Many marine mollusks live on food-rich tidal seashores. Twice a day the falling tide leaves them high and dry, which could be fatal. But these mussels survive by clamming shut to keep moist until the tide rises again, while other mollusks such as limpets and periwinkles clamp themselves tightly to rocks.

Killer cone
Tropical cone shells are predatory sea snails that creep up on fish and stab them with their highly venomous stings. The textile cone has one of the most toxic venoms, powerful enough to kill a human.

Ancient form

Most mollusks have one or two shells. But the chitons found on rocky shores have multi-segmented shells, rather like those of woodlice. Each glides on a slimy foot like a limpet, rasping algae from rocks. Chitons have hardly changed for 500 million years, so they are among the most primitive mollusks.

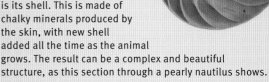

Pearly shell

The most distinctive feature of a typical mollusk is its shell. This is made of chalky minerals produced by the skin, with new shell added all the time as the animal grows. The result can be a complex and beautiful structure, as this section through a pearly nautilus shows.

Plankton

Putting a drop of cloudy ocean water under a microscope reveals all kinds of minute drifting organisms, known as plankton. Some live like plants, making food from simple chemicals. These are eaten by swarms of tiny animals, which are devoured in vast numbers by fish and other marine creatures. So plankton are the first link in the oceanic food chain, vital to all ocean life.

Hooked hunters
Long, slender, transparent arrow worms dart through the water to attack other planktonic animals. They may be tiny, but they are fearsome killers, armed with sharp hooks for seizing their prey.

Drifting eggs
The plankton is full of the drifting eggs of fish and creatures such as barnacles and mussels. Many turn into larvae that will settle, glue themselves to rocks, and become adults that never move again.

Feeding swarms
Swarms of miniature crustaceans called copepods feed on plant-like plankton near the surface at night. Their long antennae act like parachutes to help stop them sinking, but in the open ocean they allow themselves to slip into the dark depths at dawn to avoid their enemies. They swim back up at nightfall, but they are so small that the 820-ft (250-m) journey takes them three hours or more.

Bristly larva
This fuzzy-looking organism may look like part of a plant, but it is really the larva of a marine worm. Its long bristles help it drift near the ocean surface, but when it is an adult it will live on the sea bed.

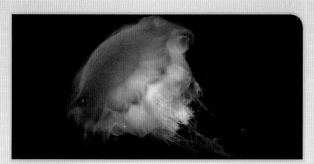

Megaplankton

Most of the animals that form the plankton are very small, but not all of them. It also includes much bigger creatures such as jellyfish, comb jellies, and salps—all simple animals that live by drifting with the plankton and feeding on smaller animals they run into. Many can swim to stay in contact with their prey.

Whale prey

When the winter sea ice in the Antarctic oceans melts in spring, planktonic algae multiply explosively to cause a "plankton bloom." This provides limitless food for shrimp-like krill, which multiply in turn to form vast swarms. These are the main prey of huge baleen whales, crabeater seals, and many penguins.

Filter feeders

Plankton is the primary food of the biggest fish—the enormous whale shark, the basking shark, and the equally spectacular manta ray (above). These giants feed by swimming slowly through the plankton with their mouths open so the food-rich water is filtered through their reinforced, sieve-like gills.

Food chain

Many small fish rely on plankton for food, especially fish that live in large shoals like these sardines. These fish feed near the ocean surface at night, but they swim deeper by day. In their turn, the small fish attract bigger fish like salmon and tuna, which are hunted by top predators such as sharks.

Long journey
No bigger than a grain of rice, and with no heavy shell to weigh it down, this crab larva may drift a very long way in the ocean currents, feeding all the time, before it turns into an adult and sinks to the bottom. This helps its species colonize new habitats. Many other marine creatures disperse in this way, so the young stages of bigger animals make up quite a large proportion of the plankton.

Food factories
Microscopic diatoms use sunlight to make sugar from water and carbon dioxide, creating food for animals. The green objects inside their glasslike shells are the structures that make the sugar.

Oxygenator
Some of the earliest living things to evolve on Earth were cyanobacteria like this—a coiled string of cells that makes food using the energy of light. In the process it also produces oxygen.

Sharks and rays

Some fish have skeletons made of gristly cartilage instead of bone. Rays generally live near the seabed, where many feed on shellfish. But typical sharks are fast-swimming, efficient hunters. Most—like this sand tiger shark—prey mainly on fish, but some species will very occasionally attack humans.

Amazing diversity

Fish come in all shapes and sizes. Some, such as the colossal 40-ft (12-m) whale shark, are among the biggest of all animals, while others are no bigger than flies. While many fish are sleek and elegant, others like this leafy sea dragon have bizarre body forms adapted for camouflage or unusual lifestyles.

Breathing underwater

A fish's gills are delicate, feathery structures attached to bony arches at the back of the head. They are made up of tiny tubes filled with blood. Oxygen dissolved in the water seeps through the thin tube walls into the fish's bloodstream, while waste carbon dioxide seeps out. The system is very efficient.

Spawning and mating

Most ray-finned fish reproduce by producing large numbers of eggs, which the males fertilize in the water. Many, like these sockeye salmon, gather at special spawning sites to do this. By contrast, some sharks and rays fertilize their eggs internally when they mate, and give birth to just a few live young.

Fish

There are at least 30,000 species of fish living in seas, lakes, and rivers all over the world. There are two main types of fish—bony, ray-finned fish like this grouper, and the cartilaginous sharks and rays. They were the first animals to evolve backbones like ours, so our distant ancestors were fish.

Folding fins

A typical fish drives itself through the water using its fins—thin membranes of skin supported by slender bones called rays, which can be folded down when they are not needed. Some fish also have strong, sharp spines protruding from some of their fins, which help protect them from enemies. The dorsal fin on a fish's back keeps it on course, while it uses its other body fins to steer and maneuver.

Buoyancy aid

The bodies of fish are slightly more dense than water, which means they tend to sink slowly. But a typical ray-finned fish has a gas-filled sac in its body called a swim bladder, which can be inflated with extra gas from a gas gland to increase the fish's buoyancy. By adjusting this, a fish can move up and down with little effort. Sharks do not have swim bladders, but they have large oily livers that help with buoyancy.

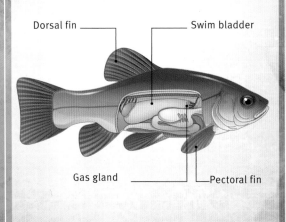

Dorsal fin

Swim bladder

Gas gland

Pectoral fin

Power plant

Unlike the other fins, the tail fin is attached to the fish's backbone and is powered by its big body muscles. It provides most of the thrust that drives a typical fish through the water.

Scaly skin
The skin of a ray-finned fish is covered with tough scales, which overlap like roof tiles to form a flexible armor. A layer of slippery mucus resists infection and helps the fish slip through the water.

Sharp senses
Fish eyes are much like ours, but adapted to see well underwater. A fish can hear well and has an acute sense of smell. Pressure sensors in the lateral line along each flank detect nearby objects in the dark.

Aqualung
A fish breathes using its gills, which are protected by tough gill covers. It draws water into its mouth, then forces it out through the gills, which extract dissolved oxygen from the water.

Sleek and speedy
Water is a very dense substance, so moving underwater is quite difficult. Most fish have smooth, streamlined bodies that slip through the water cleanly, reducing the effort needed to swim fast. This enables some specialized fish to swim at 50 mph (80 kph) or more. But other fish, which never need to move fast, may be more boxy, with lumps and bumps on their skin and long, ornamental fin rays.

Plant life

The tropical rainforests of Costa Rica are lush tangles of plant life, ranging from velvety mosses to giant trees. These green plants use the energy of the Sun to make food from simple chemicals gathered from the soil and air, and are the basis of the food chain on land. In the process they release the oxygen that we breathe, so plants are vital to all animal life.

High life

Most plants are rooted in the ground, but some cling to tall trees. These epiphytes are very common in tropical forests, where they enjoy far more light than they would on the gloomy forest floor.

Setting seed

Ferns and mosses produce spores that grow into new plants, while flowering plants produce seeds that develop into tiny seedlings. Plants also spread by sending out roots or runners that sprout new shoots.

Low life

Water is vital to all plants. Simple plants like this moss must live in places where their short roots can gather moisture. They cannot grow tall because they have no way of pumping water up their stems.

Food factories

The beautiful green leaves of plants act as solar panels, absorbing light energy from the Sun. They use the energy for photosynthesis, combining carbon dioxide with water to make oxygen and a sugar called glucose. The plant uses some sugar as fuel and stores some in the form of starch, which animals can use as food. But it turns a lot into cellulose—the tough fiber that supports its structure.

Stems and trunks
A plant loses moisture through its leaves, which sucks water up the stem from its roots. All plants need water to make food, but the water pressure in the stem also keeps many plants upright—without it they wilt and collapse. Woody plants such as trees have reinforced stems that stay standing even in a drought. They can grow very tall, with some trees reaching 330 ft (100 m) or more.

Deep roots
Simple plants soak up water from all around them, but more complex plants have root networks that absorb water from the ground. The water contains plant nutrients such as nitrates and phosphates, which the plants use to make the proteins essential for life. A plant's roots also anchor and support it, and the roots of tall trees like this one are very thick and strong to resist high winds.

Parasitic plants
A few plants cannot make their own food from air and water, so they steal it from other plants as parasites. The amazing rafflesia of Southeast Asia attacks forest vines, using their sugary sap to fuel the growth of a colossal flower that may be more than 39 in (100 cm) across—and smells like rotting meat!

Deadly trap
Most plants rely on their roots to gather nutrients from the soil. But if the soil is very poor, as in acid peat bogs, they may not gather enough. A few plants solve the problem by catching insects. This Venus fly-trap snaps shut on its victims and slowly digests their bodies to extract the nutrients it needs.

Hard times
Rainforest plants grow all year round, but many plants face cold winters or scorching summers when they cannot grow. They survive by lying dormant until better times. As winter approaches, these deciduous trees lose all their leaves and stop growing, then revive and grow new leaves in spring.

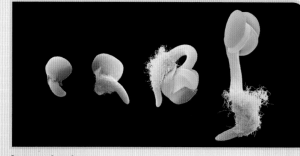

Green shoots
Most plants produce seeds—concentrated packages of energy that each contain the germ of a new plant. When conditions are right, the seed bursts open and a root emerges to soak up water. The seed swells up, loses its tough skin, and eventually sprouts a green shoot bearing its first pair of leaves.

Amphibians

Frogs, toads, newts, and salamanders are amphibians—cold-blooded animals that live mainly on land but must lay their eggs in water or moist places. These usually hatch as tadpoles that live like fish before turning into air-breathing adults. Amphibians must keep moist to survive, which is not a problem for these red-eyed tree frogs that live in the tropical rainforests of Central America.

Bright and beautiful
Many amphibians are vividly colored and patterned. The dramatic colors of some species warn predators that their skin produces powerful poisons. Others such as these tropical tree frogs use color for display purposes and reveal their bright eyes and feet only to each other. They normally spend the day crouching on leaves with their eyes shut, so their green bodies are camouflaged among the foliage.

Thin-skinned
All amphibians have thin skin with no scales, and so moisture easily escapes from their bodies. This forces them to live in damp places, where they are not in danger of drying out.

Frog lifecycle
A typical frog lays its eggs, called frogspawn, with a protective covering of jelly in a pool. The tadpoles that hatch from the eggs feed in the water until they grow legs, develop lungs, and lose their tails, and so are physically ready to live on land. Red-eyed tree frogs have the same basic lifecycle, but they attach their eggs to leaves overhanging forest pools so the hatching tadpoles fall into the water.

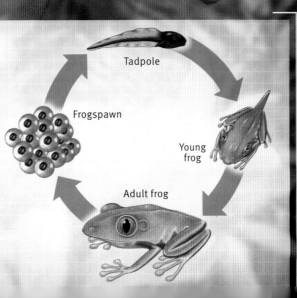

Tadpole

Frogspawn

Young frog

Adult frog

Vital adaptation

The thin, moist skin of an amphibian is able to absorb oxygen from the air, so it acts like an extra lung. In fact, many salamanders do not have normal lungs and rely on their skin to do the job. This breathing system also works underwater, allowing frogs to get through northern winters by retreating to the bottoms of ponds. As long as they do not move much, they can absorb all the oxygen they need from the water.

Keeping watch

Frogs and other amphibians are hunters that prey on smaller animals. Frogs hunt by sight, watching intently for the slightest movement before seizing their prey with a quick flick of the tongue.

Sticky feet

Tree frogs have big feet with broad, flattened toe pads that stick to glossy leaves and stems. This allows the frogs to climb high into forest trees to find their insect prey, and they rarely come down to the ground. Shady tropical rainforests are an ideal habitat for tree frogs, such as these in Costa Rica, because the moisture in the air and rainwater dripping through the foliage keeps their skins moist.

Salamanders and newts

With their long tails, salamanders and newts look rather like small lizards. But like all amphibians they have thin, moist skins, and some—especially newts—spend all or part of their lives in the water. This European fire salamander is brightly colored to warn that its skin produces dangerous toxins.

Warty toads

Frogs and toads are basically the same, but the animals that we call toads have warty skins, shorter legs, and are less agile than frogs. The American spadefoot toad is able to live in deserts by burrowing into the ground. It may spend weeks like this, emerging to hunt only after rare rainstorms.

Mating choruses

Like many male frogs, the African painted reed frog can inflate a huge vocal sac to amplify its mating calls. Each species has its own call, and in tropical forests the sound of calling frogs is often louder than birdsong. In cooler regions some male frogs and toads gather in spring to call together in chorus.

Breeding strategies

Amphibian lifecycles are extremely varied, having evolved to suit different types of habitat. This Peruvian poison-dart frog carries her tadpoles on her back while she searches for pools of water that have formed high in rainforest trees. She places each tadpole in its own pool and lays an egg for it to eat!

Flowers

Few things in nature are as beautiful as flowers. But this hippeastrum has not bloomed for our benefit; it is a device to attract an animal—in this case a hummingbird—that may be carrying pollen from another flower of the same species. The pollen will fertilize the flower and make it set seed, and once this has happened the flower will wither and fall away.

Spectacular petals
Glowing with vivid color, the petals of this flower are meant to attract animals that rely heavily on their sense of sight. Red petals tend to attract birds, which are very sensitive to the color red. Insects, by contrast, love the blues and violets at the opposite end of the spectrum. They can also see ultraviolet, which we cannot, and the petals of many flowers gleam with reflected ultraviolet light to attract them.

Powdery pollen
A cluster of stamens at the flower's center carries tiny pollen grains. Each stamen has a pollen-covered anther on the end of a slender filament shaped to brush against visiting animals. This flower attracts hummingbirds that hover to sip nectar, and the anthers are in just the right place to dust a hummingbird's breast with pollen. When the bird flies off to feed from another bloom it carries the pollen with it.

Sticky style
At the very heart of a flower lies the ovary—a container of unfertilized seeds called ovules. The ovary is extended into a long style with a sticky tip known as a stigma. When a pollen-dusted animal visits the flower, pollen sticks to the stigma and from here it fertilizes the ovules. The stigma and stamens on each flower often develop at slightly different times so the flower is less likely to fertilize itself.

Seductive scent

Some flowers have strange ways of attracting insects. The bee orchid does not offer sweet nectar, but tempts a male bee to try and mate with what looks and smells like a female bee. The insect picks up pollen and usually carries it straight to another bee orchid that is producing the same irresistible fragrance.

Blown on the wind

Many plants such as grasses rely on the wind to carry their pollen from one plant to another. They have flowers, but no showy petals or fragrant nectar. Since wind pollination is very inefficient, most of the pollen is wasted. The plants produce huge quantities to compensate, giving many people hay fever.

Juicy fruit

When a flower is pollinated and fertilized, its petals drop off and the ovary starts to swell as the seeds develop inside. In some plants like this rose the ovary turns into a juicy fruit, attracting animals to eat it. The seeds pass through the animal's system and are deposited in its droppings, well away from the parent plant.

Sugary bait

Nearly all flowers produce sugary nectar as bait for pollinating insects, birds, and even bats. The nectar oozes from nectaries at the base of the flower, forcing the animals to brush past the stamens and stigma to reach it. Some flowers are odd shapes to limit access to a few types of animal, increasing the chance that their pollen will be carried to another flower of the same type.

Fertilization

Each pollen grain contains one of the male reproductive cells of the hippeastrum. When it is carried to another flower it sticks to the stigma and grows a slender tube that burrows down through the style. When the tube reaches the ovary it penetrates one of the ovules, which contain the female reproductive cells of the plant. The male cell passes down the tube, enters the ovule and fuses with the female cell inside, fertilizing it so it grows into a seed.

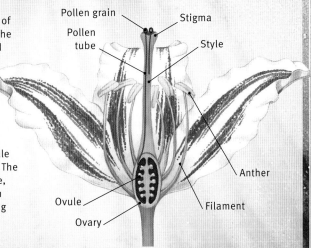

Pollen grain
Stigma
Pollen tube
Style
Anther
Ovule
Filament
Ovary

Up, up, and away

Plants have evolved many ways of scattering their seeds. The seeds of this dandelion have feathery hairs so they blow away on the breeze. Many plants in the pea family have pods that split open in hot weather, explosively ejecting their seeds. Some seeds have hooks that catch in animal hair, then drop off later.

Insects

Some of the world's most intriguing creatures are the insects that live all around us in places like this English garden. Insects belong to a group of animals called arthropods, which have armored bodies and jointed legs. But unlike other arthropods all adult insects have just three pairs of legs, and many can fly on transparent or brilliantly colored wings.

Airborne dragons
Dragonflies were among the first winged animals, and 300 million years of evolution have refined some of them into amazingly fast and agile aerial hunters. This big hawker dragonfly is resting between flights.

Winged beauties
The most gloriously beautiful of all insects, butterflies have broad wings covered with tiny colored scales that are often arranged in vivid patterns. Some, such as this holly blue, have special wing scales that scatter reflected light to create dazzling iridescent effects. The closely related moths are not so colorful because they fly by night and rely on camouflage by day. Both feed by sipping sweet nectar from flowers.

Busy bees
Ants, wasps, and bees are close relatives that are notorious for their painful stings. Many, including this honeybee, live in big colonies with hundreds of busy workers looking after a single breeding queen.

Leaping legs
Grasshoppers and crickets are easy to recognize by their long back legs, which they use for leaping. This male bush cricket cannot fly, but it has tiny, reduced wings that it rubs together to make chirping calls.

Brilliant beetles
The shiny, hard wing-cases of a ladybug identify it as a beetle—one of the most successful of all insect groups. Beetles make up at least a quarter—possibly much more—of all known animal species.

Aerial acrobats

Flies are not our favorite insects. Some may «bite, and even carry diseases. But many, such as this metallic green blowfly, are wonderfully colorful. Some two-winged "true flies" are also astonishingly agile in the air, being able to hover and even fly backward. This is because the second pair of wings has been modified into a pair of tiny "balancers" that automatically correct flight errors like an electronic autopilot.

Sap sucker

We often think of insects as bugs, but a true bug is an insect with a piercing, needle-like mouthpart. Assassin bugs use these to suck other insects dry, but this shield bug is happy to drink plant sap.

Metamorphosis

Some insects, such as crickets, lay eggs that hatch as miniature versions of the adults. But most baby insects are quite unlike their parents; many are soft-bodied, sausage-shaped larvae. They include butterfly caterpillars, which spend most of their time eating. They grow quickly and, since their skins are not stretchy enough to grow with them, they shed their skins many times. Eventually each caterpillar stops eating and turns into a pupa. Inside, its body is rebuilt into a winged butterfly that flies off to find a mate and produce more eggs. This transformation is called metamorphosis.

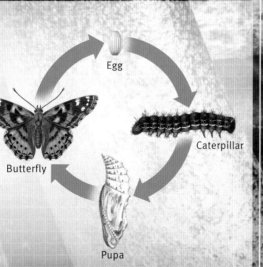

Egg

Caterpillar

Butterfly

Pupa

Arachnids

Many arthropods are not insects. The most familiar of these non-insects are the spiders, which along with scorpions belong to a group called the arachnids. A spider has eight legs instead of six, and its head forms part of the front section of its body. All spiders eat other animals, killing them with a venomous bite. Some, including this giant golden silk orb-weaver from Madagascar, make elaborate silken webs to trap their prey.

Myriapods

Some arthropods have more legs than you can easily count. They are called myriapods. This red-sided flat millipede from North America has 56 legs—typically two pairs for each body segment. But some millipedes have a lot more segments, and up to 750 legs! Centipedes have just one pair of legs for each segment, but move faster. Unlike plant-eating millipedes, they are hunters that seize prey with venomous pincers on their heads.

Crustaceans

Many arthropods live mainly underwater in oceans, lakes, and rivers. They are known as crustaceans. They come in all shapes and sizes, and include many tiny creatures that drift in the water as plankton. But the best-known are shrimp, lobsters, and crabs like this Sally Lightfoot from South America. It is one of several crabs that regularly forage for food on land, but it has to return to the water to breed.

Puffing spores

Fungus spores are microscopic, but many fungi such as puffballs produce them by the millions. The entire inside of a mature puffball is turned into spores. If it is stepped on or even hit by a big raindrop, the fungus puffs them out in billowing clouds that drift away on the breeze like smoke.

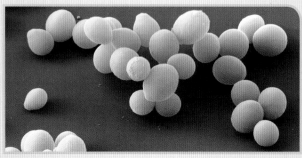

Microfungi

Most fungi are single-celled yeasts that are visible only through a microscope. They multiply by splitting in half, like bacteria, and feed on organic matter such as sugar, producing alcohol and carbon dioxide. We use this fermentation process in winemaking, and also to make bread dough rise.

Creeping mold

There are thousands of different fungi that are almost too small to see. But we do notice them when they grow in dense, furry layers of mold on decaying food like this rotten apple. The tiny dark dots are the caps of the fungi, which will pop to release masses of spores that may infect other apples.

Risky treat

Many fungi are edible, and a few are highly prized gourmet foods. Black truffles such as this grow underground and are among the most expensive foods in the world. Some other fungi, however, are lethally poisonous, and each year many people die because they eat the wrong ones by mistake.

Fungi

These fungi may look like plants, but they are quite different. Fungi form a separate kingdom of life—neither plant nor animal, but something in between. They grow like plants but feed like animals, breaking down organic matter into the simpler substances that plants can use as vital nutrients.

Fruiting bodies

Typical fungi live as thread-like root networks. The mushrooms or toadstools above ground are just the fruiting bodies, like apples on a tree, of the hidden fungus. They release spores that grow into new fungi.

Hidden network

Mushrooms sprout from a hidden network of branching, thread-like hyphae (filaments), known as mycelium. This spreads through the soil and organic food such as dead wood. In Oregon, USA, a single honey fungus like this one has taken over a colossal 3.5 sq miles (9 sq km), making it the world's largest living organism. It is also one of the oldest, having existed for at least 2,400 years.

Fungus food

Green plants use solar energy to make food from water and air. Fungi cannot do this, so they must consume ready-made food. In this respect they are more like animals than plants. They "eat" plant material like this dead wood, reducing it to simpler substances. We think of this as decay, or rot. By degrees the wood is weakened so it cracks up and turns to powder, like the core of an ancient hollow tree.

Fungus lifecycle

Each honey fungus starts life as a microscopic spore that is scattered by the parent fungus. The spore sprouts slender filaments, or hyphae, that form a branching network, or mycelium. Small buds appear on the mycelium and grow upward as young fruiting bodies, or mushrooms. At first each one is tightly closed, but as it grows its cap expands and breaks free to reveal the gills, leaving a ring around the stem. When it is mature it scatters its spores and the cycle begins again.

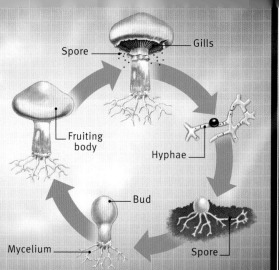

Spore — Gills

Fruiting body

Hyphae

Bud

Mycelium

Spore

Vital function

Plants such as this moss rely on fungi to turn dead organic matter into vital plant nutrients. Some plants live in partnership with a particular fungus, and cannot grow properly without it.

Perfect partners

Moss-like lichens are actually fungi that contain microscopic algae. The algae function like plants, making food from air and water using the energy of sunlight. The fungal part of the lichen absorbs some of this food, and may provide the algae with vital mineral nutrients. The partnership allows lichens to live in very hostile habitats such as bare rock, and they can survive for weeks without water.

Radial gills

Like many fungi this honey fungus has gills beneath its cap that radiate from the stem like the spokes of a wheel. They contain the spores that, when scattered, spread the fungus to new places.

Feeding

Some living things such as green plants and algae can make their own food from simple chemicals, using energy from the Sun. But animals have to eat ready-made food, break it down by digestion, and use the results to fuel and build their bodies. Different animals eat different types of food in a variety of ingenious ways.

Stealthy hunter

A carnivore like this fox preys on other animals. Since meat is very nutritious and easy to digest the fox does not need to eat much, but it spends a lot of time finding, stalking, and killing its prey.

Hungry fungi

Animals are not the only living things that need ready-made food. Fungi need it, too, because they cannot make their own. A fungus growing on a dead tree stump is basically feeding on it, even though it has no teeth!

Sweet treat

Many insects like this swallowtail butterfly sip sugary nectar from flowers. The sugar gives them energy for flight, but for the vital nutrients they need they may feed on animal dung and rotting meat.

Vegetarian diet

All land animals depend on plants to make their food. Herbivores like this rabbit eat the plants and convert them into animal tissue. Hunters such as foxes may then eat the rabbits, but they still rely on plants to feed the rabbits in the first place. Plants are tough and difficult to digest, so rabbits and many other plant-eaters are equipped with extra-strong teeth and specialized digestive systems.

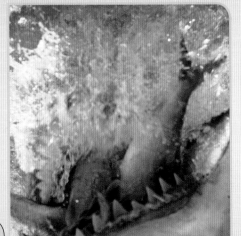

Toothy jaws

Most animals have mouths that they use to gather and swallow their food. Many hunters like this shark have powerful jaws bristling with sharp teeth that they can use to kill and bite off chunks of their prey. Plant-eating mammals such as horses have big, flattened cheek teeth for grinding their tough food to a pulp so it is easier to digest. But many animals cannot chew at all and simply swallow their food whole.

Filter feeders

Specialized diets need special feeding techniques: these flamingos gather tiny aquatic organisms by pumping water through the comb-like filters that line their odd-looking beaks. The huge basking shark on the other hand catches small sea creatures by straining seawater through its reinforced gills. And aquatic animals such as mussels attach themselves to rocks and pump food-rich water through filters inside their bodies.

Waste processors

Yellow dung flies prey on insects—especially other flies—but they gather on cowpats to mate and lay their eggs. The grubs that hatch from the eggs chew their way through the dung and any other insect grubs that they find in it. In this process they help break down the dung and turn it into substances that plants can use for nutrition, making detritivores like these a vital part of the ecosystem.

Anything goes

Some animals, called omnivores, seem to eat almost anything. Brown rats like this one are notorious for eating all kinds of waste matter, as well as eating plants and other animals. But most omnivores are quite choosy about what they eat, selecting only items that are highly nutritious such as seeds, nuts, fruit, tender shoots, and animal tissue. We should know, because we are omnivores, too!

Stealing a meal

A few animals manage to feed without the aid of a mouth or even a digestive tract. Tapeworms (left) live in the guts of other animals such as cattle and pigs. Since they are surrounded by digested food they can simply absorb the nutrients through their thin skins. Other parasitic worms known as flukes live in the blood or tissues such as the liver, seriously damaging the health of their host animals.

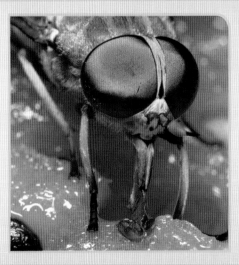

Liquid lunch

Many insects can eat only liquid foods. They are not restricted to natural fluids, though, because they can convert solid foods into liquids by smothering them with digestive juices. This fly is eating fruit in this way, using its mop-like mouthparts to soak up the resulting liquefied fruit flesh. Spiders do the same with their prey, injecting digestive fluids to turn the soft tissue into a "soup" that they can suck up.

Birds

The spectacular osprey—a dedicated fish hunter that plunges from the air to seize its victims in its sharp talons—is one of the most widespread and exciting birds of prey. Like all birds, it is basically a four-limbed vertebrate, like us. It is highly modified for flight, with a light, hollow skeleton and many adaptations for strength, stamina, speed, and aerial agility.

Flight power
Massive flight muscles anchored to a deep breastbone provide the power for each wingbeat. The breastbone is the biggest part of a specialized lightweight but extremely strong skeleton.

Vital oxygen
The lungs of birds are unlike ours, and work much more efficiently. Air is pumped through them, enabling the lungs to extract more oxygen with each breath. This is vital to a bird like the osprey, which needs a lot of oxygen to turn food into energy for flight. It also allows many birds to fly across vast oceans—and at least one bird, the Eurasian swift, can stay airborne for months or even years at a time.

Steering and braking
Most birds have long, stiff tail feathers that they can spread out to form a broad fan. This is useful for steering in flight, and makes a very effective air-brake when the bird is slowing down to land.

Feathered wings

Wings are modified "arms," with extended upper and forearm bones, and two extended "fingers." These bones and their fleshy coverings support the long flight feathers. The inner flight feathers, or secondaries, create lift while the outer primaries propel the bird through the air with each downbeat of the wings. Shorter feathers cover the leading edge of each wing and give it a sleek, aerodynamic profile.

Eagle eyes

Nearly all birds have excellent sight, which they rely on as their main sense. Hunters like the osprey have much sharper eyes than we do, so they can detect and target prey from a very long range.

Lightweight beak

The beak is made of keratin—the same material as our fingernails—and is much lighter than jaws full of teeth. The hooked end is an adaptation for ripping prey apart, but many birds swallow their food whole.

Powerful talons

The osprey's feet are modified to form powerful, strong-clawed talons for seizing prey. The soles of its feet are covered with sharp, spiny scales to give a secure grip on slippery, struggling fish.

Feathers

Birds inherited feathers from their nonflying dinosaur ancestors. Feathers provide excellent insulation, and were easily modified by evolution to form the basis of birds' lightweight wings. Each feather is a shaft, set with rows of filaments called barbs. These have many smaller branches called barbules—more than a million per feather—that interlock with the barbules of the neighboring barb. Rows of tiny, flexible hooks on the barbules zip the barbs together to form a continuous vane with very high air resistance—perfect for the demands of flight.

Barbule — Barb

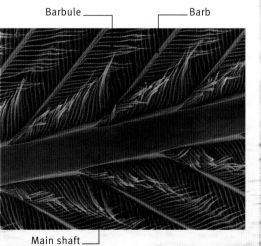

Main shaft

Flightless birds

All modern birds have evolved from flying ancestors. This includes flightless birds like these ostriches, which retain many features of flying birds, including wings. However, their "flight muscles" and breastbones are much reduced, and their plumage is entirely made up of fluffy down feathers.

Underwater birds

Some birds are adapted for hunting fish underwater. The most specialized are the penguins, which propel their streamlined bodies through the water with short, highly modified wings, and cannot fly at all. Auks such as puffins use the same technique, but their wings are just long enough to work in the air as well.

Peacock plumes

Feathers can be dazzlingly attractive. The male peacock has long plumes and brilliant colors, which it displays to attract mates and compete with male rivals. Some colors are created by pigments in the feathers absorbing light, but blues and purples result from scattered reflections that produce shimmering iridescence.

Eggs and nests

All birds lay eggs, which they keep warm until they hatch. Most, like this great crested grebe, incubate them in nests beneath their warm bodies. The nests of some birds are very elaborate, protecting the nestlings which, in many cases, hatch blind and naked and so need constant care by both parents.

Movement

Unlike most other organisms, animals can move—often rapidly. This lion is having to move very quickly to bring down its kudu prey. Like many animals it relies on muscles that are linked to the bones of its strong legs and flexible spine to propel its attack run. Other animals use muscles in different ways to swim, fly, or crawl.

Powerful legs
A lion's muscular legs are built for strength, giving it the power to accelerate into a lethal high-speed charge within a second or two. But it cannot keep up this speed for long before it gets exhausted.

Flexible spine
A lion increases its stride-length and speed by using strong back muscles to flex its spine. Its long tail aids balance, and altering the tail's angle helps the lion swerve in the right direction to keep track of its fleeing prey.

Lean body
High-powered movement burns a lot of energy, so fast movers like this lion will never get fat, no matter how much they eat. Since an animal gets all of its energy from its food, though, using too much energy to secure a meal is a big mistake. Most hunters instinctively know when to give up, so if this kudu slips out of its grasp the lion may let it escape rather than waste more energy than the meal will provide chasing after it.

Fast mover
The kudu is built for speed. It runs on tiptoe on long, slender legs. Each foot is a lightweight two-toed hoof, and its powerful leg muscles are high up near its center of gravity to improve agility.

Snake in the grass
A snake slithers through the grass by contracting its flank muscles to send waves of movement down its long body toward its tail. These push against the ground and plants to drive the snake forward. It can climb through trees and bushes in the same way, and many snakes—and eels—swim using exactly the same technique. It is surprisingly efficient, enabling snakes to move much faster than their four-legged lizard ancestors.

Rippling waves
The underside of a snail's body is one big muscular "foot," lubricated by slimy mucus. Waves of muscle contraction ripple along the foot toward the snail's head like waves on the sea. Each wave lifts part of the snail's foot off the ground—or twig—and reattaches it slightly further forward. Since this is happening constantly, the whole foot glides along, carrying the snail forward. Slugs and most sea snails move in the same way.

Flying
A bird's wings are powered by the same basic mechanism as the lion's legs, with big muscles pulling on the limb bones. But their broad feathered surfaces ride the air and provide thrust (a force that pushes the bird forward) during active flight. Some birds such as vultures also soar on updrafts of warm air, gliding from one updraft to another. They cover huge distances without beating their wings at all.

Lung power
Big lungs ensure the kudu gets enough oxygen to fuel its muscles and help it to keep running for longer. This ability to keep running over long periods of time is called stamina.

Swimming
Most of the power that propels a typical fish through the water is provided by its big flank muscles. These flex its body and tail, pushing the water back and forcing the fish forward.

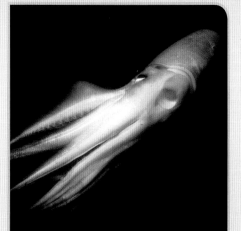

Jet-propelled
A few animals have evolved really exciting ways of moving about. Squid are marine mollusks that respire by drawing water into a muscular chamber lined with oxygen-absorbing gills. When it wants to move fast, a squid squirts the water out through a fleshy nozzle to drive its streamlined body in the opposite direction. This jet-propulsion technique works so well that some squid can shoot right out of the water and fly through the air.

In the loop
Most caterpillars move about by crawling on their short legs, but some types use a different method. Clinging to a twig with its six front legs, this moth caterpillar draws its body up into a loop. It then grips the twig with the four fleshy "prolegs" at its tail end, lets go with its front legs and straightens itself out. It reattaches its front legs and repeats the sequence, looping and straightening to inch forward along the twig.

Mammals

All the animals around this African waterhole are mammals—furry or hairy creatures that feed their infant young on milk. They make up a surprisingly small proportion of animal species, but they live all over the world and include humans as well as the biggest animal that has ever lived—the mighty blue whale.

Warm blood
Like all mammals, this Cape buffalo is warm-blooded—the temperature of its body is always the same. This means that some mammals can live in places that are freezing cold for much of the year.

Mother's milk
Unlike most other animals, newborn baby mammals do not have fully developed digestive systems so they cannot eat solid food. Instead, their mothers convert some of their own food into nutritious milk that the young can drink and digest. The olive baboon seen here suckling her baby is a type of mammal known as a primate—a group that includes lemurs, monkeys, apes, and humans.

Nibbling rodents
Almost half of all mammal species are rodents—mainly small animals that include squirrels, cavies, and mice such as this grass mouse. All rodents have sharp front teeth for nibbling tough plant foods.

Egg layers
Nearly all mammals give birth to active babies, but a few very primitive mammals called monotremes lay eggs, just like birds do. These monotremes are the platypus—famous for its duck-like bill—and four species of spiny echidnas. Their soft-shelled eggs hatch within about 10 days of being laid and then the tiny, half-developed young depend on their mothers' milk for another six months.

Snug pouch
A typical mammal is born after spending a long time growing inside its mother's body. But marsupials such as kangaroos are born when they are little more than tiny embryos. Despite this, each manages to climb into a pouch on its mother's belly, where it is fed enriched milk while it develops into a normal baby. This young kangaroo is old enough to eat grass and will soon leave the pouch for good.

Safety in numbers
Small mammals can hide from predators, but big mammals such as kudu antelope are built for speed so that they can escape their enemies. Many live in herds, with many eyes to watch for danger.

Powerful hunters
Some mammals such as lions are among the biggest and most powerful of all hunters. They belong to a group called the carnivores, which includes cats, dogs, bears, and hyenas, as well as smaller predators such as weasels and mongooses. Many feed almost exclusively on meat, but a few such as bears have a broader diet—one type of bear, the giant panda, has even become a vegetarian.

Specialized grazers
Zebras and many other hoofed mammals are herbivores that specialize in eating low-value food such as grass. They have to eat a lot of it, and have big, complex digestive systems for processing it.

Airborne
One group of mammals has conquered the air. Bats can fly just as well as most birds, on wings made of skin stretched over extended finger bones. An insect-eating bat like this one flies at night, relying on an amazing sonar system that uses echoes of its calls to create a mental image of its surroundings. A bat can use this echolocation technique to target an airborne moth in total darkness.

All at sea
The earliest mammals all lived on land, but some mammals have become equipped for life in the water. They include seals, which must return to land to breed, and whales and dolphins, which spend their entire lives at sea. Like all mammals, dolphins must breathe air, so they return to the surface to do this. Apart from this they are superbly adapted to their way of life, swimming like fish and even giving birth underwater.

Living together

All living things interact, but some live together in a very close association known as symbiosis. Sometimes both species profit: the oxpeckers removing bloodsucking ticks from this African buffalo do it a service as they feed. But frequently only one organism benefits—and very often at the expense of the other.

Not welcome
The oxpecker is searching for ticks hidden in the buffalo's coarse hair. These tiny relatives of spiders cling to big animals and suck their blood, swelling up like peas as they fill their stomachs. They are parasites, stealing from their living "hosts" and giving nothing in return except pain and—sometimes—nasty diseases. So this is one form of symbiosis that the buffalo could definitely do without.

Low trick
Sometimes an oxpecker changes roles. Instead of helping an animal by removing bloodsucking parasites, it pecks at wounds to make the blood flow and laps up the blood itself—so the bird becomes a parasite, too. This confusion of roles is common among organisms that live together. True partnerships are probably quite rare, because each partner will try to take advantage of the other if it can.

Aphid farmers

True mutualism is rare, but you might find it in your backyard. Tiny aphids eat sugary plant sap, and as they feed they exude surplus sugar as sweet honeydew. Black garden ants love this, so they round up herds of aphids and protect them from their enemies in return for a steady supply.

Brood parasite

The Eurasian cuckoo is a parasite on small songbirds. It lays its eggs in their nests and, when a cuckoo egg hatches, the new nestling destroys any other eggs and young in the nest. It also takes all the food brought by the parent songbirds, growing far bigger than they are before it fledges and flies off.

No problem

Some animals benefit from others without harming them— a relationship called commensalism. This shark is accompanied by several remoras that cling to the shark's skin with strong suckers. They get free transport and a chance to finish off any food scraps, and the shark doesn't mind at all.

Internal parasites

Wild animals are preyed upon by an alarming variety of internal parasites. Some are quite big, like the worms that live in their guts. Others are microbes that multiply in their bodies to cause diseases. This highly magnified image of red blood cells shows that the animal's blood has been invaded by the trypanosomes (single-cell parasites) that cause African sleeping sickness. They are carried by the bloodsucking tsetse fly. Most African wild animals are not badly affected, but humans who are infected can suffer fever and fatal brain damage.

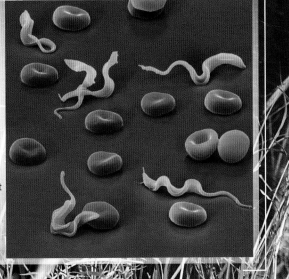

Eaten alive

True parasites never kill their hosts, because they need them alive. But parasitoid wasps lay eggs on caterpillars and similar living insects, and when the eggs hatch the wasp grubs eat the caterpillar and eventually kill it. This dead moth caterpillar is covered with the silken cocoons of the tiny wasps that killed it.

Attack and defense

This mantis is a predator—an animal that attacks other animals, kills, and eats them. It has developed special adaptations, such as sharp senses and fearsome weapons, that make it a more efficient hunter. But the mantis's prey has also evolved some very effective defenses.

Deathtrap
The mantis is a living trap. It sits motionless on a plant, waiting for other insects to come within range. Then it suddenly shoots out its powerful spiked forelegs to seize its victim. It moves so quickly that it may even snatch a passing fly out of the air. Massive forelimb muscles ensure that there is no escape from its spiny grip, and its victim can only hope for a quick end as the mantis calmly eats it alive.

Slicing jaws
The jaws of a mantis are quite small, but very sharp and can slice through the armor of its insect prey very efficiently. It often starts by biting its victim's head off to stop it struggling.

Flight option
Long wings give the locust the option of flying out of trouble—although this one would be very lucky to escape. Like the mantis it is camouflaged, but its movement has betrayed it.

Chemical defense
If the mantis attacks this locust, it may get a nasty surprise. Like many of its relatives, the green milkweed locust can defend itself by squirting a noxious froth from near the base of each hind leg. It advertises this by revealing vivid warning colors on its hind wings. The colors also work another way: showing brightly in flight but vanishing when it lands. Since its enemy would still be looking for a brightly colored target, the grasshopper effectively disappears.

Keen eyesight
Huge compound eyes, set widely apart on its very mobile triangular head, give the mantis excellent binocular vision for judging when it is within range of its victim. Each eye is made up of many hundreds of lenses covering its surface—the dark spots are just dots of color. These compound eyes are very sensitive to movement, and if a nearby insect stays quite still the mantis may not recognize it as prey.

Hidden menace
This particular mantis has green camouflage that conceals it among the leaves. The locust does not know it is there and walks straight into the trap. Other mantids are vividly colored to resemble flowers, and they lurk in wait for nectar-feeding insects. Their camouflage also conceals them from their own enemies—larger predators such as lizards and insect-eating birds that hunt mainly by sight.

High jump
The locust's main defense is its ability to leap away using its powerful hind legs, jumping high in the air and landing well away from its enemy. Its hind legs are also armed with defensive spines.

Joining forces

Predators tend to be quite intelligent, and some regularly work together to outsmart their prey. These humpback whales have joined forces to round up fish by creating a "net" of bubbles around them. Apparently trapped by the bubbles, the fish form a tight shoal that makes an easy target for the hungry whales.

Giveaway glow

Some predators have evolved with astonishing hunting adaptations. The pits on the snout of this eyelash viper contain infrared sensors that can "see" the heat of a warm-blooded animal in total darkness. This allows the snake to target mice and similar prey in the dead of night.

Safety in numbers

Some prey animals such as these fish defend themselves by seeking safety in numbers. This can be a mistake if their enemy is big enough to eat many of them at a time, but most hunters will only take a few, so their chances of survival are greater in a school. Many eyes also reduce the risk of being taken by surprise.

Spiny armor

The stout spines and armored scales of the Australian thorny devil make it a very prickly mouthful for any predator. Many other animals such as armadillos and porcupines have similar defenses. Skunks on the other hand can produce vile smells, and some tropical tree frogs are protected by incredibly powerful poisons.

Reptiles

With its scaly skin and dragon-like appearance, this chameleon is clearly a reptile—a group that includes tortoises, crocodiles, lizards, and snakes. These are all cold-blooded animals, which rely on the temperature of their surroundings to keep them warm. As a result, most are tropical, and only a few live in cool climates.

Energy saver

The flap-necked chameleon moves very slowly, creeping up on insects until they are within range of its long tongue. But many reptiles are quite nimble, provided the climate is hot enough to keep their bodies warm. In fact, cold-bloodedness can be an advantage; since a reptile does not turn food energy into body heat, it can live on very little food compared to a warm-blooded animal of the same size.

Prehensile tail

Strong muscles in the chameleon's tail enable the animal to curl it up tightly or wrap it around a twig for extra support. This grasping type of tail is very useful to a creature that lives in bushes and trees.

Vice-like grip

Typical lizards have five separate toes on each foot. But the toes of a chameleon's foot are partly fused to form two strong hooks. These squeeze together like clamps to grip twigs and slender branches.

Lizards

The most diverse group of reptiles are the lizards, with some 4,560 species ranging from tiny geckos to the giant Komodo dragon. Most, including this anole lizard, hunt insects and similar animals. But a few, such as the seaweed-eating marine iguana, are herbivores. Many have astonishing adaptions, such as the eyes of chameleons, and the sticky feet of geckos that allow some to run across ceilings.

Tortoises and turtles

Instantly recognizable by the massive shells that encase their bodies, tortoises and turtles are the most ancient surviving reptiles. They evolved 230 million years ago, along with the earliest dinosaurs, and have not changed much since. Tortoises are famously slow-moving animals, but sea turtles such as this hawksbill turtle are graceful swimmers that regularly travel vast distances across oceans to lay eggs on traditional breeding beaches.

Scaly skin

The tough scales covering the chameleon's skin do more than protect it from minor scuffs and scratches: the scales waterproof it, so it retains vital body moisture. Reptile eggs are waterproof, too, so the animals can lay them in dry places. This allows reptiles to thrive in permanently dry terrain—unlike soft-skinned amphibians—and since they do not need much food they can survive in deserts where food is often scarce.

Trick of the eye

Chameleons are very specialized lizards with many unique features. These include weird scaly lidded eyes that swivel independently in their sockets, so one eye can look up while the other looks down.

Lightning strike

A chameleon seizes prey with the sticky tip of its amazingly long tongue. It can flick it out, latch onto a fly, and haul it back into its mouth in a split second, giving its victim no chance of escape.

Changing color

Chameleons are famous for changing color. These are all flap-necked chameleons in different disguises—some are for camouflage, when stalking prey or hiding from enemies such as birds, but chameleons also use color for display, and it often reflects their mood. A courting male is vividly patterned, but if he loses a fight with a rival his color may fade to drab gray.

Snakes

The most specialized reptiles are the snakes, with their long, legless bodies, refined senses, and, in some snakes—but not this red mountain racer—powerful venom. They are superbly adapted for tracking and killing their victims, but since they have no limbs to pull prey apart they must swallow it whole, engulfing it with their amazingly stretchy mouths. A large python can swallow a whole gazelle in this way.

Crocodilians

The crocodiles and alligators include the biggest of all living reptiles—powerful predators like the Nile crocodile that may attack almost anything. They are highly adapted for life in the water, living in mainly tropical lakes and rivers where they ambush their prey, although the saltwater crocodile also swims out to sea. Unlike other reptiles they have complex social lives and are attentive parents.

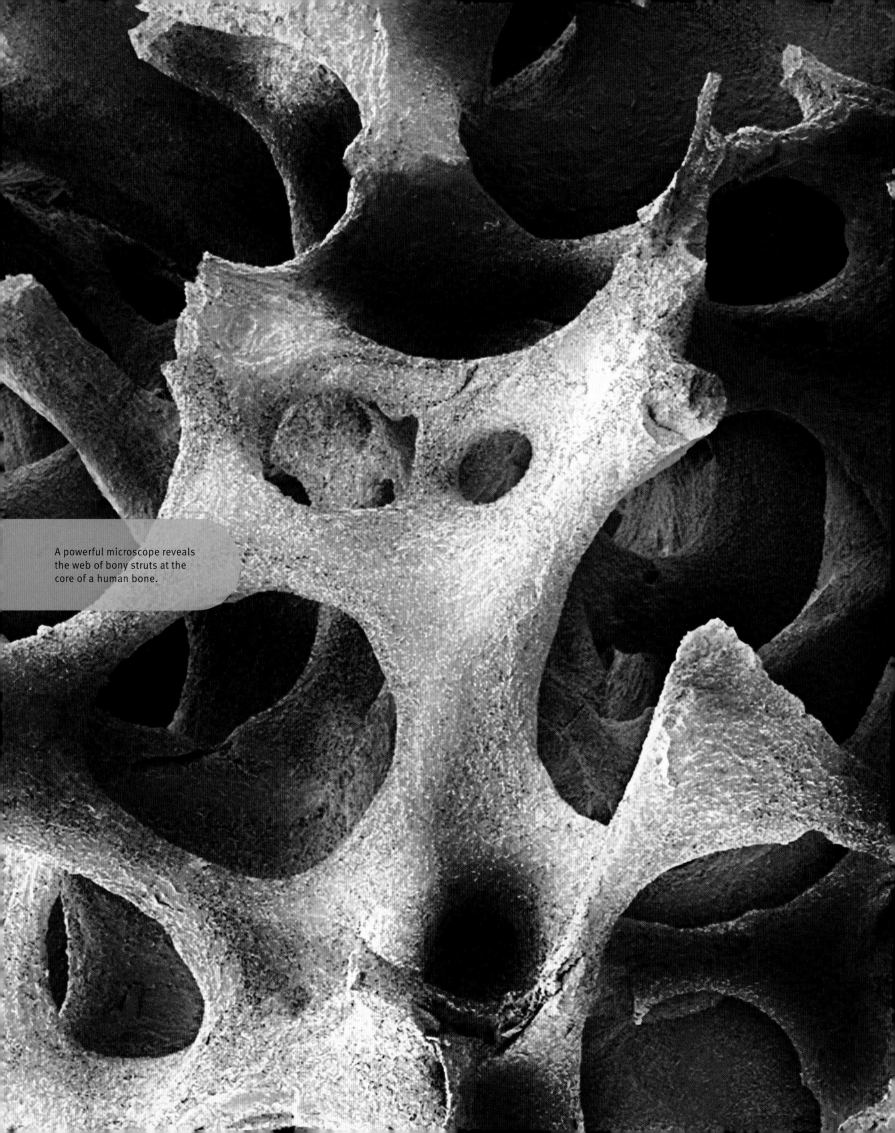

A powerful microscope reveals the web of bony struts at the core of a human bone.

HUMAN BODY

Built up from millions of microscopic cells, each specialized for its particular purpose, the human body is an astonishing creation. As long as we stay fit and healthy, every element of our anatomy works together with seamless efficiency—from the tirelessly beating heart to the mysterious electrical networks of the brain.

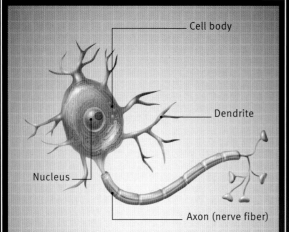

Cell body

Dendrite

Nucleus

Axon (nerve fiber)

Nerve cells

The brain and nerves are built from nerve cells, also called neurons. There are probably more than 100 billion of them in the brain. A typical nerve cell receives messages along short finger-like dendrites, analyzes them in its cell body, and passes the results along its bigger axon or nerve fiber to other nerve cells. Nerve messages take the form of tiny pulses of electricity, many hundreds every second.

Premotor cortex
This narrow strip works with the motor cortex to control movement. It receives feedback about how an action is progressing, and advises the motor cortex about ongoing adjustments.

Motor cortex
Voluntary movements—those made by conscious thoughts—are under the planning and control of the motor cortex. It works in conjunction with the cerebellum at the base of the brain.

Prefrontal cortex
Personality traits and aspects of behavior, such as always being in a hurry, planning ahead, or tending to stay cool and calm, seem to be based in various regions of the prefrontal cortex.

Broca's area
Toward the front of the brain, Broca's area is involved in choosing words, making them into sentences, and speaking them out loud. It also helps other areas to understand received words. This image shows the left hemisphere of the brain; the right hemisphere is its mirror image. Here you can see the left Broca's area. Like all the other regions shown here, it has a mirror-image partner on the brain's right side.

Brain and nerves

Every thought we have, and each sensation we experience, all happen in the brain. This gray, unmoving organ is the body's chief control center. The main part of the brain, the cerebrum, is split into the left and right hemispheres (halves). The different areas of its wrinkled covering, the cerebral cortex, each have their own important tasks—but they all work together, too.

Primary auditory cortex
In the mid area of the brain, just beneath the ear itself, is the auditory cortex. It sorts, recognizes, and gives meaning to sounds of all kinds, even when they are jumbled together.

Auditory association cortex
Situated around the primary auditory cortex, this association area has two-way communications with it, and identifies familiar sounds, such as a dog's bark or a baby's cry.

Somatosensory cortex
This is the brain's "touch center."
Nerve signals from different
regions of the skin arrive for
sorting and analysis, so we sense
not just touch but heat, cold,
pressure, and pain.

Sensory association cortex
This region does not deal with
information coming along nerves
from a particular part of the body,
but with how sensory data is
shared, passed among other brain
areas, and used to make decisions.

Wernicke's area
Working with Broca's area,
Wernicke's area is the main center
for understanding words and
sentences, both spoken and
written. It works out the sense
and meaning of language.

Visual association cortex
Like the sensory association
cortex, this region processes
information from other brain areas.
Data from the primary visual cortex
comes here for analysis, so we can
recognize the things we see.

Primary visual cortex
This "sight center" is the main
destination for nerve messages
from the eyes. It forms a mind's
eye image of what we see, aided
by details worked out by the visual
association cortex.

Cerebellum
At the lower rear, the cerebellum
is like a mini-brain. It fills in the
details for movements planned by
the motor cortex. The cerebellum
helps to make actions smooth,
precise, and balanced.

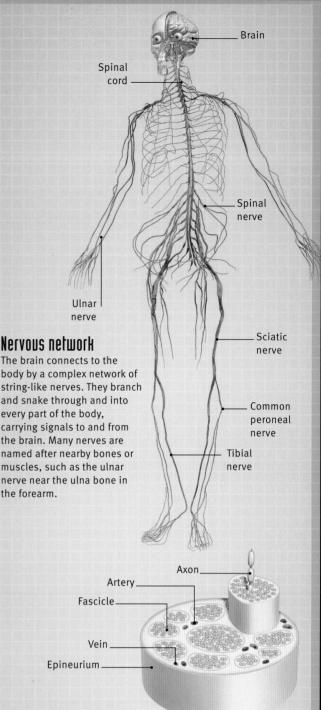

Nervous network
The brain connects to the
body by a complex network of
string-like nerves. They branch
and snake through and into
every part of the body,
carrying signals to and from
the brain. Many nerves are
named after nearby bones or
muscles, such as the ulnar
nerve near the ulna bone in
the forearm.

Bundle of nerve fibers
Nerves vary from those as thick as your thumb, such as the
sciatic nerve in the hip and thigh, to some that are thinner
than a hair. A nerve is formed from a tough outer casing, the
epineurium, which is packed with fascicles—bundles of long
axons—as well as tiny artery and vein blood vessels.

Spinal cord
The main nerve is the spinal
cord, which is protected in
a tunnel within the backbone
(vertebral column). It has
31 pairs of branches called
spinal nerves that run out to
the arms, main body, and
legs. The top of the spinal
cord connects to the base
of the brain. Connected to
each side of the spinal cord
are chains of nerve junctions
called ganglia, which are
packed with nerve cells.

Shoulder muscle
The deltoid is a large, curved triangle of muscle wrapped over the shoulder. It lifts and twists the upper arm, moves the arm out to the side, and makes the shoulder move forward or backward.

Tendons
Most muscles taper at each end into tough tendons, the ends of which are embedded in the bone. Tendons from the muscles in the forearm pass through the wrist to pull on the finger bones.

Types of muscles
The muscles that work the skeleton, and which we control at will, are known as skeletal or voluntary muscles. They make up more than four-fifths of all the body's muscle tissue. There are two other kinds of muscle. Involuntary or visceral muscle is in the walls of the guts and other internal organs, and cardiac muscle forms the walls of the heart. Both work automatically, without our need to think about controlling them.

Quadriceps femoris
This muscle has four parts and is one of the strongest muscles in the body. Its parts come together into one tendon that pulls on the knee to straighten the leg. An opposing muscle pulls the knee to bend it.

Skeleton and muscles

Without its strong skeletal framework of 206 bones, the body would flop down helpless. As well as structural strength, bones also contain valuable mineral stores and make blood cells. Without the 400-plus muscles that pull on the bones and each other, the skeleton would be still and lifeless. Together the muscles and bones make up about two-thirds of the body's weight.

Skull
The upper dome or cranium of the skull consists of eight curved bones joined firmly to protect the brain. Another 14 smaller bones form the face, and one large U-shaped bone, the mandible, is the lower jaw.

Rib cage
The ribs are attached to the spine. There are 12 pairs of ribs in total: the upper 10 pairs join to the breastbone or sternum at the front to make a moveable cage that protects the lungs and heart.

Hip bone
Wide and strong, the pelvis or hip bone joins to the base of the spinal column at the rear. Each thigh bone, or femur, links to the lower side by a ball-and-socket joint that lets the leg move and twist in most directions.

Knee
The knee is an example of the biggest type of joint, a hinge joint. It only allows the lower leg to move forward and backward, not sideways. It is protected at the front by the kneecap, or patella.

Ankles, feet, and toes
Each ankle is a complex joint of eight small bones, the tarsals. In the sole of the foot are five long metatarsals. Oddly the first or big toe has two bones, while the other smaller ones have three each.

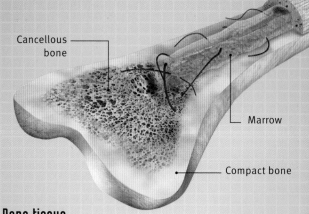

Cancellous bone

Marrow

Compact bone

Bone tissue
Most bones have a strong, dense, shell-like outer layer known as compact bone. Inside is lighter, honeycomb-like cancellous or spongy bone. In the middle of many bones is marrow, a jelly-type substance. Depending on the bone, the marrow either makes new red and white blood cells, or stores nourishment, mainly in the form of fat.

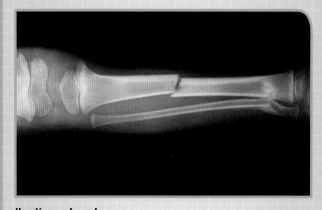

Healing a break
A broken or fractured bone may have a crack, split, or complete gap, like this break in the tibia (shin bone). To treat a break, the pieces must first be moved back into their correct positions. This is known as reduction. The bone is then immobilized by some kind of casing around it to take the strain, so that the broken ends gradually grow and knit together.

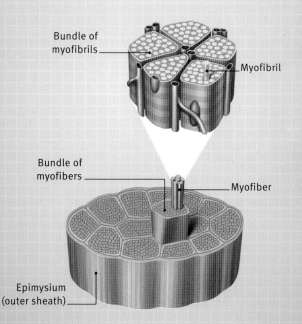

Bundle of myofibrils

Myofibril

Bundle of myofibers

Myofiber

Epimysium (outer sheath)

Muscle fibers
Skeletal muscle conains bundles of long, slim, hair-thin threads known as myofibers. In turn, each of these fibers is a bundle of even thinner myofibrils. These contain long filaments called actin and myosin. To make muscle contract, each of the millions of actin filaments slides past its myosin partner, making the myofibrils shorter, and so shortening the myofibers.

Balance

Not so much a single sense, balance involves the brain receiving information from many different sources, and sending nerve messages to the muscles to keep the body steady and well positioned. Information comes from the semicircular canals, which track head movements, the eyes, which see what is level, and parts of the body, especially the feet, that detect leaning by the pressure placed on them.

Ear protection

Parts of the ear—especially the delicate hair cells in the cochlea—can be damaged by too-loud sounds. If the sounds continue, these cells can even die. People who work in noisy places such as factories, quarries, construction sites, and airports must wear ear protectors to protect their hearing. These have cups to fit snugly over the ears and keep out the worst of the noise.

Aids to hearing

Some people are born with hearing disabilities, and for others hearing deteriorates as they get older. There are several ways to help hearing problems. A behind-the-ear aid (above) gathers sound waves using a small microphone, amplifies them, and beams them to the eardrum. A cochlear implant can take over the cochlea's job and convert sound waves into electrical signals that go straight along the auditory nerve to the brain.

Ears

The ear is much more than the curly flap on the side of the head. This part, the outer ear, is simply a funnel to gather sound waves. The waves travel along the ear canal to the eardrum and make it shake very fast, or vibrate. The vibrations then pass along three tiny bones and into the snail-shaped cochlea, where they produce nerve signals for the brain.

Outer ear

Known as the pinna or auricle, the ear flap guides sound waves into the ear canal. It is made of springy cartilage covered by thin skin. The hollow part, the concha, is named after the Greek word for shell.

Ear canal

The canal is a slightly S-shaped tunnel that leads from the outer ear flap into the skull bone, ending at the eardrum. The outer part of the canal is made of cartilage; the inner part is a channel in the bone. It is covered in thin skin and lined with hairs and wax that trap dust and debris. As the jaws move when eating and speaking, the wax moves along the canal and out of the entrance, cleaning as it goes.

Semicircular canals

These three C-shaped canals, each at right angles to the other, are for balance rather than hearing. Head movements make fluid inside them swirl around and move microscopic hairs that stick out from hair cells in their linings. As the hairs sway to and fro, the cells generate nerve signals in the form of tiny electrical pulses, which travel along the vestibular nerve to the brain.

Ear bones

The three ear bones, or ossicles, are named for their shapes. The hammer connects to the eardrum and the anvil, which in turn links to the stirrup. As vibrations pass along the bones, the stirrup presses against the oval window of the cochlea and transmits the vibrations to the fluid inside.

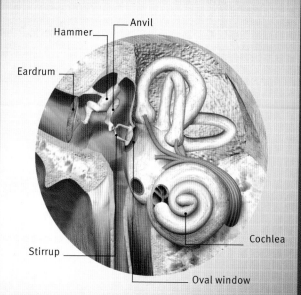

Hammer
Anvil
Eardrum
Stirrup
Cochlea
Oval window

Middle ear space

This air space is a chamber well protected and surrounded by the temporal bone of the skull. It is bridged by the three tiny ear bones that link the eardrum to the inner ear (see panel above).

Cochlea

As small as the little fingertip, the cochlea converts vibrations into nerve messages that go to the brain. Vibrations cause hairs to shake on hair cells—more than 15,000 of them along the cochlea's length.

Eardrum

The eardrum, or tympanic membrane, is about the same size as a fingernail but much thinner. It is a very flexible sheet of skinlike material that bends when even the smallest sound waves bounce off it.

Eustachian tube

This tunnel connects the air space inside the middle ear to the back of the throat, and so to the air outside. General air pressure changes with the weather. If the middle ear were a sealed chamber, the changes would make the eardrum bend and disrupt hearing. The tube allows changes to reach the middle ear space, so the pressures either side of the eardrum are equal.

in, hair, and nails

is both the body's barrier against the outside world, and its biggest sense organ.
tects aspects of touch, from light contact to heavy pressure. As a barrier it continually
ws itself to protect the delicately moist inner parts from drying out and guards them
nst rubbing, knocks, dirt, and germs. Surface skin cells are toughened with the strong,
-resistant protein substance keratin, which also forms the nails and hair.

Head hair

A typical head has about 110,000 scalp hairs, although people with light-colored hair tend to have more, and those with very dark or reddish hair have fewer. Each one grows for two to four years, initially by 0.1 in (2.5 mm) each week. Then it falls out and a new hair grows in its place. This hair-growth cycle happens at different times for different hairs, so they do not all fall out at once!

Inside skin

Skin has two main layers. The outer epidermis makes new cells at its base, which gradually move up, harden, die, and reach the surface, where they continually wear away. Below the epidermis, the dermis contains nerves and microscopic touch sensors, hair follicles, hair-erecting muscles, oil glands, and sweat glands.

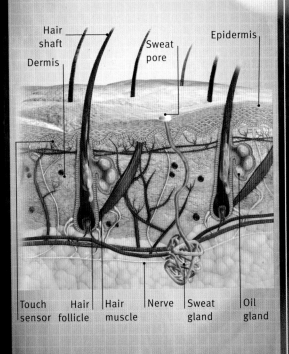

Hair shaft | Sweat pore | Epidermis
Dermis

Touch sensor | Hair follicle | Hair muscle | Nerve | Sweat gland | Oil gland

Sensitive skin

Under the skin's surface are touch sensors that are connected to nerves and send information to the brain about physical sensations. Close to the skin's surface are sensors that detect light touch. Deeper down, larger sensors respond to heavier pressure and to being stretched. Some areas of the body are more sensitive than others—the lips, fingertips, toes, and soles of the feet are particularly rich in sensors.

Fingernails

The sensitive tips of the fingers and toes are protected by nails. These hard plates are made from tough keratin and grow constantly forward from under a fold of skin, called a cuticle, at the nail's base.

Forehead skin

As on most parts of the body, the skin on the forehead is 0.04–0.08 in (1–2 mm) thick. Forehead skin, along with skin on the armpits, hands, and feet, contains plentiful sweat glands.

Eyebrow hair

Hairs on the eyebrows are similar in thickness to those on the scalp and have a growth cycle of 12–14 weeks. Along with the brow ridge on the skull bone just underneath them, the eyebrows help to prevent forehead sweat from trickling into the eyes. As with all hairs on the body, oil glands, also called sebaceous glands, make oil called sebum. The oil makes the hair flexible and soft.

Body hair

Fine hair called vellus covers most of the body. In most people the hairs are hardly noticeable. There are about five million of them in total and they have a growth cycle of one to two years. When touched by movement, the hairs alert us by stimulating nerves around their base. Only a few areas of skin have no hairs at all—chiefly the palms of the hands, soles of the feet, back of the ear, and lips.

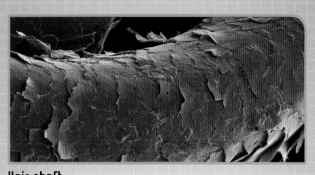

Hair shaft

A hair grows at its base, or root, in a tiny pit in the dermis called the hair follicle. The visible hair is completely dead, made of glued-together, flattened cells filled with the tough substance keratin, which look like peeling scales. New hairs grow upward from the base and push out old hairs.

Skin ridges

On the hands and feet, especially the fingertips and toes, skin is folded into swirling patterns of small ridges. These give a better grip than smooth skin. The patterns are different on each finger of every body, so people can be identified from prints, called fingerprints, that the patterns make on hard surfaces.

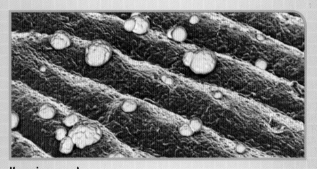

Keeping cool

Up to three million sweat glands cover the body and make tiny amounts of sweat, a watery fluid containing waste products and salt. If the body becomes hot, they produce more sweat, which draws heat from the skin as it evaporates (dries). The skin's blood vessels also widen to lose excess heat and cool the body down.

Skin color

Skin color comes from micrograins of the dark pigment melanin, made by melanocyte cells in the epidermis. These cells are more active in people with darker skin. In light skin, small patches of more active melanocytes form freckles. In sunlight, all melanocytes are more active and can tan the skin.

Eyelid
The upper and lower eyelid muscles tighten to close the lids over the eye. A blink lasts about one-third of a second and smears lachrymal (tear) fluid over the eye to moisten it, kill germs, and wipe away dust.

Sclera
Apart from the transparent cornea at the front of the eye, the rest of the eyeball has a tough, stiff, pale casing up to 0.04 in (1 mm) thick, known as the sclera. This casing gives the eyeball protection, retains its fluids inside, and maintains the rounded shape. We see the sclera at the front as the "white" of the eye, although it extends all around the sides and back of the eyeball, too.

Eyes

The eyes send almost as much information to the brain as all the other senses added together. Each eyeball is about 1 in (2.5 cm) across and is well protected in a rounded socket in the skull called the orbit. From the front we see the parts that protect the eye, bend or focus light rays to give a clear view, and control how much light enters the eyeball.

Cornea
The clear, dome-shaped front of the eyeball is known as the cornea. Its curved shape provides the main focusing power for light rays. The cornea's very thin, sensitive surface layer is the conjunctiva.

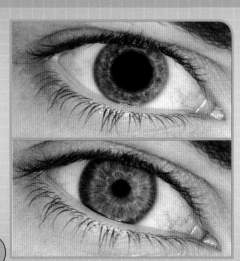

Shutter action
The iris muscles adjust the size of the pupil by a reflex (automatic) action, according to surrounding light levels. In dim conditions they widen or dilate the pupil (left, above) to allow in as much light as possible, so we can see better. In bright light the iris muscles make the pupil smaller or constricted (left, below) to prevent too much light from entering the eye and damaging the delicate retina.

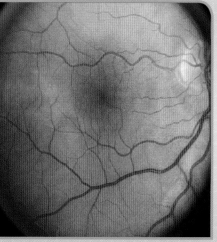

Retina
A close-up view through the pupil shows the paper-thin retina lining the inside of the eyeball. It contains light-sensitive cells called rods and cones. The greatest concentration of cone cells is in a darker central zone known as the fovea or yellow spot. This is where the center of the image falls, so we can see this part in greatest detail. Blood vessels branch across the retina's surface to supply energy and nutrients.

Eyelashes

Amongst the body's thickest hairs, eyelashes have a short growing cycle of just five to eight weeks. They work with the eyelids to swish dust and other debris away from the surface of the eye.

Iris

The iris is a ring of colored muscles around its central hole, the pupil. The muscles are in two groups. When one group contracts, the iris becomes thinner and flatter so that its area increases, spreading inward to make the pupil smaller. The other group does the reverse so the pupil enlarges. Like fingerprints, the color and pattern of the iris is different for each eye in every body.

In focus

Light rays entering the eye are bent, or refracted, by the curved cornea and finely adjusted by the lens. This produces a clear, sharply focused, upside-down image on the light-sensitive retina. The image is sent via the optic nerve to the brain, which corrects it to look the right way up.

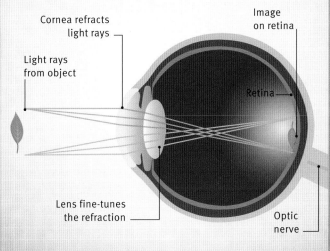

Cornea refracts light rays

Light rays from object

Image on retina

Retina

Lens fine-tunes the refraction

Optic nerve

Pupil

This looks like a black spot, but in fact it is a hole leading into the mostly dark interior of the eyeball. Just behind it is the clear, pea-sized lens that makes fine adjustments when focusing.

Rods and cones

The retina has more than 120 million rod cells (shown as pale threads in this false-color image) and about six million cone cells (green). Most cells in the fovea are cones, which respond to different colors of light, and see fine detail. But they only work in high light levels. Rods are more numerous in the rest of the retina. They do not respond to colors, so they produce images in shades of gray, but they work in dim light.

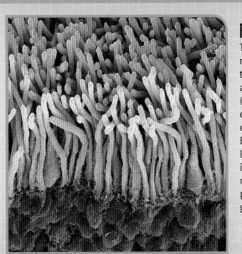

Correcting vision

If the cornea and lens are not quite the correct shape, or the eyeball is too large or small for their focusing power, then the image on the retina is blurred. Contact lenses or glasses provide an extra lens, which refracts the light rays so they focus correctly. Alternatively, tiny amounts of the cornea can be removed and its shape sculpted using a very precisely aimed laser beam.

Mites

Tiny eight-legged cousins of spiders, mites of several kinds live on or in the skin. The eyelash mite, just 0.01 in (0.3 mm) long, dwells and lays eggs in the pit-like follicle from which an eyelash grows. It eats skin cells, skin oils, and hair fragments and about half of all people unknowingly have them.

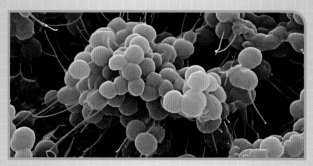

Bacteria

Some bacteria cause illnesses, but most kinds are harmless, and some are helpful, such as *Staphylococcus* (shown here)—a skin bacteria that makes substances to deter harmful ones. Other "friendly" or symbiotic bacteria are necessary for our health, such as *Bifidobacterium*, which live in the gut and help food digestion.

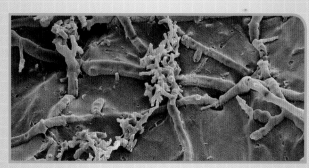

Fungal spores

Fungi, or molds, grow from microscopic seed-like structures called spores. They sometimes infect nails or skin, especially where it is moist, sweaty, or folded. Athlete's foot, or tinea pedis, is a fungal infestation between the toes by *Trichophyton* (shown here). This fungus also causes ringworm, an itching skin disease.

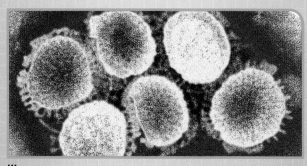

Viruses

Hundreds of times smaller even than bacteria, viruses are obligate parasites. This means they must invade the cells of other living things and use up their energy to make copies of themselves, destroying those cells in the process before breaking out and infecting other cells. Pictured here are the H1N1 flu viruses that cause swine flu.

Body invaders

The human body hosts many thousands of life forms on its outer surface. Occasionally there are small parasites such as lice, fleas, and ticks. Often there are microscopic mites. Always there are microbes, invisible to the naked eye. These can include bacteria, fungi, and viruses, ready and waiting to invade the body.

Hair
Adult lice are up to 0.1 in (3 mm) long and live among human hairs, usually on the scalp where it's warmer and favoring the back of the neck and behind the ears where it's dark. They hold onto hairs and can also dig their claws into the skin, but they do not burrow into the skin. They spread from person to person by direct contact and also through shared items such as towels, hairbrushes, combs, and hats.

Egg opening
A female louse lays eggs from her rear end and can lay up to four eggs daily, just one or two days after mating with a male. She lays a total of more than 100 eggs during her average adult life of one month.

Legs and claws
Each head louse has three pairs of legs that extend from its body and curve around like pincers. Each leg ends in a sharp claw plus a stubby "thumb," ideally designed for a tenacious grip on human hair.

Mouthparts
A louse uses its tiny, needlelike mouthparts to pierce human skin and suck up blood and body fluids. As it does so it dribbles saliva, which contains anticoagulant chemicals that prevent blood from clotting, into the wound. This keeps the blood liquid and flowing. Hungry lice feed up to five times daily, but they can survive without a meal for several days. When not feeding, the mouthparts withdraw under the head.

Head
The louse's head bears two eyes, which cannot form detailed images but see patterns of light and dark. The two antennae are sensitive to touch, air movements, and scents such as human sweat.

Abdomen
As in other insects, this large rear part of the louse's body contains its digestive, excretory, and reproductive parts. As the louse feeds, the incoming blood makes its abdomen swell to twice its normal size.

Louse eggs

The eggs of lice, known as "nits," look like tiny, pale salt grains. When they are laid, the mother secretes a sticky substance that glues them to hair shafts, making them very difficult to remove. After about a week the immature form, or nymph, hatches from the egg and sheds its outer skin three times over 2–3 weeks before maturing into an adult.

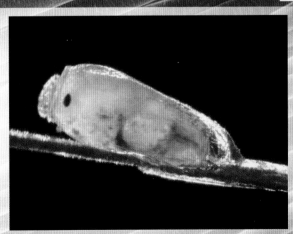

Egg cell
At more than 0.004 in (0.1 mm) across, the egg cell is one of the largest cells in the human body and would be just visible to the human eye. Whereas most body cells contain a double set of genes, egg cells contain only a single set of 23 chromosomes. An egg is formed in one of the two ovaries of a mature female, and ovulation (when one egg is released from one of the ovaries) occurs about every 28 days.

Egg surface
The surface of the egg may be covered with a layer of tiny cells called the corona radiata, left over from the egg's development. These cells provide nourishment to the egg but soon die and fall away.

Successful sperm
About 200 to 500 million sperm from the father enter the mother's reproductive system following sexual intercourse. But probably only a few hundred swim strongly and long enough to reach the egg cell. When one sperm penetrates the egg, the egg surface hardens to prevent any more sperm from getting in. The successful sperm then releases its genetic material to join with the egg's and make a complete set.

New life

Each human body consists of billions of cells but began as a single cell smaller than a pinhead. That cell was a fertilized egg—an egg cell (ovum) from the mother that was joined by a sperm cell (spermatozoon) from the father. The fertilized egg then took nine months to develop in the mother's uterus, or womb, into a baby ready to be born.

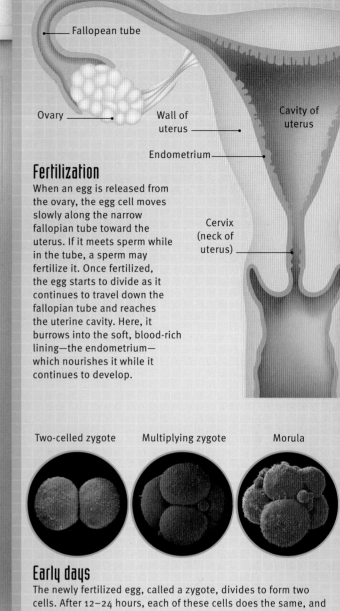

- Fallopean tube
- Ovary
- Wall of uterus
- Cavity of uterus
- Endometrium
- Cervix (neck of uterus)

Fertilization

When an egg is released from the ovary, the egg cell moves slowly along the narrow fallopian tube toward the uterus. If it meets sperm while in the tube, a sperm may fertilize it. Once fertilized, the egg starts to divide as it continues to travel down the fallopian tube and reaches the uterine cavity. Here, it burrows into the soft, blood-rich lining—the endometrium— which nourishes it while it continues to develop.

Two-celled zygote | Multiplying zygote | Morula

Early days

The newly fertilized egg, called a zygote, divides to form two cells. After 12–24 hours, each of these cells does the same, and so on. No longer a large egg cell, the newly multiplied cells are normal body-cell size. Each cell continues to divide at its own rate to create a ball of cells known as a morula. As it enters the uterus, it changes into a hollow ball of cells called a blatocyst.

Sperm cells
These tiny cells are just 0.002 in (0.05 mm) long. Each sperm has a bulbous head that contains genetic material, a middle piece to provide energy for swimming, and a long tail that thrashes to propel the sperm toward the egg at a rate of 0.1 in (3 mm) per hour. Like eggs, sperm are made by the special kind of cell division called meiosis, which halves the usual double set of genes to just one set.

DNA and genes

Most body cells have 46 thread-like chromosomes arranged into 23 pairs, onto which are packed the instructions for the body's development and life processes. Chromosomes are made up of extremely tightly twisted coils of DNA (deoxyribonucleic acid)—a long molecule of two strands that looks like a twisted ladder. A gene is a small section of DNA that controls a certain trait or aspect of development. The rungs of the DNA ladder are made of pairs of chemicals called bases. The sequence of these chemicals is the code that holds the genetic information.

Two bases link to form a base pair

DNA backbone

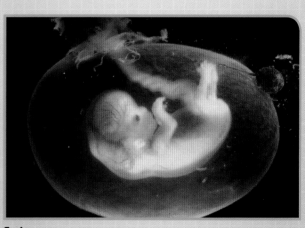

Embryo

As cell division continues, some of the blastocyst's cells become the embryo and the rest become the placenta. New cells take on specialized forms to make muscle, skin, nerves, and blood. The brain develops fast, and so the head is proportionately large. Eight weeks after fertilization, the embryo is grape-sized, all main body parts have formed, and it floats in a protective pool of fluid. From now until birth it is known as a fetus.

Breathing

The human body can survive for several days without food, and a day or so without water—but it would only last a few minutes without oxygen. The body uses oxygen to break apart food nutrients and release their energy for life processes. Getting oxygen is the task of the respiratory system—the nose, airways, and lungs.

Trachea
Also called the windpipe, the trachea is a wide tube linking the throat with the lungs. Its upper section is the larynx or voicebox, which uses the airflow of breathing to make speech sounds.

Bronchial tree
The base of the trachea divides to form two airways: the left and right bronchi, one to each lung. These branch in turn into slightly thinner tubes called secondary bronchi, which split into tertiary bronchi, and so on. This pattern produces an upside-down "tree" of gradually narrowing airways inside the lungs. Like the trachea, the bronchi are held open by hoops of springy cartilage in their walls.

Bronchioles
After several divisions the airways are only a few millimeters wide and are known as bronchioles. They continue to divide another five or six times until they form terminal bronchioles (see opposite).

Diaphragm
This sheet of muscle under the lungs separates the chest from the abdomen. It is shaped like an up-curved dome when relaxed, and contracts to become flatter for breathing in.

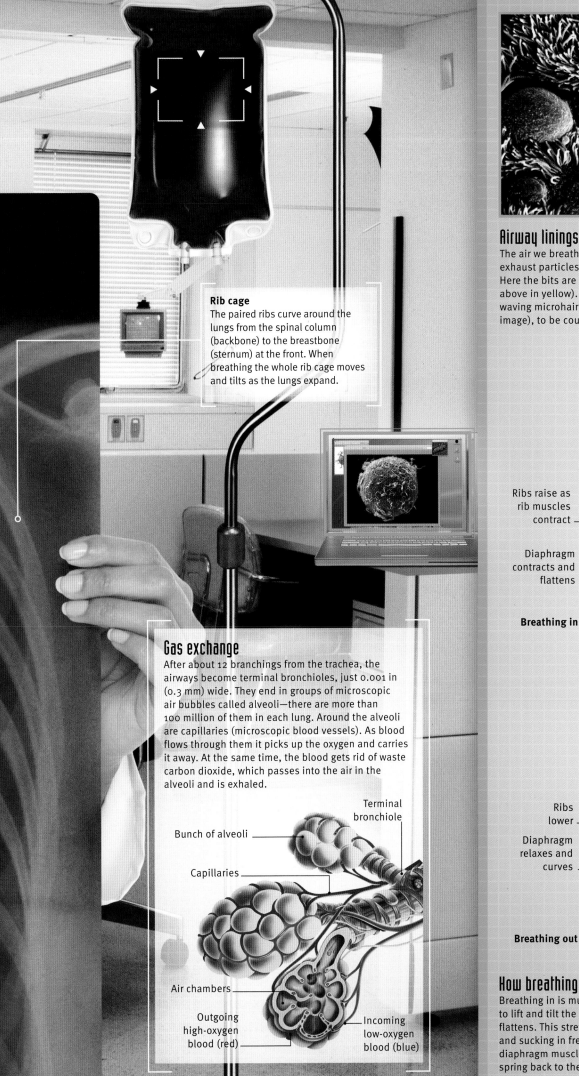

Rib cage

The paired ribs curve around the lungs from the spinal column (backbone) to the breastbone (sternum) at the front. When breathing the whole rib cage moves and tilts as the lungs expand.

Gas exchange

After about 12 branchings from the trachea, the airways become terminal bronchioles, just 0.001 in (0.3 mm) wide. They end in groups of microscopic air bubbles called alveoli—there are more than 100 million of them in each lung. Around the alveoli are capillaries (microscopic blood vessels). As blood flows through them it picks up the oxygen and carries it away. At the same time, the blood gets rid of waste carbon dioxide, which passes into the air in the alveoli and is exhaled.

Terminal bronchiole

Bunch of alveoli

Capillaries

Air chambers

Outgoing high-oxygen blood (red)

Incoming low-oxygen blood (blue)

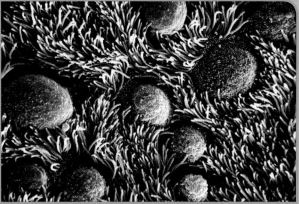

Airway linings

The air we breathe, especially in cities, is far from clean. Dust, exhaust particles, and other debris is sucked into the airways. Here the bits are trapped by blobs of sticky mucus (shown above in yellow). These are swept steadily up to the throat by waving microhairs called cilia (the colored threads in this image), to be coughed up and swallowed.

Ribs raise as rib muscles contract

Lungs stretch larger, sucking air in

Diaphragm contracts and flattens

Breathing in

Ribs lower

Lungs squash smaller, pushing air out

Diaphragm relaxes and curves

Breathing out

How breathing works

Breathing in is muscle-powered. The rib muscles contract to lift and tilt the ribs, while the diaphragm contracts and flattens. This stretches the spongy lungs, making them larger and sucking in fresh air. Breathing out is passive. The rib and diaphragm muscles relax and the stretched, elastic lungs spring back to their smaller volume, pushing out stale air.

Blood

The average body contains 8.5–10.5 pints (4–5 liters) of endlessly flowing blood, with an average heart-to-heart round trip lasting 40–50 seconds. Under the microscope, blood teems with billions of microscopic cells of three main kinds: red cells, white cells, and platelets. Blood delivers oxygen, nutrients, and hormones to the body, collects carbon dioxide and wastes, spreads heat around the body, and clots to seal cuts and leaks.

Platelets

More cell fragments than whole cells, oval-shaped platelets are the smallest blood components. Also known as thrombocytes, they are mainly involved in thrombosis (clotting). There are about 200,000 to 400,000 platelets in a pinhead-sized droplet of blood, and they live for about one week. Like all three kinds of blood cells, they are made in bone marrow.

Blood components

If a blood sample is allowed to settle, it forms three main layers. At the top is plasma, constituting just over one half of the total volume, and itself more than 90 percent water. At the bottom are red cells, making up about 45 percent of the total volume. In the middle, at about 3 percent, are the white cells and platelets. Changes to these proportions can indicate illness. For example, fewer red blood cells may be due to a form of anemia, an iron deficiency that causes tiredness.

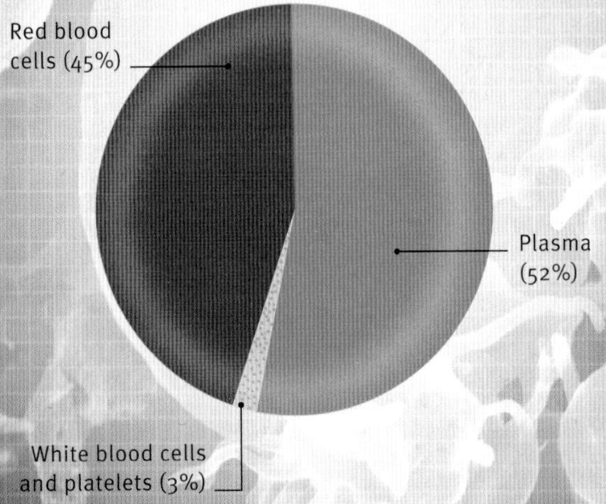

Red blood cells (45%)

Plasma (52%)

White blood cells and platelets (3%)

Red blood cell

Also called erythrocytes, red blood cells carry oxygen and carbon dioxide in the blood. Each one is seven-thousandths of a millimeter across, shaped like a doughnut with the hole filled in, and contains up to 300 million molecules of the oxygen-carrying substance hemoglobin. Every second, two million new red blood cells are created by the marrow inside bones, and each one can live for up to three months.

White blood cell

There are several kinds of white blood cells, with the overall name of leucocytes. Their main functions are to clean the blood of bits of dead cells and other unwanted matter, and to attack invaders such as bacteria. They can be any shape, and change shape easily like flexible bags. Small projections help them latch onto germs. Some kinds of leucocytes—such as lymphocytes and macrophages—live for many years.

Plasma

The fluid part of blood is called plasma. It is a complex cocktail of dissolved substances including sugars, salts, hormones, dozens of minerals and nutrients, and oxygen, carbon dioxide, and nitrogen gases.

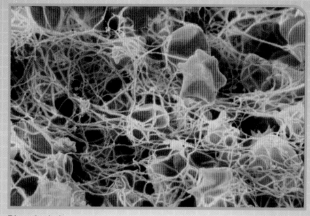

Blood clot

When a blood vessel is damaged by injury, its contents leak into the blood and trigger the process of clotting. Platelets begin to stick together in clumps. A protein substance called fibrin, normally dissolved in plasma, starts forming nets of sticky threads. Red cells soon get caught up in the fibrin and platelets, and as the tangled mass spreads as a clot or thrombus, it blocks the leak.

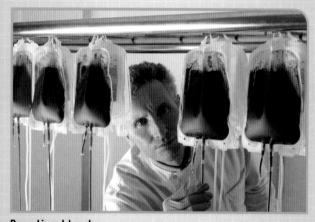

Donating blood

Blood can be taken from one person, called a donor, and put into another person, called the recipient. The donor's body soon replaces the missing blood naturally. When taken, the blood is processed and stored in bags (above). Because there are different groups of blood, each donor and recipient is tested for their group. If the wrong group of blood is transfused, it could clot and kill the recipient.

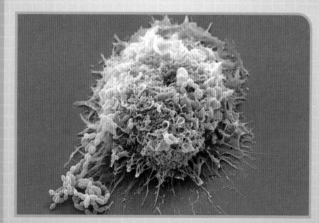

Battle in the blood

Some white blood cells, called macrophages, specialize in "eating" germs. Here a frilly-surfaced, flexible macrophage has captured a chain of bacterial germs (yellow blobs, mainly lower left) to engulf and dissolve them. One macrophage can consume several hundred bacteria during its life. White cells known as B-lymphocytes make natural chemicals called antibodies that stick to and disable germs.

Heart

Nestling between the two lungs, slightly left of center, the heart is a powerful, high-stamina pump for the blood. It beats on average 70 times each minute, which could add up to almost three million beats over a lifetime. The heart is in fact two pumps, side by side. Each has a small, thin-walled upper chamber, the atrium, and a much larger thick-walled lower chamber, the ventricle.

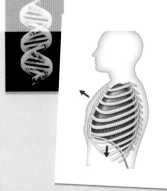

Aorta
The body's main artery carries high-oxygen blood away from the left ventricle to most of the body. Like all arteries, which take high-pressure blood away from the heart, it has thick, strong walls.

Superior vena cava
Veins carry low-pressure blood from the organs and tissues back to the heart and have thin, floppy walls. The main vein of the upper body brings blood from the head, neck, and arms to the right atrium.

Atria
These thin-walled chambers rest like flappy pockets on their ventricles. They contract during each heartbeat to force blood through the atrioventricluar valve into their corresponding ventricle below.

How the heart beats

For each heartbeat, the heart relaxes and the atria fill with blood. The right atrium fills with used blood from the body; the left atrium fills with oxygen-rich blood from the lungs. In the second stage, the atria contract, and blood flows into the ventricles (below left). Then the ventricles contract, pushing the blood into the aorta (from the left ventricle) and pulmonary arteries (from the right ventricle). The sounds of the heartbeat, "lub-dup", are the valves slamming shut to stop the blood going the wrong way.

Ventricles
The right ventricle receives the returning low-oxygen blood and pushes it out through the pulmonary valve into the pulmonary arteries and on to the lungs. The left ventricle receives high-oxygen blood from the lungs via the left atrium. The thick muscles in its walls contract powerfully to pump the blood out through the aortic valve into the aorta and all around the body.

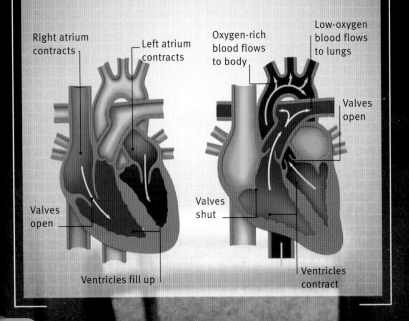

Right atrium contracts

Left atrium contracts

Oxygen-rich blood flows to body

Low-oxygen blood flows to lungs

Valves open

Valves open

Valves shut

Ventricles fill up

Ventricles contract

Inferior vena cava
This is the main vein from the lower body—the abdomen and legs. It brings low-oxygen blood to the right atrium, opening into this chamber below the opening of the superior vena cava.

Pulmonary arteries
One short artery, the pulmonary trunk, carries blood away from the right ventricle. It divides into the left and right pulmonary arteries, one to each lung, that carry dark, low-oxygen blood.

Pulmonary veins
Bright red, high-oxygen blood returns on the short journey from the lungs along these veins to the left atrium. There are two veins on each side, the superior (higher up) and inferior pulmonary veins.

Valves and "heartstrings"
On each side of the heart, between the atrium and ventricle, is a large, flexible valve known as the atrioventricular valve. This has flaps or cusps that bend open to allow blood from the atrium to the ventricle. When the ventricle contracts, the flaps bulge together under the blood's pressure to close the gap and prevent backflow. The valve flaps are prevented from turning inside out by long, string-like cords.

Pulmonary circulation to the lungs

Heart

Systemic circulation to the rest of the body

Systemic arteries (red) carry oxygenated blood

Systemic veins (blue) carry low-oxygen blood

Circulation
The body has a two-part circulation. The smaller, shorter route is the pulmonary circulation from the heart's right ventricle to the lungs and back to the left atrium. Much larger is the systemic circulation from the left ventricle, through arteries branching all around the body, then back along veins to the right atrium.

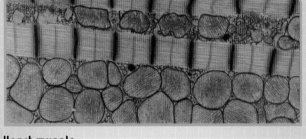

Heart muscle
Heart or cardiac muscle forms the walls of the atria and ventricles. It has a specialized structure with a network of branching, Y-shaped muscle fibers. Containing numerous energy-providing mitochondria (shown as ovals in the picture above), its chief feature is stamina—it works all day, every day, without becoming fatigued like skeletal muscle does.

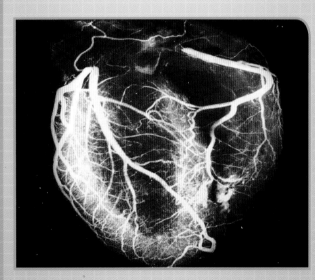

Heart's blood
Heart muscle has its own mini-system of arteries and veins known as the coronary circulation. The coronary arteries are wide and numerous, to supply the hardworking cardiac muscles with sufficient oxygen, energy, and nutrients. The arteries branch from near the start of the aorta and divide over the heart's surface, sending smaller branches into the muscle.

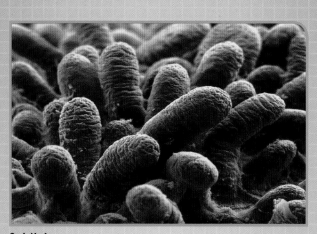

Gut lining

The highly folded lining of the small intestine is covered with more than three million microscopic villi, each about 0.04 in (1 mm) long. They form a huge surface area, more than 2,153 sq ft (200 sq m), to absorb as many nutrients as possible from digested food.

Healthy eating

The human digestive system works best when fed plenty of fresh fruits and vegetables (especially for vitamins and minerals), sufficient carbohydrates (starches)—such as bread, rice, pasta, and potatoes—for energy, plus smaller quantities of dairy produce and meats for proteins.

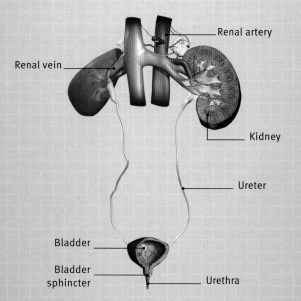

Renal artery

Renal vein

Kidney

Ureter

Bladder

Bladder sphincter

Urethra

Bladder and kidneys

Like the guts, kidneys get rid of unwanted material—in their case urine, which is dissolved wastes and excess water filtered from blood. It flows down the ureters to the bladder. To expel urine, the bladder's exit sphincter (muscle ring) relaxes and its wall muscles contract to push urine along the urethra.

Mouth and esophagus
In the mouth, teeth crush and chew food. The tongue moves this food toward the muscular-walled tube of the esophagus (gullet). Here, peristalsis (muscle contractions) pushes food down to the stomach.

Liver
The liver, just under the lungs, is the second-largest body part after the skin. It stores many kinds of nutrients, including high-energy supplies such as sugars in the form of glycogen (body starch).

esophagus

Gall bladder
This small bag under the liver stores bile, a fluid made by the liver. As part-digested food leaves the stomach, bile flows into the small intestine to help with further digestion, especially of fats.

Duodenum

Stomach
Swallowed food enters this J-shaped bag, which has strong, muscular walls that contract to churn the contents. The stomach lining makes digestive juices, including acid and enzymes, to break down food.

Pancreas
Just below the stomach, the pancreas gland produces powerful digestive enzymes. These flow along the pancreatic duct into the small intestine to break food into smaller and smaller pieces.

Jejunum

Digestive system

The human body needs regular supplies of energy-containing food for movement, to power its inner workings, and to keep warm. It also needs nutrients and raw materials for growth, maintenance, and to replace worn parts. The digestive system breaks down—digests—these substances into tiny pieces that the blood can deliver to all organs and tissues.

Appendix

Branching from the large intestine, the finger-sized appendix seems to have no vital role in our digestion. Yet in plant-eating animals it is big and important, so it may have been essential in the past.

Large intestine

The colon or large intestine is wider than the small intestine, at about 1.6–2.8 in (4–7 cm), but shorter, at 4.9 ft (1.5 m) long. As leftovers pass through, it absorbs excess water, body salts such as potassium, and useful vitamins. The leftovers gradually become firmer and compact as feces. They are stored in the last part of the colon, the rectum, until it is convenient to get rid of them via the anus.

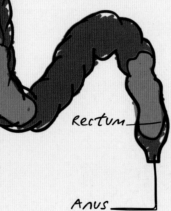

Ileum

Rectum

Anus

Small intestine

The small intestine is the longest part of the digestive tract, at 16 ft (5 m) long. Coiled into the middle of the abdomen, it has three sections: the duodenum, where most chemical breakdown happens, the jejunum, which digests fats, and the ileum, where most nutrients are absorbed. The small intestine receives digestive juices from the liver, gall bladder, and pancreas. Its lining has tiny villi to absorb digested nutrients.

Taste and smell

Taste and smell are chemosenses—they detect chemical substances, "flavorants" in foods and drinks, and "odorants" in air respectively. Both senses are well placed to check if foods and drinks seem "off" or bad, and therefore harmful. Smell and taste seem to combine as we appreciate foods and drinks, but they are separate until their perceptions merge in the brain.

Nostrils

These holes are the entrance to the nasal chamber. Muscles in their walls make them wrinkle and narrow if there are bad smells in the air, and widen or flare when breathing hard after exercise.

Teeth

An adult has 32 teeth of four main kinds. From front to back in both the upper and lower jaws, and on each side, left and right, are two incisors, one canine, two premolars, and three molars. The incisors have a straight, sharp edge for cutting. The canine (indicated here) is slightly taller and more pointed, to tear. The premolars and molars are wider and flatter, to crush and chew.

Tongue

The tongue is the body's bendiest muscle, and one of its most active. It has 12 groups of muscle fibers inside that can flex it up and down, make it wide or narrow, and poke it out or draw it in. The tongue has taste buds to detect flavor, moves food around inside the mouth for thorough chewing, and works with the lips and cheeks to form and clarify the sounds of speech.

Lips

The lips' thin skin is extremely sensitive to touch, temperature, and pressure. Underneath is the two-part orbicularis oris muscle. When this contracts it pulls the lips together so that they seal to prevent dribbles when chewing. About 30 surrounding muscles in the face help the orbicularis oris to make a huge variety of lip shapes for biting, facial expressions such as smiles and grins, and speech.

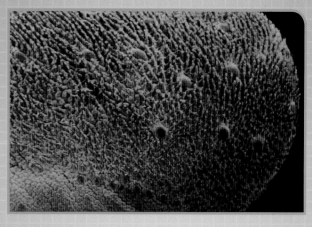

Tongue surface

The tongue's upper surface is covered with hundreds of small projections called papillae. These provide a rough surface to grip and manipulate food when eating. Around the larger papillae (the ones that look rounded in this image) are microscopic bunches of cells called taste buds—about 10,000 in total. Gustatory cells in the taste buds have microhairs that respond to particular flavorants in foods and drinks.

Nasal lining

Like the lining of the trachea and lung airways, the lining of the nasal chamber has thousands of tiny mucus glands. They continually produce sticky, slimy mucus to trap dust and debris. This mucus is steadily swept to the rear by tiny, waving, hair-like cilia, and down into the throat, where it is swallowed by an automatic reflex action. Infection by cold viruses makes the lining produce excessive mucus that is thinner than normal.

Nose
The framework of the nose is made from bendy cartilage rather than bone. Inside is the nasal chamber, divided by a cartilage plate called the septum. To heighten the sense of smell, air is sniffed in through the nose rather than being breathed in as usual. The sniff brings more air through the nasal chambers and swirls it around so that more odorant particles come into contact with the smell receptors.

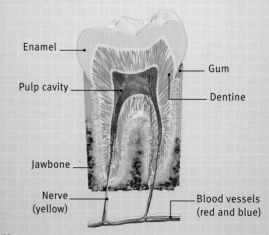

Enamel
Pulp cavity
Gum
Dentine
Jawbone
Nerve (yellow)
Blood vessels (red and blue)

Teeth

Each tooth is covered by the body's hardest substance, enamel, to withstand years of biting, crunching, and crushing. Under the enamel is slightly softer, shock-absorbing (but still very tough) dentine. At the tooth's center is the pulp cavity with tiny blood vessels and nerves. The upper visible part of the tooth is the crown. Its lower parts, firmly cemented into the jawbone, are the roots.

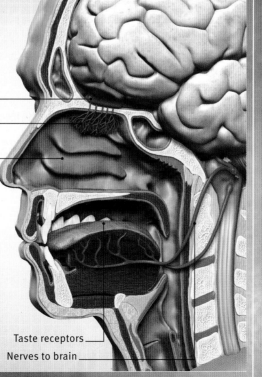

Olfactory bulb
Olfactory epithelium
Nasal chamber

Receptors and nerves

Smell microreceptors are grouped as a thin sheet, the olfactory epithelium, in the roof of each side of the nasal chamber. Nerves link to the olfactory bulb above, which carries the signals or message to the brain. Taste microreceptors are spread over much of the tongue's surface, on the taste buds, and send messages along branches of three nerves to the brain.

Taste receptors
Nerves to brain

Cells

Many huge structures are built up from small parts such as bricks and blocks. The living body has its building blocks too, more than 100 million million of them, known as cells. An average body cell is so small that 30 in a row would stretch just 0.04 in (1 mm). There is no such thing as an average cell, however. There are more than 200 different cell shapes and designs, each suited to its own task.

Epithelial cells
Many cells of the same kind arranged together form groups called tissues. Each one of these red surfaces is an epithelial cell, arranged in sheets or layers to make epithelial tissues. These tissues form the outer coverings and inner linings of many body parts, including the surface of the tongue (shown here), and the inside linings of the guts, blood vessels, and reproductive tubes. The biggest epithelial tissue is the skin.

Bacteria
These yellow wisps are bacteria, single-celled organisms smaller than most body cells. They enter the body via air, food and drink, and through cuts and wounds, and are attacked by white blood cells.

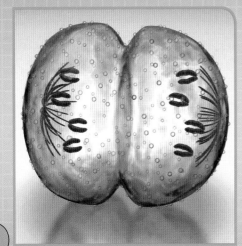

How cells divide
Before a cell divides, its set of genes—in the form of the chemical deoxyribonucleic acid (DNA)—copies itself to make two sets. These coil into chromosomes and line up in the middle. The cell membrane forms a furrow around the middle, as the sets of chromosomes move to opposite ends (left). The furrow deepens and finally nips the cell into two new cells. This kind of division is known as mitosis.

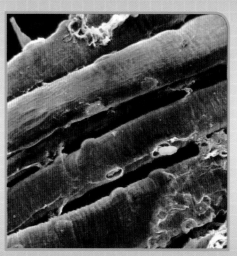

Muscle fibers
Among the biggest cells in the body are muscle fibers inside muscles (shown left). In fact, each fiber is a multicell with many nuclei (control centers). They are formed by the merging or fusion of separate cells called myoblasts, during an early stage of muscle development. In big muscles, the fibers can be more than 12 in (30 cm) long, yet they are hardly as wide as hairs.

Cell structure

The cell's control center, the nucleus, contains instructions for life in the form of genes. The outer cell membrane surrounds the cell fluid, or cytoplasm, and controls what goes in and comes out. Mitochondria break apart sugars to release their energy for cell processes. Multilayers of endoplasmic reticulum make new parts and products for the cell.

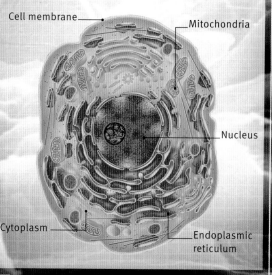

Cell membrane

Mitochondria

Nucleus

Cytoplasm

Endoplasmic reticulum

Dead cells

On outer surfaces, epithelial cells usually become flat and hard, to resist wear and tear. As they are gradually scraped and worn away, they are replaced by more cells from below by cell division. This rapid turnover of cells is an important feature of epithelial tissues. Cells on the inside lining of the mouth last for only one or two days, but other body cells can live for months.

Stem cells

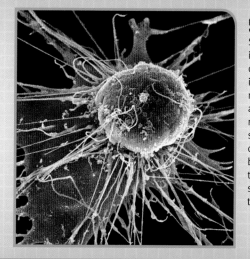

Stem or progenitor cells are cells in an early, unspecialized stage of development. They have instructions or genes for making many different kinds of cells, such as nerve cells, epithelial cells, or muscle cells, but one particular set has not yet been "switched on." In medicine, stem cells can be triggered by various chemicals to develop into particular specialized cells, for example to become new skin or nerves.

Fat cells

Fatty or adipose cells are specialized for energy and nutrient storage. They become swollen with droplets of fat, which are so plentiful that adipose tissue can be 95 percent fat. These droplets are a valuable store for times when the body cannot take in sufficient food, when they are broken down to release their energy. They also cushion organs such as the kidneys, and insulate the body.

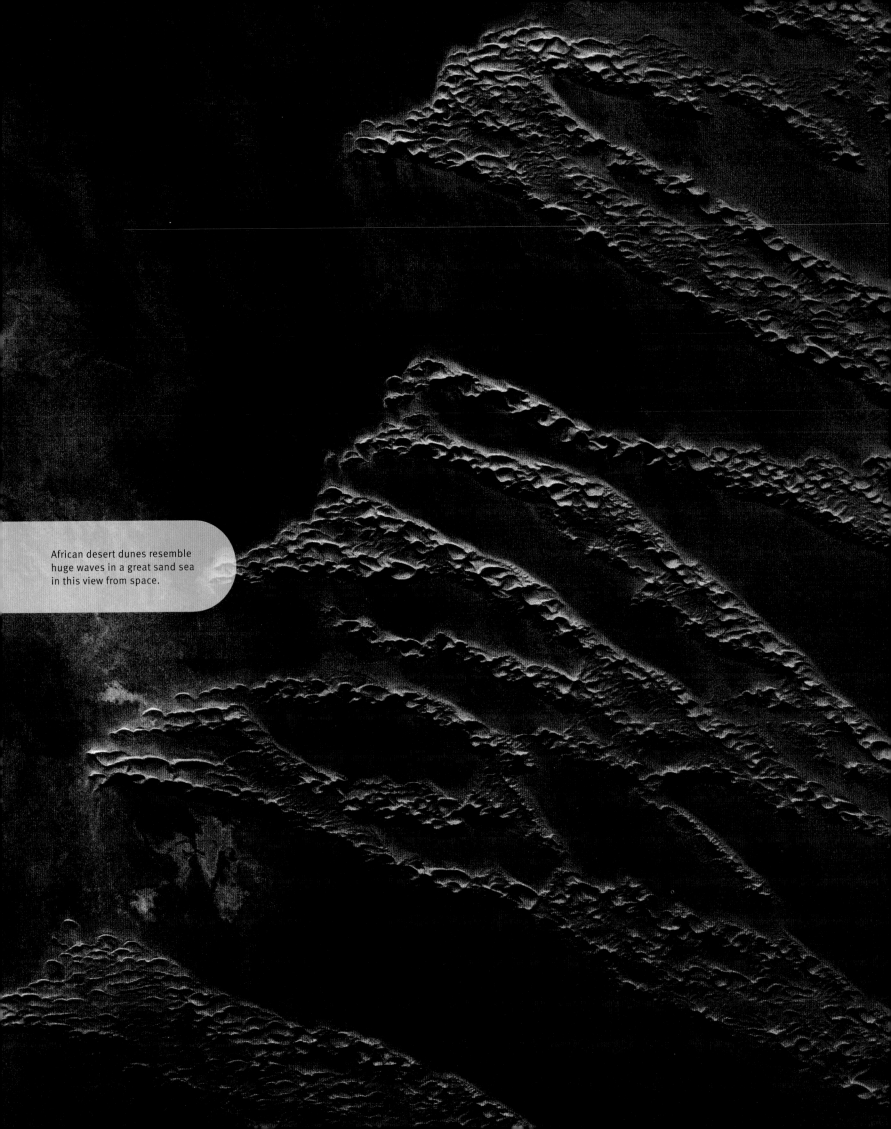

African desert dunes resemble huge waves in a great sand sea in this view from space.

EARTH

Our dynamic planet is a world of constant change. Titanic forces within the Earth keep the fragile crust continually on the move, building mountains while triggering earthquakes and volcanic eruptions. The turbulent atmosphere generates the weather that wears away the continents, and rivers carry the rocky debris into the vast, restless oceans.

Sinking peak
Kauai is the oldest of the main Hawaiian islands. Its volcano has been extinct for more than four million years, and is slowly sinking as the rock deep beneath it cools. It is one of the wettest places on Earth.

Prevailing wind
The wind in Hawaii nearly always blows from the east. It brings heavy rain that makes the east-facing slopes of islands such as Molokai much wetter and greener than the western slopes.

Capital island
Most of the Hawaiian population lives on the island of Oahu, and especially in the Hawaiian capital city of Honolulu. This lies at the far southeastern end of a broad plain between two extinct volcanic peaks. Just west of Honolulu is Pearl Harbor, headquarters of the US Pacific Fleet, and site of the mainly aerial attack by the Japanese in December 1941 that brought the United States into World War II.

Hotspot chain

The Hawaiian islands form a long chain, created by volcanoes erupting from a hotspot beneath a plate of the Earth's crust. The hotspot is stationary, but the Pacific plate is slipping slowly northeast. This carries each island off the hotspot so its volcano becomes extinct. As it cools it subsides, and the oldest islands northeast of Kauai have sunk below the waves.

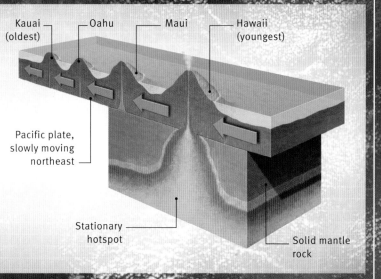

Kauai (oldest)   Oahu   Maui   Hawaii (youngest)

Pacific plate, slowly moving northeast

Stationary hotspot

Solid mantle rock

Islands

Lying in the middle of the vast Pacific, the Hawaiian islands are among the most remote on Earth. Like most oceanic islands they were formed by volcanoes erupting from the ocean floor, although most of these are now extinct. Similar volcanoes support the coral atolls that dot the tropical oceans, while other islands are basically isolated fragments of continents.

Dormant threat
Maui is formed from two volcanoes. The bigger eastern one last erupted in 1790, but it is not officially extinct. The three nearby islands are part of the same volcanic group, separated by shallow seas.

Tropical seas
These islands lie in the trade wind belt of the tropical Pacific, where steady easterly winds build huge waves that crash on the windward shores. More sheltered coasts are fringed by glorious coral reefs.

Mighty volcanoes
The big island of Hawaii is dominated by two colossal volcanic peaks, Mauna Kea and Mauna Loa. Measured from its base on the ocean floor, Mauna Kea is more than 33,000 ft (10,000 m) high, which is higher than Mount Everest. Mauna Loa—the island's dark central peak—last erupted in 1984, but Kilauea on its southern flank has been erupting continuously since 1983 and is one of the most active volcanoes on Earth.

Continental islands
Most of the islands that lie just off continental coasts are parts of the continents themselves. They have been created by waves destroying weaker rocks that linked them to the mainland, or cut off by rising sea levels. This island off southern Ireland was once attached to the headland in the foreground, and during the last ice age Ireland itself was attached to mainland Europe, along with the rest of Britain.

Coral atoll
In the tropics, volcanic islands become surrounded by reefs of living coral. When their volcanoes stop erupting, the islands cool and start sinking, but the coral keeps growing to stay near the surface, forming low coral islands. Over time, the coral forms a barrier reef around a shallow lagoon with just the peak of the original island visible—as here at Bora Bora, Tahiti. Eventually even this peak will disappear, leaving a ring-shaped coral atoll.

Islands and evolution
Living conditions on an island favor particular features of the animals and plants that live there, so over time these features become more common. Since the animals and plants are cut off from their relatives on the mainland they cannot interbreed with them, so they gradually evolve in different ways. Eventually this process may result in the evolution of unique island species like this 550-lb (250-kg) Galapagos giant tortoise.

Volcanoes

Boiling up from below Hawaii, this cascade of molten lava is helping to build one of the biggest volcanoes on Earth. These fiery mountains erupt over hotspots beneath the crust, from spreading rifts, or from earthquake zones where the plates of the crust grind together. Some erupt like this one, but others explode with catastrophic violence.

Fire fountain

A searingly hot mixture of gas and molten basalt erupts from Kilauea like soda from a shaken bottle. The lava is squeezed up by the colossal weight of Earth's crust, and blown into the sky by gas pressure.

Molten rock

Volcanic craters are enlarged fissures that allow molten rock to erupt from the mantle below the crust. The mantle is very hot, but normally kept solid by the extreme pressure at depth. If a fissure or rift releases some of the pressure, the rock melts and is squeezed up to the surface. Water carried down into the mantle by the moving plates of the crust has a similar effect, because it makes the hot rock melt more easily.

Shield volcano

The volcanoes of Hawaii are created from layers of liquid lava that erupt from a deep magma chamber and flow a long way before they cool to solid rock. The layers form shallow slopes that cover a broad area, like a shield. Volcanoes that erupt stickier lava, solid rocks, and volcanic ash form the much steeper cones typical of regions such as Central America and Indonesia.

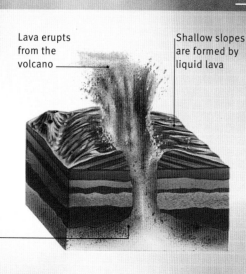

Lava erupts from the volcano

Shallow slopes are formed by liquid lava

Magma chamber

Gas clouds

Erupting volcanoes release vast quantities of gas, especially water vapor, carbon dioxide, and sulphur compounds. Here, water vapor is turning to steam as it billows into the cold air.

Scorched earth

Molten lava spilling out over the landscape incinerates everything in its path. As it cools the lava from this oceanic hotspot volcano turns to black basalt, creating broad, bleak lava fields of bare rock.

Red-hot river

The lava that erupts from Kilauea and similar oceanic volcanoes is molten basalt from below the ocean floor. It is very liquid, flowing down the flanks of the volcano in fast-running rivers of fire. Lava from other types of volcano tends to be stickier, so it does not flow far. Gas cannot escape through it so easily, so pressure builds up and causes explosive eruptions that are far more dangerous than the lava flows seen here.

Pyroclastic flows

Some eruptions produce red-hot avalanches of rock and dust called pyroclastic flows. They travel at deadly speed and have destroyed several cities with huge loss of life, including Pompeii in 79 CE and St. Pierre on Martinique in 1902. This flow is cascading down Soufrière Hills volcano on nearby Montserrat.

Ash clouds

Explosive volcanoes blast huge amounts of volcanic ash into the air. Its heat can make it rise high into the atmosphere, to be carried around the globe. Ash and gas from the 1815 eruption of Tambora in Indonesia affected world climates for three years, causing cold summers, crop failures, and famine.

Hot geysers

In volcanically active regions, groundwater often comes into contact with scorching hot rock. High pressure at depth stops it boiling, so it is heated to well over 212°F (100°C) until the water eventually explodes out of the ground as a geyser. Similar processes create hot springs and bubbling mud pools.

Undersea eruptions

The ocean floors are made of basalt rock that has erupted from submarine volcanoes. As each lava flow hits the near-freezing water it instantly solidifies on the outside. But the pressure of molten rock makes it burst open and squeeze out more lava, creating a series of rounded "pillow lavas" like these off Hawaii.

Storm surge
As a hurricane approaches land it pushes ocean water up into a storm surge that breaks over the shore like a tsunami. This usually causes far more damage than the wind and rain of the storm itself.

Hurricane Flossie
This satellite image of Hurricane Flossie in August 2007 clearly shows the huge clouds spiraling around the central eye of the storm, generating torrential rain and winds of up to 140 mph (230 kph) at its peak on August 12. Luckily the hurricane had weakened by the time its fringes brushed the southern shore of Hawaii on August 14, and within two days it had drifted west and blown itself out.

Weather

This hurricane building up over the Pacific Ocean near Hawaii is an extreme form of weather—the atmospheric turmoil that brings us wind, rain, snow, and more dramatic events such as thunderstorms. The weather is powered by the heat of the Sun, which drives the air currents that set the whole complex, chaotic mechanism in motion.

Heavy snow

Much of the moisture in clouds is made up of microscopic ice crystals that bond together to form snowflakes. As these fall into warmer air they generally melt into raindrops, but in cold climates or seasons they fall as snow. If this settles in deep layers and drifts, it can make normal life very difficult.

Electric charge

Where solar heating generates masses of water vapor, this can condense into huge storm clouds up to 9 miles (15 km) high. Powerful air currents toss ice crystals around inside the clouds, generating static electricity that builds up in the cloud until the multimillion-volt charge sparks to earth as lightning.

Storms and floods

Giant storm clouds contain a colossal weight of water, and if this falls in a concentrated area it can cause floods. Sometimes the water rises steadily as rivers overflow their banks, as here, but it can also rage down a valley in a torrential flash flood that carries off vehicles and buildings in a wave of destruction.

Inside a hurricane

The maelstrom of a hurricane is triggered by intense tropical sunshine heating the ocean and generating vast amounts of water vapor. This billows upward and condenses into enormous storm clouds. The rising air creates a zone of extremely low atmospheric pressure, and surrounding air swirls into this at high speed like water pouring down a drain. It spirals up around the core, or eye, of the storm creating a rising wall that spills out in the opposite direction at the top, but the eye of the hurricane is eerily calm.

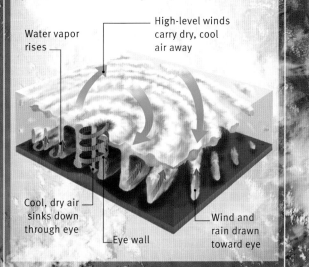

Water vapor rises

High-level winds carry dry, cool air away

Cool, dry air sinks down through eye

Eye wall

Wind and rain drawn toward eye

Tornadoes

The most violent weather events are the tornadoes that rip through the prairie states of the American midwest. They are spawned by rotating thunderstorms that suck air upward in a spinning vortex. As this tightens, the wind speed can build to 310 mph (500 kph) or more, destroying anything in its path.

Earth

Our planet began about 4.6 billion years ago as a ball of hot rock orbiting a young star. Luckily, Earth's gravity enabled it to retain an atmosphere, and its ideal distance from the hot Sun gave it just enough warmth to have oceans of liquid water. Between them, the rock, air, water, and solar energy provide the raw material of life—the thing that makes Earth so special.

Living planet

Life on Earth began some 3.8 billion years ago, but for 3 billion years it consisted of simple microbes such as bacteria. The first complex organisms appeared in the oceans 800 million years ago, and another 330 million years would pass before the first plants started to colonize the land. The earliest land animals evolved some 420 million years ago, and since then life in all its diversity has taken over the planet.

Vital clouds

Water evaporating from oceans forms clouds in the mobile lower atmosphere. This carries them over land, where they spill their moisture as rain. Without weather there could be no life on land.

Inside Earth

When Earth melted soon after it formed, most of the heavy iron and nickel in the molten rock sank to the center to form a metallic core. This is mainly molten, but intense pressure keeps the inner core solid. The mass of the core gives Earth enough gravity to hold on to its atmosphere. Most of the remaining rock formed the thick, hot, but solid mantle. The upper mantle is fused to the relatively thin, cool, brittle crust to form the lithosphere, which is kept constantly on the move by heat currents rising from near the core.

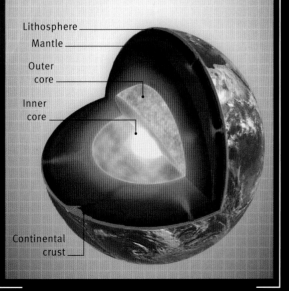

Lithosphere

Mantle

Outer core

Inner core

Continental crust

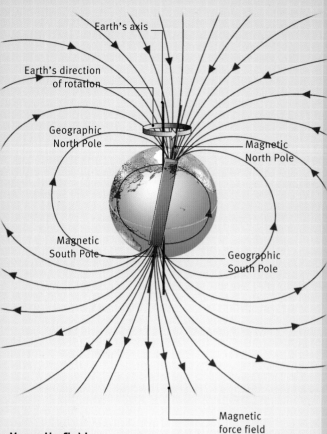

Earth's axis

Earth's direction of rotation

Geographic North Pole

Magnetic North Pole

Magnetic South Pole

Geographic South Pole

Magnetic force field

Magnetic field

Earth behaves like a giant bar magnet with a magnetic field that encircles the planet. This makes a compass needle point north—but not to the geographic north pole because the field is tilted at a slight angle to Earth's axis. The magnetism is probably generated by the mobile molten iron of the planet's outer core acting like an electromagnetic dynamo.

Atmosphere

The blue glow in this view of the horizon from the International Space Station is the densest part of the atmosphere—the air that we breathe. Mostly nitrogen and oxygen, it also contains carbon dioxide that retains heat and fuels the growth of plants. Without this insulating blanket, Earth's average temperature would be 86°F (30°C) lower and we would freeze each night.

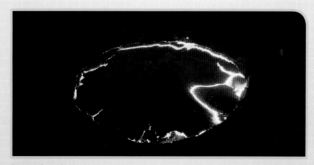

Deep heat

The crater of Erta Ale volcano in Ethiopia contains a lake of molten lava with a temperature of at least 1,832°F (1,000°C). The heat that keeps it liquid comes from deep inside the planet, which is still hot from its formation—and where the radioactive decay of heavy elements such as uranium generates energy like a huge natural nuclear reactor.

Light and heat
Sunlight warms the surface water and provides
microscopic plankton with energy to make food.
The warm water is lighter than the cold water
below, and floats above it. In cooler oceans the
surface water cools and sinks each winter, mixing
with deeper water containing the minerals also
needed by plankton. This does not happen in the
tropics because the surface water is always warm,
so there is far less plankton in tropical oceans.

Salty seas
Dissolved mineral salts have been
draining off the continents into the
oceans for billions of years. This is
why seawater is salty. Some of
these mineral salts are essential
nutrients for marine life.

Full support
Water is a very dense material, so animals such
as these killer whales float in it, and do not
have to support their own weight. This enables
some sea creatures to grow to colossal sizes.
The blue whale, for example, is the biggest
living animal and is twice the weight of the
largest known dinosaur. It weighs as much as
30 big African elephants. But in the water it
behaves as if it were practically weightless.

Oceans

The oceans cover two-thirds of the globe, to an average depth of more than
2 miles (3.5 km). They form a huge 3D living space, with a volume of about
319 million cubic miles (1,330 million cubic km). But they are not just vast
pools of water. The ocean floors, filling the gaps between the continents,
are made of different rock that erupts from deep within the planet.

Light zones

In the sunlit zone, from the surface to 650 ft (200 m) deep, light does not penetrate far before some is absorbed by the water, turning it blue. The blue light dims with depth, until there is not enough to support plantlike plankton. Fewer animals live in this twilight zone, although many visit daily from the sunlit zone. Below 3,280 ft (1,000 m) lies the dark zone, where any remaining sunlight fades out and the water is very cold. Many animals here are highly specialized.

Sunlit zone

Twilight zone

Dark zone

Sea and air

The oceans are rich in food. Most of the animals that eat it are marine creatures that live underwater, such as fish and squid. But they are also hunted by squadrons of seabirds like these gannets, which plunge headlong into the waves to seize their prey. Like most seabirds, they only return to land to breed.

Wind and wave

The waves that break on seashores are whipped up by winds dragging on the ocean surface. The broader the ocean and the stronger the winds, the bigger they get. Some of the biggest build up in the stormy Southern Ocean, but the record is held by a 88-ft (27-m) wave measured in the Gulf of Mexico in 2004.

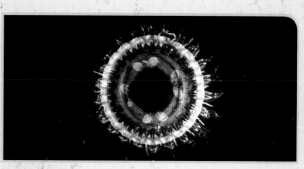

Living light

In the deep ocean, where little or no light filters down from the surface, many sea creatures provide their own. Animals like this deep-sea jellyfish glow with inner light produced by a chemical reaction within their special luminous organs. They use this bioluminescence to communicate with each other or attract prey.

Swirling currents

The surface waters of the oceans swirl around the globe in powerful currents driven by the winds. Near the poles, cold salty surface water also sinks to drive deepwater currents that flow over the ocean floors. All these currents are linked together in a complex pattern, which carries ocean water through all the oceans of the world. It continuously transfers heat from the tropical oceans to the polar regions.

Black smokers

The ocean floors are split by spreading rifts at mid-ocean ridges along the tectonic plate borders. Submarine volcanoes erupt vast quantities of molten basalt that freezes into cushion-shaped pillow lavas, while hydrothermal vents called "black smokers" spew plumes of mineral-rich water, heated by contact with the hot rock.

Permafrost

In the warmer parts of the Arctic much of the surface snow and ice melts in summer, so plants can grow in the thawed-out surface soil. But below the surface the ground stays frozen all year. Meltwater cannot drain through this permafrost layer, so the defrosted ground above stays swampy until it freezes again.

Glaciers

A glacier is made of snow that has become compacted into solid ice. Despite this, its weight exerts so much pressure that the ice deforms and cracks, allowing it to flow very slowly down slopes and valleys. It moves so slowly that it freezes to the rock, then rips it away as it moves on.

Icy past

Moving ice transforms the landscape, gouging deep valleys through mountains. At the height of the last ice age 20,000 years ago, ice sheets covered vast areas of northern Eurasia and North America, eventually retreating to leave ice-scoured terrain like this U-shaped glacial valley in Oregon, USA.

Ice-core analysis

Polar ice sheets are built up over thousands of years from layers of compressed snow that include bubbles of trapped air. A core sample drilled from deep within an ice sheet contains a record of the changing atmosphere. Analysis provides evidence of air temperature, and links between the atmosphere and climate.

Iceberg factories

In the coldest parts of the world many glaciers flow right down to the coast. As the ice pushes out over the sea, the glacier tends to crack up. Great slabs break off and tumble into the water to become icebergs.

Sea ice

This pancake ice is forming on the sea as the surface water freezes. Eventually, these ice rafts may freeze into a solid sheet, forming the thick pack ice that covers the polar oceans in winter.

Ice

In high mountains, and in the cold regions of the far north and south, the landscape is dominated by ice. Some forms as water freezes on contact with cold air, creating sheets of ice that cover rivers and seas. But most of the world's ice has formed from compacted snow, which builds up over many centuries to create glaciers and ice caps.

Snow to ice

Here in the Arctic—and on the frozen continent of Antarctica—only some of the snow that falls in winter melts away in summer. So each year the snow in the coldest places gets thicker and heavier, compressing the deeper layers into solid ice. Over thousands of years the ice builds up into glaciers that creep downhill under their own weight. In the coldest regions it forms huge ice sheets that smother whole landscapes.

Snowy peaks

The higher you climb, the colder it gets, so high mountains are often capped by snow that forms icy glaciers, even in the tropics. These flow downhill, often melting when they reach lower, warmer altitudes.

Drifting icebergs

The icebergs that drift away from crumbling coastal glaciers float with just one-ninth of their bulk above the surface. This means that they are much bigger than they look. Some are truly colossal, especially the broad tabular icebergs that break off Antarctic ice shelves. All icebergs eventually melt into the sea, but this takes a long time in near-freezing polar oceans, so they may drift a long way on the currents.

Highest peak

The biggest mountain range on Earth is the Himalayas, a massive crumple zone in the planet's crust created by the collision of India with Asia. The range includes all 100 of the world's highest mountains—including Mount Everest, the highest of all at 29,029 ft (8,848 m) above sea level.

Mighty half dome

Amazingly, some mountains such as Half Dome in California, USA originally formed deep underground, as molten magma boiled up and slowly solidified into very hard, granitic rock beneath layers of softer rock. Over time these softer layers wore away to reveal the granitic rock, which is more resistant to erosion.

Mountain wildlife

Although food is scarce at high altitudes, some animals such as this American mountain goat and the Eurasian ibex are specialized for life in the mountains. They have thick coats to resist the cold, and are extremely sure-footed. They are preyed upon by high-level hunters such as the Asian snow leopard.

Blue water

The lakes that form high in the mountains are generally very cold and pure, with few of the dissolved minerals that support microscopic life. As a result the water is often a beautiful clear blue, as in this lake high in the Peruvian Andes. Like many such lakes, it was gouged out of the rock by a glacier.

Shattered peaks
The highest peaks and crags are slowly crumbling away as they are splintered and shattered by the icy climate. But where mountains are still being pushed up, they may actually be getting higher.

Rocky remains
A long trail of dark rubble marks where two glaciers have merged on their way down the mountains. The mass of ice will carry the rubble down to valleys and seashores, and dump it to form layers of sediment. Under pressure, these layers will eventually turn into rock, which may be uplifted to create more mountains. They too will be ground down by ice and other forces of erosion in the relentless rhythm of the rock cycle.

Mountains

The world's mountain ranges are created by the same forces that trigger earthquakes and volcanoes. Rocks that formed on sea floors are buckled and thrust high into the sky. But even as they are being raised, mountains such as these in Alaska, USA, are ground down again by the relentless forces of erosion.

Mountain chill
The air is always colder high in the mountains, so in the near-Arctic climate of Alaska it is very cold indeed, especially in winter. Clouds swept in off the north Pacific Ocean spill their moisture as snow, which lies on the high peaks throughout the year. These barren snowfields are the birthplaces of spectacular glaciers that carve their way through the mountains, eroding their rocks and carrying the debris to the sea.

Living green
Conditions on the mountain slopes are so tough that only the hardiest plants can grow. In winter, they are buried by snow, but for a few months in summer plants can grow, flower, and set seed.

Lava layers
The Alaskan Wrangell Mountains are the remains of huge volcanoes that erupted less than 5 million years ago. Glaciers have sliced deep valleys in their flanks, revealing the layers of volcanic lava and ash that built their slopes. The peaks of the nearby St. Elias range are fold mountains, rucked up by the colossal force of the Pacific Ocean floor steadily plowing beneath the North American continent.

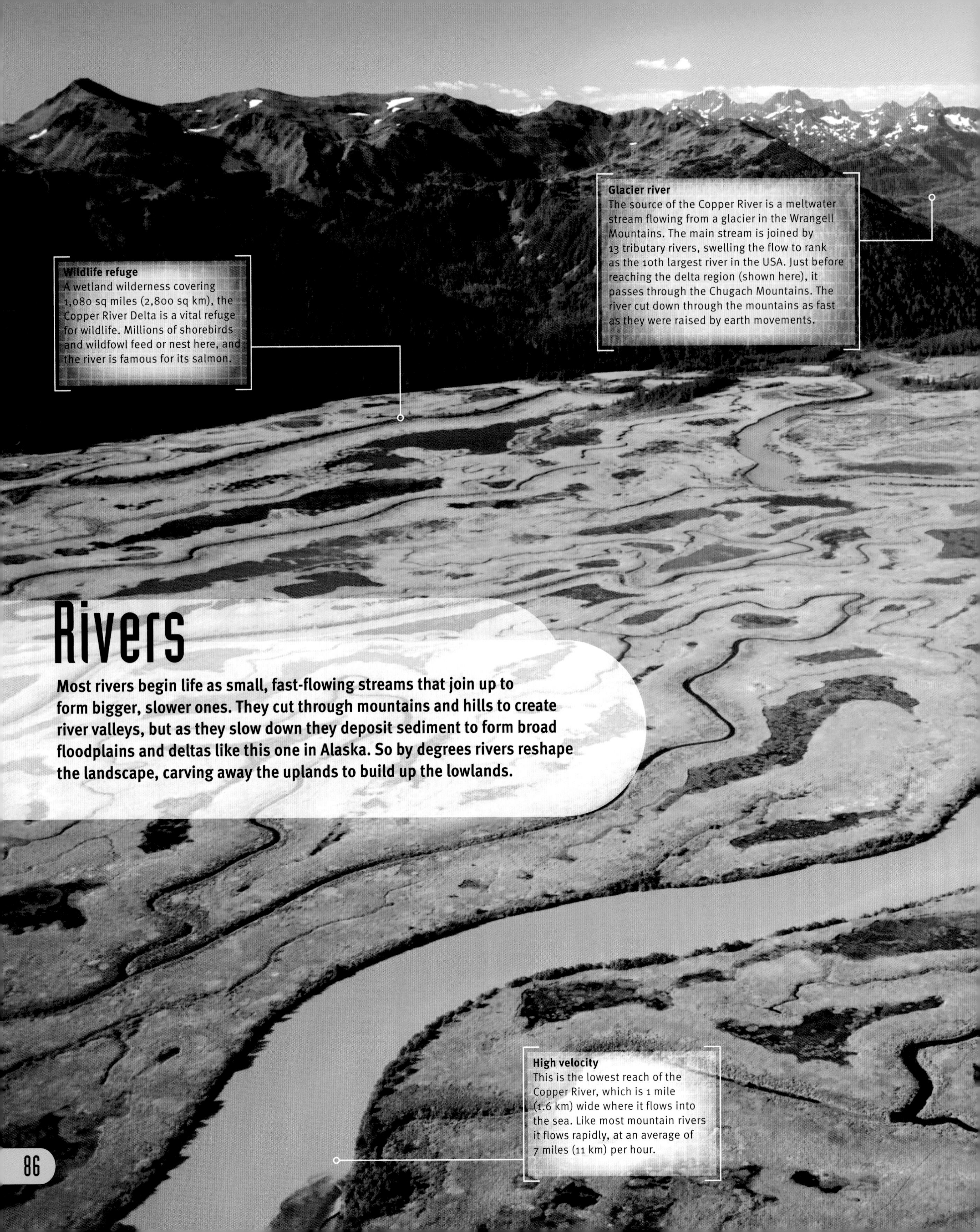

Rivers

Most rivers begin life as small, fast-flowing streams that join up to form bigger, slower ones. They cut through mountains and hills to create river valleys, but as they slow down they deposit sediment to form broad floodplains and deltas like this one in Alaska. So by degrees rivers reshape the landscape, carving away the uplands to build up the lowlands.

Wildlife refuge
A wetland wilderness covering 1,080 sq miles (2,800 sq km), the Copper River Delta is a vital refuge for wildlife. Millions of shorebirds and wildfowl feed or nest here, and the river is famous for its salmon.

Glacier river
The source of the Copper River is a meltwater stream flowing from a glacier in the Wrangell Mountains. The main stream is joined by 13 tributary rivers, swelling the flow to rank as the 10th largest river in the USA. Just before reaching the delta region (shown here), it passes through the Chugach Mountains. The river cut down through the mountains as fast as they were raised by earth movements.

High velocity
This is the lowest reach of the Copper River, which is 1 mile (1.6 km) wide where it flows into the sea. Like most mountain rivers it flows rapidly, at an average of 7 miles (11 km) per hour.

Spring torrents

Torrents pouring off the Alaskan mountains and foothills during the spring thaw carry masses of sand and silt into the river. This then deposits the sediments in its lower valley, or carries them out to sea.

Fertile plains

Rivers naturally overflow their banks after heavy rain or when deep snow is melting. The floodwater spilling out over the landscape stops moving, and all the sediment carried in the flowing water settles out. Over the years this builds up a broad, fertile floodplain that fills the river valley. Near the coast a similar process can create a delta, with many streams running over its surface toward the sea.

White water

Some rivers tumble over cliffs in spectacular waterfalls. These are often created when a river flows from hard rock to much softer rock. It cuts down through the soft rock, but the hard rock survives and the river cascades over the precipice—as here at Iguazu Falls on the border of Brazil and Argentina.

Deep gorges

All rivers create valleys, but some flow through dramatic sheer-sided gorges. They may be eroded by floodwater torrents carving the rock into sculpted formations like these on the Galana River in Kenya. Others form when the land surface is slowly pushed up, forcing the river to cut down through it.

Meanders

As a river wanders over a plain, its flow cuts away the banks on the outside of bends while building them up on the inside. The bends become more acute, creating a series of meanders. Eventually the river may cut through an extreme meander, isolating it as an oxbow lake like this one on the Amazon.

Tidal estuaries

Ultimately most rivers flow into the sea. A fast-flowing river may build up a delta at its mouth, but many rivers flow more slowly and are stopped altogether by the rising tide. Combined with the effect of salt water, this makes them dump sediment to form the broad, gleaming mudflats of a tidal estuary.

Soil

Most plants such as these trees grow in a mixture of rock fragments and organic remains that we call soil. This supplies them with the water and dissolved chemicals that are vital to their survival. Some types of soil have more of these plant nutrients than others. This influences the plants that can grow in them, and the whole character of the living landscape.

Rich grassland soil

Prairies and steppe grasslands have naturally deep, fertile soils. They formed over the course of thousands of years from the decaying remains of dead grasses and other plants. Most of this natural grassland is now used for growing farm crops such as wheat, barley, or maize, but since the crops are harvested before they can decay and feed the soil with nutrients, the fields need to be fertilized artificially.

Bog peat

In wet climates where the ground is waterlogged, dead vegetation cannot rot down properly. It builds up, forming layers of half-decayed peat instead of normal soil. If this is kept wet by rainwater, it forms acidic peat bogs, which are so infertile that only specially adapted plants such as bog mosses can grow in them. On this Irish bog, peat is cut and dried so it can be used as fuel.

Taking root

When plants of some kind have taken root and soil starts forming, other plants can move in. The first plants' roots stabilize the young soil, and their leaves fall and decay to build up its depth and fertility.

Soil formation

Most soils are a mixture of mineral fragments and the remains of dead organisms. The mineral fragments are either broken-up bedrock or transported sediment such as sand or gravel. Most of the organic remains are plants broken down by fungi and bacteria. This organic matter collects on the surface, and is mixed into the soil by burrowing earthworms. Rainwater carries dissolved nutrients downward, while rising groundwater may carry them up from the bedrock.

Organic matter

Mixed topsoil

Infertile subsoil

Rainwater

Mineral layer

Groundwater

Bedrock

Fertility boost

Fine silt particles suspended in river water are normally carried far downstream. But if the river floods it forms a broad, shallow lake of virtually still water. The silt sinks to settle on the land, and when the flood recedes the silt is left behind. This usually increases the fertility of the soil by adding plant nutrients, and is one reason why the plant growth in a river valley is relatively lush and green.

Starting over

Flash floods can carry away soil, stripping the landscape back to barren sand or rock. Then the whole soil-forming process starts over again. But the stripped soil may add to soil depth elsewhere.

Heathland soil

If the soil contains a lot of sand or gravel, rainwater drains through it easily, carrying along dissolved plant nutrients with it. This creates a barren, acid soil that most plants cannot thrive in. It is taken over by specialized plants such as the colorful heather and gorse in flower on this coastal heath in Britain. The natural vegetation found in an area is often the best indicator of soil type.

Volcanic soil

Unlike heathland soil, soil derived from mineral-rich volcanic lava is usually very fertile. This makes it ideal for crops such as these grapevines. So although the slopes of volcanoes can be dangerous places, they are often intensively farmed. The vineyards on the flanks of Mount Etna in Sicily are considered the best on the island, though many have been destroyed by lava flows.

Total breakdown

When an earthquake hits a city, it doesn't just make buildings fall down. It brings down power lines, ruptures water and gas supply pipes, and disrupts road and railway access. This makes rescue much more difficult, and often forces people to leave their houses even if they are still intact. Leaking gas pipes can also cause disastrous fires, like those that swept through San Francisco after the earthquake of 1906.

Earthquake-proof?

New buildings, bridges, and other structures in earthquake-prone cities are built with strong steel frames to resist collapse. But even these may fall over if the ground subsides beneath them.

Repair bill

The Kobe earthquake lasted just 20 seconds, but it caused more than $101 billion worth of damage. It was many months before the rubble was cleared away and rebuilding began.

Earthquakes

The plates of the Earth's crust are always moving, causing earth tremors along the fault lines that divide them. But if a fault is locked firmly together so it cannot slip easily, the tension builds up over many years. Eventually something snaps, causing a catastrophic earthquake like the one that devastated the the busy port city of Kobe, Japan, in 1995.

Demolition day
More than 200,000 buildings were destroyed by the 1995 Kobe earthquake. Most of these were timber-framed buildings that gave way as the ground shifted beneath them. Many had heavy tiled roofs that collapsed on the occupants, and altogether more than 4,600 people died. During earthquakes few casualties are caused by the earth movement itself. Most of the dead and injured are crushed by collapsing buildings.

Aftershock
After the Kobe earthquake ended, people were afraid to return home because of the many aftershocks that struck the city. Kobe has now been rebuilt, but it has never regained its former importance.

Anatomy of an earthquake

The focus of an earthquake is deep underground, at a point on a locked fault. Here the rock on the right of the fault is being forced up, but the fault was locked. Suddenly it has given way, so all the upward movement happens within a few seconds instead of gradually over many years. This generates the shock waves that we experience as an earthquake.

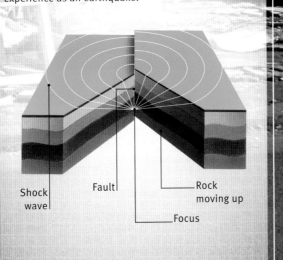

Shock wave — Fault — Rock moving up — Focus

Tsunami

Earthquakes often occur beneath the sea, shifting parts of the seabed. As the rocks lurch up or down they transfer the shock to the water, creating a huge wave that sweeps ashore as a tsunami. It can swamp vast areas with catastrophic effects, as here on the coast of Thailand after the 2004 Asian Tsunami.

Cracking up

During an earthquake, one part of Earth's crust moves relative to another along a fault line. This generates the shock waves that shake the land, but also physically cracks up the ground surface. Some cracks pull apart, as here, but others shift sideways, or move up or down to create steps in the landscape.

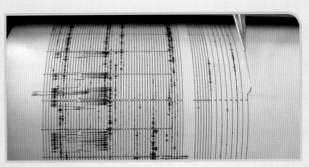

Shock waves

Earthquake shock waves are recorded by instruments called seismographs. These are so sensitive that they can even detect tremors on the other side of the globe. The intensity of an earthquake is usually measured on the Moment Magnitude Scale, which has replaced the less accurate Richter Scale.

New horizons

Some earthquakes have dramatically changed the landscape. During the 1964 Alaskan earthquake the Pacific floor slid 66 ft (20 m) beneath Alaska, raising the shore by up to 33 ft (10 m). It lifted an offshore reef right out of the water, complete with this ship that was wrecked on the reef in 1942.

Plate tectonics

Slicing across the arid Carrizo Plain of California, the San Andreas Fault marks a boundary between two moving plates of the Earth's crust. As they slip past each other they reshape the landscape while unleashing the forces that cause earthquakes. Over millions of years, similar tectonic movements have built mountains, fueled volcanoes, and dragged continents around the globe.

Fold mountains
The uplands around the San Andreas Fault have been raised by the same titanic earth movements that make the tectonic plates grind past each other at the fault line itself. The pressure squeezes the crust so it buckles and folds, pushing up long mountain ranges. These are etched with stream beds and valleys that hide the original fold pattern, but this can be seen within the rock strata.

Sliding fault
The San Andreas Fault is a transform fault—a boundary where two tectonic plates slide past each other. The land to the west of the fault is part of the Pacific Plate, which is sliding northwest relative to the land on the east, on the North American Plate. Where the fault creeps steadily, it causes frequent small earth tremors. But where it has locked, the tension builds until it is released by a big earthquake.

Crumpled ground
The rocks on this side of the fault line have been rucked up into a series of ridges by the force of the fault movement. The same is happening on the other side, in the opposite direction.

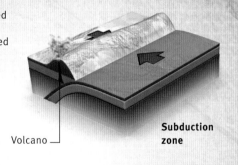

Offset valley
This stream once flowed straight across the fault. But the section on the right has been shifted (toward the camera) by the fault movement, so the stream bed now has a big kink following the fault line.

Plate boundaries

The plates of the Earth's crust are dragged around by heat currents in the mantle below. At mid-ocean ridges they are pulled apart to form spreading rifts. In other places the plates are pushing together—one grinds beneath another to form a subduction zone, which pushes up mountains and volcanoes. They can also slide past each other at transform faults such as the San Andreas Fault.

Volcano

Subduction zone

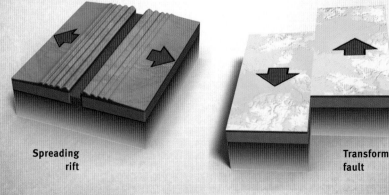

Spreading rift

Transform fault

Continental drift

As the plates that make up Earth's crust shift slowly around the globe, they carry the continents with them. Over millions of years they crash together and pull apart, changing the face of the planet. Some 250 million years ago they came together to form the supercontinent of Pangaea. During the dinosaur era this split up (right) and eventually the continents we know today took shape.

Tectonic world

The Earth's crust is a shifting jigsaw of tectonic plates. Some are immense while others are too small to show up on this map. Green lines show boundaries where the plates are moving apart at spreading rifts, and red lines show where they are pushing together. Blue lines mark sliding transform boundaries.

Spreading rift

This rock wall on Iceland marks one side of the Mid-Atlantic ridge, a spreading rift in the ocean floor that is pushing the Americas away from Europe and Africa. Here the ocean floor has been thrust up above sea level by the rising plume of heat that also fuels the island's volcanoes and geysers.

Subduction zone

This view from space shows part of the Aleutian Island chain that curves across the globe from Alaska to Siberia. It marks a plate boundary where the Pacific Ocean floor is pushing under the Bering Sea. The subduction of one plate beneath the other has triggered the eruption of volcanoes, forming the island arc.

Climate zones

Different regions of the world have dramatically different climates. This is partly because the Sun's rays are most intense in the tropics, making them much warmer than regions nearer the poles. The difference in temperature drives air currents in the atmosphere that make some regions very wet, while others like this North American desert barely get enough rain to support life.

Joshua tree
The tough water-retaining foliage of the Joshua tree is typical of many desert plants, which must survive months without rain. It only grows in the Mojave Desert—a region cut off from moist Pacific winds by the Sierra Nevada mountains, creating a rain-shadow desert. Other deserts like the vast Sahara don't receive much rain because they lie in zones where global airflow creates sinking dry air, which stops clouds forming.

Spiny survivors
Unlike some deserts, the Mojave does get some rainfall. This supports woody, slow-growing shrubs such as sagebrush and creosote bush, as well as the Joshua tree. The American deserts are also famous for their cacti— spiny plants that soak up water during rare rainstorms and store it in their fleshy stems. The plants provide food for animals such as jack rabbits and tortoises.

Tropical rainforest
Near the equator, intense heat evaporates huge amounts of water from the oceans, forming giant storm clouds that move over land and spill torrential rain. This fuels the growth of dense rainforest like this, in Borneo. The forests also produce vast quantities of water vapor, forming more clouds and rain. Life flourishes in the warmth and moisture, making rainforests the most populated and richly diverse habitats on Earth.

Oceanic air
The cool, rainy climate of western Ireland is created by moist winds sweeping in off the Atlantic ocean, which encourage the growth of lush green grass. Further east, the natural vegetation of this oceanic temperate climate is deciduous woodland, with trees such as oak, beech, and hazel. This forest zone extends east across Europe until the effect of the oceans fades and the trees give way to dry grassland.

Desert skies

The cloudless sky allows the Sun to beat down all day, evaporating the moisture in the ground. By night the lack of cloud allows heat to escape into space, so desert nights are surprisingly cold.

Barren rock

Most deserts have large areas of bare rock, and some have vast "sand seas" of drifting dunes. This is because the climate is too dry for the dense plant growth that would create a stable soil.

World climates

The world's climate zones tend to lie in distinct bands around the globe. Tropical rainforest near the equator is flanked by tropical grasslands and then deserts. Temperate zones support forests that fade to grasslands in drier regions. In the north there is a broad band of mainly evergreen taiga forest, which gives way to treeless tundra and permanent ice in the high Arctic.

- Tundra and ice
- Taiga forest
- Mountains
- Temperate forest
- Arid scrub
- Desert
- Temperate grassland
- Tropical grassland
- Tropical forest

Steppes and prairies

Where the climate is too dry for dense forests to grow, the natural landscape is taken over by grass. Outside the tropics this dry prairie or steppe develops in the heart of great continents, such as here in the landlocked country of Mongolia in Asia. This type of land covers vast areas, but in many countries much of it has been turned into farmland. The summers can be baking hot, but temperatures plummet as the continents cool down in winter.

Arctic tundra

Beyond the northern limit of the evergreen taiga forest lies the tundra—a region of dark, freezing winters where big trees cannot grow. Much of the ground is rocky and barren, but tough mosses, grasses, and low-growing "arctic-alpine" plants manage to cling to life and flower during the brief summer. On higher ground, and in Greenland, the ground is buried beneath sheets of ice, preventing any plant growth at all.

Mineral crystals

Rocks are made up of natural chemical compounds called minerals. If these are melted or dissolved and allowed to cool or dry slowly, they tend to form gemlike crystals. These are natural crystals of quartz, which is a major ingredient of continental rocks and the main component of sand.

Igneous rocks

When molten lava or magma cools and solidifies, it forms hard rock made of interlocking crystals. The longer this igneous rock takes to cool, the bigger its crystals. The big pink feldspar crystals in this granite show that it cooled very slowly, deep underground. It also contains a lot of quartz and dark mica.

Cemented grains

Sedimentary rocks are composed of separate grains cemented together, instead of interlocking crystals. They often erode easily, as shown above in Bryce Canyon, Utah, USA, since the "cement" is rarely as strong as mineral grains. In time, the rocks become stronger and ancient sedimentary rocks are much harder.

Heat and pressure

Volcanic activity or massive earth movements can transform rocks by subjecting them to intense heat or pressure. These metamorphic rocks include marble, which was once limestone, and very hard gneiss (above), which originated as soft, stratified sedimentary rock. The dark bands are compressed strata.

Rocks

Earth's crust is made of the mixtures of minerals we call rocks. Many rocks form as molten lava or magma cools and crystallizes. Others, such as these rocks in the Mojave Desert, USA, are hardened sediments such as sand. Some are transformed by heat and pressure into metamorphic rocks studded with crystals.

Rock strata
Sedimentary rocks start as layers of soft sediment such as mud or sand, often created by the erosion of other rocks. Sediment may be blown on the wind, but usually it is laid down by flowing water or on seabeds. As conditions change, different layers are deposited on top of each other. These are compressed over millions of years into solid rock, but the layers survive as different types of rock strata.

Stream sediments
This layer of red rock was once the sandy bed of an ancient river. Channel sandstones like this often preserve clues to their formation, such as ripple marks that were created by the water flow.

Volcanic ash
The grains within most sedimentary rocks are all much the same size because they were sorted by the water flow that deposited them. Yet some rocks contain big particles as well as small ones. This pale rock formed from river sand mixed with very fine ash and lumps of hot rock blown from the crater of a long-extinct volcano. The mixture has become cemented into a mass of rock made up of many thin layers.

Wind-blown sand
Some sedimentary rocks form on dry land. If this sandstone were put under a microscope, it would show that it is made up of sand grains with the distinctive "frosted" look of wind-blown sand.

Ancient dunes
This sandstone made of wind-blown sand was once a desert sand dune, formed when the region was even drier than it is now. These dunes creep slowly across the landscape as sand grains are blown up from behind and tumble down the face of the dune. This creates curved sand layers that are preserved in dunes that turn to solid rock, making them easy to recognize.

Fossils

All fossils are the remains or traces of dead animals or plants that have survived the normal process of destruction and decay. They are usually found in sedimentary rocks, where they have been turned to stone over millions of years. Normally only tough tissues fossilize, such as the skull of this extinct marine reptile, but sometimes soft tissues are preserved too.

Giant skull
Preserved almost intact in the rock, this is the fossilized skull of *Mosasaurus*, an immensely powerful marine reptile that lived toward the end of the age of dinosaurs. Skulls are particularly strong, so they tend to survive when other parts of the skeleton are destroyed. Comparing it with the skulls of modern reptiles allows scientists to work out how the animal would have looked in life, and how it lived.

Killer teeth
Teeth fossilize well, and are often all that is left of an extinct animal. Luckily they also tell scientists a lot about how the animal lived. In this case the sharp teeth are those of a fearsome hunter.

Fossil record
Most of the fossils that are found are of sea creatures like this ammonite—an extinct, shelled relative of cuttlefish and squid. Such fossils are so common that geologists can see how their shell details changed with time. They can then use this knowledge to date the rocks the fossils are found in. The first-ever geological map was created in 1815 by using fossils to work out which rocks were the same age, older, or younger.

Trace fossils
Some fossils are not the actual remains of living things, but traces of where they have been. They include dinosaur footprints such as this one, originally left in soft mud in what is now northeast Spain. Such prints tell us not only about the animals' feet, but also how long their stride was, and how fast they could move. Some even show big and small dinosaurs walking together, possibly in families.

Intact skeleton

These neck bones are all joined together as they would have been in life. But fossil bones are often scattered, with many missing, which can make reconstructing a skeleton far more difficult.

Fossil-bearing rock

Most fossils are found in rocks that originally formed underwater as beds of soft sediment in lakes and seas. This is why fossils of aquatic animals are more common than those of land animals.

Turned to stone

Most animal remains are destroyed by other animals and decay organisms. But sometimes an animal dies and its body is rapidly buried by mud or similar sediment. The airless conditions slow down the decay process, and dissolved minerals seep into the tissues and slowly turn them to stone. Over time, the soft sediment around them turns to rock too, protecting the fossil until it is exposed by erosion.

Mosasaurus

One of the most powerful hunters that ever lived, *Mosasaurus* was a giant oceanic relative of modern monitor lizards, and grew to at least 49 ft (15 m) long. It lived at the same time as *Tyrannosaurus rex*, and its colossal jaws and teeth would have made it an equally terrifying predator. It probably hunted other marine reptiles, as well as big fish and other sea creatures.

Deep, flat-sided tail made the reptile a powerful swimmer

Long, powerful jaws lined with broad, sharp teeth

Lucky survival

Usually all the soft tissue in an animal's body decays before it has time to become fossilized. But sometimes some is preserved, especially if the animal falls into soft mud where there is no oxygen to support decay organisms. This fossil of the small dinosaur *Archaeopteryx* shows clear evidence of feathers, and their form makes it almost certain that the animal could fly, making it one of the first birds.

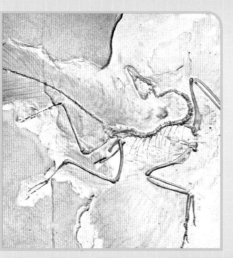

Rebuilding the past

Most fossils are stored away in boxes and drawers, but the best are displayed in museums. Some fossils can be reconstructed into whole skeletons, like this spectacular *Tyrannosaurus rex*. Careful examination of the bones shows how they fitted together. It can also reveal how the muscles of the living animal were arranged, meaning that scientists can work out and rebuild its original appearance.

Erosion

This towering cliff on the coast of Corsica has been created by the forces of erosion—the process that wears away the land and steadily reduces even the highest mountains to low-lying plains. Here, most of the erosion has been caused by the sea, but the land can also be eroded by flowing water, ice, and even the wind.

Shattered by ice

In cold climates, water that seeps into rock fissures freezes at night, expanding and forcing the cracks apart. By day the ice melts, so more water gets in, freezes and expands, until eventually the rock shatters. The moving, rock-studded ice of glaciers has an even more erosive effect, gouging huge scars in the landscape.

Wind and sand

Desert winds pick up sand grains and hurl them at exposed rock like an industrial sand-blaster. This carves away the softer strata faster than harder layers, sometimes creating strange rock sculptures like these in Utah, USA. Wind by itself has no effect, so wind erosion occurs only in dry, sandy terrain.

Tumbling water

Flowing water etches deep valleys, especially where it is flowing fast, but it gets much of its erosive power from rocks and sand that are suspended or tossed around in the flow. These potholes in a South African riverbed have been ground out of the rock by stones swirled round and round by floodwater torrents.

Soil erosion

It's not just rock that is affected by erosion; storms and floods can sweep away soil as well, especially where it is left exposed by the removal of the plants that hold it together. This catastrophic soil erosion in Brazil was a direct result of the destruction of the tropical rainforest by cutting down the trees.

Rockfall
The horizontal layers in the cliff are formed of slightly different sedimentary rock strata. Some are harder than others, so they resist erosion for longer. Over time the softer layers are worn away, undercutting the harder ones, which are left jutting out and eventually collapse for lack of support, tumbling down the cliff to the shore below. Even the hardest rocks are gradually destroyed by this process.

Crumbling strata
The softer strata are often reduced to fine sand, which constantly falls away as the rock is pounded by the waves. Fossils made of harder minerals are gradually exposed as the surrounding rock crumbles.

Wavepower
During storms waves break on the shore with a force of up to 5,000 lb per sq ft (25,000 kg per sq m). Water driven into fissures in the rock compresses the air inside, and as each wave retreats the air expands again with explosive force, blasting fragments of rock off the crevice walls. The waves pick up the fragments and hurl them at the cliff, adding to the demolition effect.

Boulders and pebbles
Big boulders are tossed around by storm waves until they break into smaller ones. Their sharp corners are worn away by the constant battering, creating the rounded pebbles of a stony beach.

Coasts

The seashore is a dynamic frontier, relentlessly reshaped by the action of the sea. In some places the land is cut back as wave-exposed shores like this Mediterranean coastline are battered by storms. In other places the debris dislodged by waves is swept into beaches and banks that extend the shore, building up the land and leaving former coasts cut off from the sea.

Wildlife refuge
The maritime plants that grow on sea cliffs are specially adapted to survive the salty spray that would kill most plants. In spring and early summer the cliffs are also colonized by breeding seabirds.

Rocky cliffs
Hard rock like this limestone often forms high cliffs that are slowly cut back by wave action. The rock debris falls into the sea, which eventually carries it away and builds it up into beaches elsewhere.

Shallow seas
As the waves cut back the cliffs, the rock beneath the sea surface survives as a wave-cut platform, often covered by debris. Over millions of years this process has created the continental shelves that fringe the world's landmasses. The water on the shelves gets deeper offshore, but is never more than 490 ft (150 m) deep. These shallow, sunlit shelf seas are much richer in wildlife than the deep, dark oceans beyond.

Battered headlands

The most exposed parts of the shore are the headlands of very hard rock that survive the battering of stormy seas. Everything soft or detached is stripped away, and only the toughest marine wildlife can survive as the full force of the waves scours the rock and tosses the boulders around. But these headlands provide shelter for other parts of the coast, creating quiet havens that are often used as natural harbors.

Sheltered bay

This beautiful bay on the south coast of England has been created by waves breaching a wall of hard rock and eroding the softer rock behind it. Some of the hard rock survives as two headlands, sheltering the waters of the bay within. Sand and shingle have been able to build up to form a beach because there is less wave energy inside the bay, and the calm, sheltered, shallow water makes a fine anchorage for small boats.

Losing battle

Cliffs of soft rock are easily cut back by the waves, and this can be a problem for coastal communities. This house was originally built a long way from the cliff, but many years of cliff falls have brought it closer to the edge until it has finally started collapsing into the sea. Massive concrete sea defenses

Stacks and arches
Breaking waves soon find the weaknesses in cliffs, crumbling the softer or fractured rock first. This often leaves harder rocks isolated as headlands or promontaries. Since these are more exposed they are attacked too, and as the weaker parts crumble they sometimes leave isolated stacks and rock arches. They make ideal nesting sites for seabirds, since land predators such as foxes cannot get at them.

Tidal shores

On most coasts the water level rises and falls twice a day. These tides are caused mainly by the gravity of the Moon, which pulls ocean water into a very slight oval shape. As the Earth spins on its axis, any point on the seashore passes through both tidal bulges every day, causing two high tides separated by two low tides. These can dramatically change the appearance of the shore as the water level rises and falls.

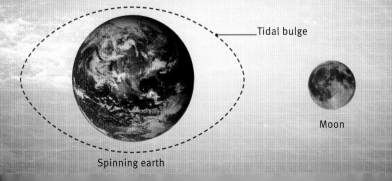

Tidal bulge

Moon

Spinning earth

Dissolving rock
All rainwater is slightly acidic. When it seeps down through cracks in alkaline limestone, it slowly dissolves the rock to form potholes. Streams tumble into these and keep flowing below ground, enlarging fissures into complex cave systems. Narrow passages link yawning caverns opened up by rockfalls. Spectacular natural sculptures created by mineral-rich water dripping into the caves adorn these caverns.

Dark refuges
Many caves were used as shelters by people during the last ice age. We know this because they left tools and other artifacts in them, as well as wonderfully graphic paintings on the cave walls.

Caves

Some of the most dramatic natural landscapes lie in places that never see the sunlight—deep underground in caves. Limestone caves such as this one are extraordinary places with vast, echoing caverns festooned with strange rock formations. Yet caves can form in many other ways, in solid rock, ice, or even the molten lava that erupts from volcanoes.

105

Caving in

Limestone caves usually form deep underground, but over time parts of the cave may open up, allowing sunlight to flood in. Sometimes a whole cave network collapses, creating a deep limestone gorge.

Chemical reaction

As water erodes limestone caves it becomes saturated with dissolved lime, or calcite. When it drips into an airy cavern, a reaction with the air makes the water deposit some of the calcite as a solid mineral. This gradually builds up into floor-standing stalagmites, hanging stalactites, flowstones such as these, and other formations. The process is very slow and may take tens of thousands of years.

Crystal cave

Mineral-rich water flowing into caves may evaporate to leave glittering crystals of pure calcite or other minerals. Deep in the Naica silver mine in Mexico, miners discovered a natural cave containing huge gypsum crystals up to 36 ft (11 m) long—the largest ever found—and up to half a million years old.

Coastal caves

Caves often form on rocky seashores as waves undermine the cliffs. On tidal shores they are usually flooded at high water, but as the tide level falls many become accessible from the beach. Some sea caves are now high above even the highest tide, because the sea level has fallen since they were formed.

Glacier caves

Meltwater flowing from beneath glaciers creates long tunnels through the ice. Sunlight filtering through the ice turns the walls of these glacier caves a glorious translucent blue, so they are among the most beautiful of all caves. However, shifting ice and meltwater torrents make them very dangerous to explore.

Lava tubes

Molten rock erupting from volcanoes, such as those on Hawaii, pour down the slopes in rivers of fire. These can solidify on the outside while lava is still flowing through them. If all the lava flows out, it leaves long, tubular lava caves. Some contain weird rock formations created by the torrents of lava.

A bustling city scene is reflected by Anish Kapoor's giant *Cloud Gate* sculpture in Chicago.

PEOPLE AND PLACES

Thanks to our amazing adaptability and ingenuity, we humans have colonized virtually every part of the planet. In the process we have created a colorful kaleidoscope of nations, each with its own character and customs.

▲

Cities

Cities are centers of government, culture, and commerce, and home to more than half of the world's people. With 20 million residents, Shanghai is the largest city in the world's most populous country, China. In the 1980s, the Pudong area was mainly farmland, but it has been rapidly developed into an ultra-modern business district that towers over nearby residential zones.

Space-age icon
The Oriental Pearl is part of Shanghai's famously futuristic skyline. This 1,535-ft (468-m) tower houses viewing platforms, museums, restaurants, and the city's most expensive apartments.

Trading history
Cities are often located near rivers. Shanghai's position at the mouth of the Yangtze helped it to grow from a fishing village to an international trading hub and one of the world's busiest ports.

International heritage
In the early 1900s, Shanghai became a magnet for European trading companies, who brought their architecture with them. The Customs House clock tower is modeled on the UK's Big Ben.

Green spaces
City planners are developing green areas to improve quality of life for Shanghai's residents. Trees and plants filter pollution, cool the urban environment, and capture carbon dioxide.

Bustling Bund
Cities are collections of districts, each with a distinct identity. The Bund has been developed as a tourist zone, with a 1.2-mile (2-km) riverside promenade that offers sweeping views of Pudong.

Building boom

Every year Shanghai's housing and office space increases by an area the size of Amsterdam. The pace of this development is fastest here in Pudong district, where cranes litter the landscape.

Making money

The Lujiazui Financial and Trade Zone is a center for international business in China. Many companies have headquarters here, helping this to become one of the world's wealthiest areas.

Vertical city

City land is expensive, so the best way to get more space is to build upward. The Shanghai skyline features more than 30 super-tall skyscrapers—buildings more than 656 ft (200 m) tall—including many futuristic designs. The 127-floor Shanghai Tower will be the world's third tallest building when completed in 2014. Shaped like a twisted triangle, the building will have a "double skin"—two glass walls that work like a thermos flask to reduce energy use. Nine large sky gardens will house trees and plants, and the walls will collect rainwater for the air-conditioning system.

Twisting edge controls wind flow

Atrium, one of nine sky gardens

Glass and steel "double skin"

Getting around

Many people live on the outskirts of cities, so traveling is a defining part of urban life. Fast and affordable transportation systems keep cities running smoothly. Tokyo's subway system carries 8 million people to work every morning and white-gloved attendants are employed to push passengers on to the trains.

Pollution traps

Large populations make cities prone to pollution. Poor air quality is a big problem in Mexico City, where choking smog caused by exhaust fumes threatens public health. Cities worldwide are tackling pollution by creating walking and cycling zones and investing in green transportation, such as trams.

Cultural capitals

From the fashion on the streets to a wealth of galleries, theaters, and public art, cities are often at the cutting edge of culture and the forefront of new trends. Chicago's *Cloud Gate* sculpture reflects the city skyline in its polished surface. Originally controversial, "the bean" is loved by both tourists and residents.

Urban innovation

New cities find innovative solutions to the problems created by so many people living in one place. Gwanggyo, South Korea, mixes housing, offices, shops, and leisure facilities in a cluster of hill-shaped buildings, with plant-filled terraces bringing outdoor life to the heart of the city.

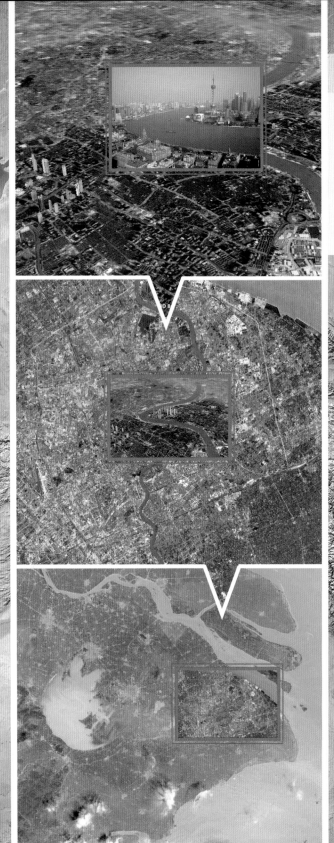

Countries

Every country has its own government, a permanent population, and recognized borders. The world's 194 countries are often defined by their differences, but there can be great diversity within their borders. Shaped by more than 40 centuries of history, China has many landscapes and ways of life, from the bustling cities in the east to the high mountains of the west.

Roof of the world
The high Tibetan plateau is home to fewer than 4.5 million people. Tibetans share a distinct culture and lifestyle adapted to the harsh climate. Many are nomads who move around with their yak herds.

Formidable border
The Himalayan mountains form a natural border with India. China also shares land borders with 13 other countries. These political boundaries have often been agreed after years of dispute.

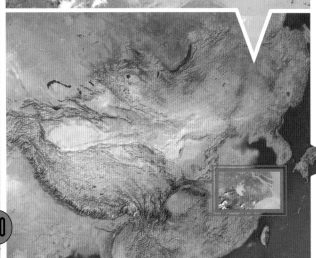

Bright lights of Beijing
Every country has a capital—a city or town that is home to the main government buildings, and other organizations that help to run the country. China's capital Beijing is a sprawling megacity of high-rise buildings, shopping districts, eight-lane highways, and the world's largest city square, Tiananmen Square. Beijing is also a center of tradition and culture, with more than 2,000 years of history on show.

Crowded coasts
Most of China's people live in the eastern third of the country. Economically developed coastal areas, such as Shandong province, attract millions of migrants from rural regions seeking work.

China's pantry
China's fertile river plains are devoted to agriculture. Crops such as rice, wheat, and corn are grown on a huge scale to meet the challenge of feeding China's 1.35 billion people.

Autonomous island
Hong Kong is one of China's two special administrative regions. Like a country within a country, it has its own currency, laws, and political systems, which reflect its history as a British territory.

Creating new countries
More than 30 new countries have been created in the last two decades. The European nation of Montenegro declared its independence in 2006, after 90 years as part of the former Yugoslavia and in union with Serbia. Prime Minister Djukanovic led the move, supported by just over half of his citizens.

Who owns the oceans?
The United Nations' Law of the Sea says that countries with a coast can extend their borders up to 12 nautical miles (22 km) into the ocean. Beyond these territorial waters, countries can negotiate exclusive economic zones, so that they have the right to control fishing and exploit resources such as oil.

Overseas territories
Many African, Asian, and South American countries used to be controlled from Europe. Today, just a handful of these overseas territories remain. Reunion Island is 12,000 miles (19,000 km) from Paris, but has the same status as any French region, and its citizens celebrate French national holidays.

The smallest country
With an area of 0.17 sq miles (0.44 sq km) and just 500 citizens, Vatican City is the world's smallest independent state. Like other countries, it issues passports, and is recognized by international law. The elected Pope, currently Pope Benedict XVI, leads the Vatican as well as being head of the Catholic Church.

Continents

The description "European" or "African" brings to mind the cultural characteristics of each group of countries, not just the landmass. Asia has a third of the world's land and almost two thirds of its people, but the diverse Asian populations have more in common with one another than they do with people on other continents.

Africa
The Sahara Desert divides Africa in two. People living in northern Africa share parts of their culture with the Middle East. Countries south of the Sahara are home to many diverse ethnic groups, and the most ancient cultures in the world. In these countries most people still work in farming, producing their own food. Africa has rich natural resources but is industrializing more slowly than other continents.

Continents of the world
The world's seven continents are almost entirely surrounded by oceans. Thousands of years ago, these natural barriers meant that amazingly diverse cultures developed in different areas of the world. The movements of people, goods, and media across the globe help these different cultures to spread, but also make the world less diverse.

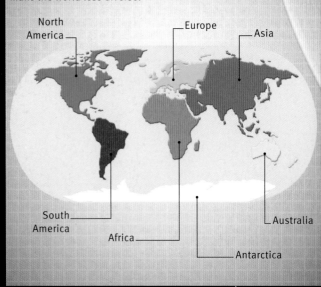

North America

Europe

Asia

South America

Africa

Antarctica

Australia

Middle East
The countries of western Asia are part of a crosscontinental region known as the Middle East. Some of these nations are the source of a large proportion of the world's oil and are very wealthy.

India
India is one of Asia's fastest growing economies. Asia has been a global center of manufacturing and export for centuries. Now, booming populations, a rapid rise in city-living, and improving living standards are creating enormous demand for goods within the region too. By the middle of this century, the Chinese and Indian economies are expected to be the biggest in the world.

Living at extremes

People have found ways to live in Asia's most extreme landscapes, including the frozen grassy plains of Siberia in northern Russia. Peoples such as the Yamal-Nenets survive by regularly migrating to find grazing grounds for their reindeer herds. Their culture has evolved to support this nomadic lifestyle, and is helping them to survive the pressures of climate change and gas drilling in the area.

Singapore

Asia is home to 30 of the world's 50 biggest cities. Singapore, an island city-state, is an important global financial center, with foreign workers making up almost a quarter of its population.

Australia

Australia is both a country and the world's smallest continent. Its native peoples have a 50,000-year history, but most Australians are descended from relatively recent settlers from Europe and Asia.

Antarctica

Antarctica is bigger than the USA, but as the temperature can dip to below -112°F (-80°C), it has no permanent population. Scientists from 29 countries visit research stations there to carry out experiments, often year-round. Antarctica also has more than 46,000 adventure tourists every year.

Across continents

The boundary between Europe and Asia is not precise, and the city of Istanbul, Turkey, is considered to be in both continents. Europe is small but its 44 countries have distinct ethnic groups and languages. Many have come together politically under the European Union, and share a single currency—the euro.

Oceania

The region known as Oceania includes thousands of tiny islands that are not part of any continent, spread out over a vast area of the Pacific Ocean. Palau is a collection of islands that are home to an amazing variety of unique plants and animals. Scuba divers visit from around the world.

Panama canal

The man-made Panama Canal divides the continents of North and South America. Both are home to a diverse mix of cultures, from Amazon peoples who have had no contact with the outside world, to urban New Yorkers who are descendants of immigrants who moved to the US in the last 500 years.

Maps

Maps show us things in relation to each other. Mapping the locations of places and objects has helped us to navigate and understand the world. Anything and everything can now be mapped. Complex concepts, events, and processes become easier to understand when they are presented as pictures, and technology is helping map users become map makers.

Interactive maps
Computers are changing what maps can do. This digital map of an area of São Paulo, Brazil, layers aerial photographs, transportation data, and other information onto a set of underlying coordinates. People can customize the map by choosing which layers are displayed, and interact with it by tagging coordinates with text, images, and videos. Linking data to geographical locations is a powerful tool.

Squaring a circle
Globes are the only truly accurate geographical maps. Flat maps distort the Earth's curved surface to represent it in two dimensions. Different ways of doing this change the countries' proportions.

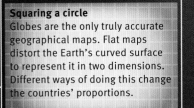

21st-century navigation
The Global Positioning System (GPS) uses radio signals from satellites to pinpoint the location of anything in the world. Handheld GPS receivers can be used alongside digital or paper maps to track exactly where you are and where you are going. GPS has also revolutionized the way that maps are made. Surveyors can collect data in seconds, and use powerful software to assemble the information.

Mapping politics
Information about how humans divide the world into political territories can be combined with physical data, such as the shape of coastlines. A vast amount of data is delivered by a simple image.

Iconic design
The London Underground map is famous for making a complex system easy to navigate. It shows how stations are connected, but ignores non-essential data such as the distance between stops.

Which way is up?
Historically most maps have placed the North Pole at the top, but this is a man-made concept. Upside-down maps that place Australia at the top are just as accurate. They are often used to encourage people to look at the world in a different way. The focus shifts from the continents to the water that covers 71 percent of the Earth's surface. They also show that most of the world's land is in the Northern Hemisphere.

The Earth is not flat
The UK's Ordnance Survey mapmakers have begun using lasers to produce futuristic 3D maps that can be rotated and viewed from any angle. This computerized map of Bournemouth seafront was made by bouncing laser beams off buildings, vegetation, and terrain to record every object in breathtaking detail. The information was combined with 2D maps and overlaid with aerial photographs to make it look lifelike.

Mapping cyberspace
Mapping something that changes daily and can't be seen is a challenge, but several groups are trying to map the Internet. This image was created by the Opte Project, and shows the entire Internet on a single November day. Using a unique software program, researchers traced the flow of information through the Internet to highlight all of the connections between different networks around the world.

Quality of life

Levels of health, education, and income vary greatly from place to place. Brazil has lifted millions of people out of poverty in recent years, but the gap between rich and poor is still one of the largest in the world. The huge differences in wealth and quality of life are easy to see in São Paulo, where slums sit in the shadow of luxury homes. However, a closer look reveals that economic well-being is only part of the picture.

Stress busters
Access to nature and leisure activities like tennis is proven to reduce stress and boost mental health. Wealthy neighborhoods, like Morumbi, are often designed with large communal grounds.

Crowded world
One-third of São Paulo's people live in unplanned *favelas* (shanty towns), often moving here from rural areas to find work. In Paraisópolis, 17,000 houses are crowded into an area the size of 70 football fields.

Self-built life
In low-income areas, quality of life is strongly linked to basic needs. Paraisópolis' 80,000 residents live without many of the facilities often taken for granted, such as trash collection and proper sewage systems. With no planning regulations, houses are built out of waste wood, tin, or even cardboard, and large families share crowded rooms. High crime rates add to the feeling of insecurity.

Walled in
Morumbi is one of São Paulo's wealthiest and fastest-growing suburbs. Security is a big concern for residents, so super-high walls surround the apartment buildings, and journeys by foot are rare.

Revolution
Life in the *favelas* is improving as the government and community organizations upgrade services and build schools. Most homes here have running water, and electricity allows access to satellite television.

High living
Every square foot of these luxury apartments is worth $700. Buyers benefiting from Brazil's economic growth have improved their quality of life by swapping polluted city air for greenery and swimming pools.

Feeling well

Health is a key quality of life indicator, and is improving around the world. The average person now lives 15 years longer than 50 years ago, but there are huge differences between developed and developing countries. Public health campaigns like this measles program in Kenya are helping to close the gap.

Learning for life

Better education leads to a better quality of life—not only for the person educated, but for their family and community too. Education for all remains one of the world's greatest challenges. In many developing countries, such as Nepal, children can miss out on school because they are working to help their families.

Free and fair

People are happier if they feel in control of their lives. This ranges from the security to walk through city streets to freedom of speech. In open societies, like France, citizens can protest against government policy without fear of punishment. The political and legal systems are seen to be mainly fair.

Social bonds

Latin American countries, such as Cuba, have happier residents than would be expected from their income alone. Strong bonds with family and community are significant in shaping quality of life. Most elderly Cubans live with their families rather than in care homes, and community activities are central to their lives.

Industry

Industry turns raw materials into something more useful. This might be goods that people want to buy, or an energy source such as electricity. In developed countries, most industry takes place in large plants or factories, such as this printing press. The raw materials are put through processes that turn them into the finished product.

The printing process
Printing is a manufacturing industry, which means it turns materials, such as paper, into finished products, such as books. As in many modern factories, the same machinery can be used to manufacture a wide variety of things. The printing press can be set up to print an entirely different poster, book, or magazine simply by switching the inked plates that leave an image on the paper passing through.

Bulk buying
The cost of producing each poster depends on the cost of the paper, ink, energy, labor, and everything else put into the process. Buying these things in large quantities helps to keep the price down.

Factory personnel
Various industrial workers carry out different roles to help the manufacturing process to run smoothly, from assembling and maintaining the machines to moving goods around the factory.

Raw materials
Mining, farming, and forestry are known as primary industries. They provide raw materials that can be changed into useful goods or commodities. These harvested logs may be turned into timber for the building industry, paper for the printing industry, or burned by the energy industry to generate electricity. Countries rich in natural resources may also have large, related manufacturing industries, or may export the raw materials to other countries for processing.

Mass production
The more cars that can be made by these car factory workers in a set time, the cheaper the overall cost of making each one will be. This is called an economy of scale and is very important for all industries. To speed up production, the cars are passed through a production line, a set sequence of processes carried out either by hand or machine. Conveyor belts move the cars from one worker or robot to the next so the same tasks can be repeated on each vehicle.

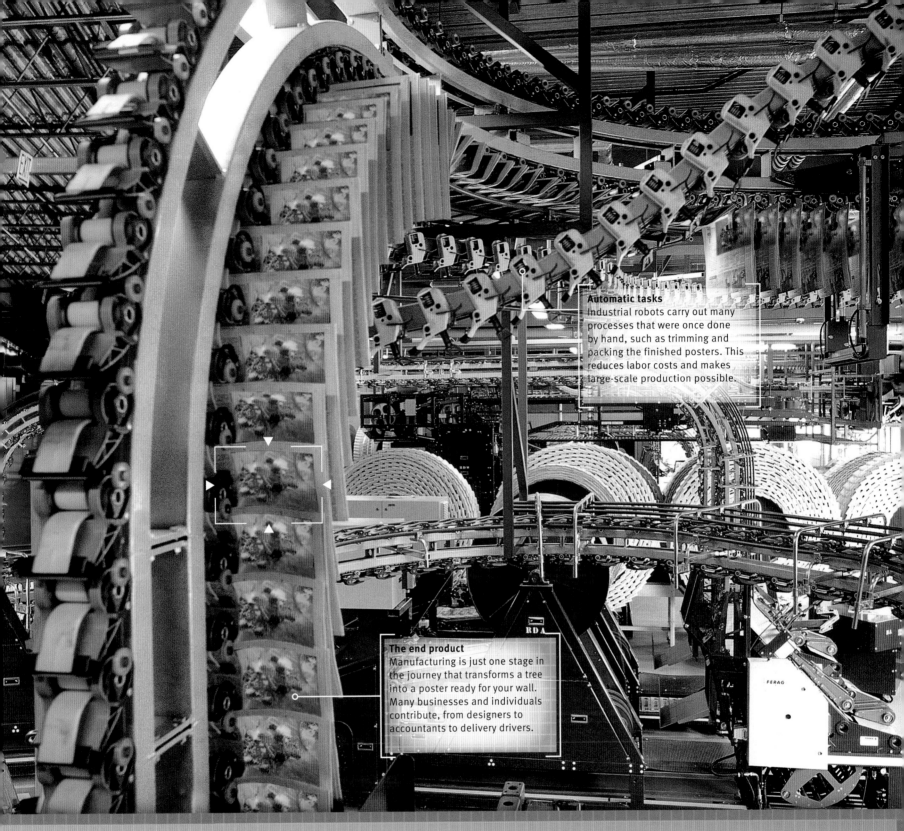

Automatic tasks
Industrial robots carry out many processes that were once done by hand, such as trimming and packing the finished posters. This reduces labor costs and makes large-scale production possible.

The end product
Manufacturing is just one stage in the journey that transforms a tree into a poster ready for your wall. Many businesses and individuals contribute, from designers to accountants to delivery drivers.

Cottage industry
Small-scale manufacturing carried out in people's homes is known as cottage industry. It was the main form of industry before the Industrial Revolution in the 1800s. It is still very important in some areas of the world, such as Rajasthan, India. A dry climate makes the region unsuitable for building large factories that use lots of water and energy. Instead, families make handicrafts such as patterned dhurrie carpets that are sold around the world.

Distribution
Goods tend to be manufactured near sources of raw materials, energy, or a skilled or affordable workforce. The people who will buy the finished products often live elsewhere. Logistics experts ensure that the right products get to the right places at the right times. Most are transported in containers that can be loaded on and off trains, trucks, and ships with ease. Every year, 220 million container-loads of materials and goods are transported around the world.

Seasonal cheer

Before clocks and calendars scheduled life, festivals were an important way to mark the seasons. Chinese New Year is a spring festival celebrated across north and east Asia. The date varies with the Chinese lunar (moon-based) calendar. Dragon dances are thought to bring luck for the season ahead.

Dance of the Fools

Many festivals mark historical events. Japan's Awa-Odori folk dance festival began in 1587 with the opening celebration of the Tokushima Castle. More than four centuries later, up to 1,000 dance groups parade through Tokushima every August to the beat of drums and traditional musical instruments.

Famous fests

Contemporary festivals or "fests" bring people together to enjoy a shared interest, such as music, food, or film. They often celebrate the best of popular culture, past and present. The UK's Glastonbury festival unites more than 100,000 music fans and 700 acts for a three-day party.

Harvest feasts

Almost every culture has a celebration to give thanks for successful harvests. Many of these ancient festivals have been adopted by the world religions. Some Christians in Germany celebrate with feasts of seasonal food and processions of floats that are decorated to represent ancient harvest rituals.

Festivals

Life, family, and community are celebrated at festivals. Many of the world's oldest festivals mark events in religious or seasonal calendars. The Holi festival takes place at full moon in the Hindu month of Phalguna (February or March). Streets across the Indian subcontinent celebrate the start of spring with chanting and color.

Krishna's colors

Many Hindu legends are linked with Holi, but the festival has special meaning for followers of the god Krishna. The color-throwing ritual is based on the story of Krishna playfully splashing *gopis* (milkmaids) with colored water. It also symbolizes the love between Krishna and his friend Radha. Some Hindus begin Holi by smearing statues of Krishna with colored powder as an act of worship.

Gulal powders

During Holi, markets sell vast quantities of *gulal* (richly-colored powder). People "play Holi" by sprinkling it from rooftops, making kaleidoscopic water bombs, or smearing it over faces and clothes.

Flame of the forest

Holi powders were traditionally made at home. The fiery red flowers of spring-blossoming tesu trees were dried in the sun and ground into powder. These natural dyes are becoming popular again.

Festival of colors

Revelers traditionally dress in white cotton *kurtas*, or tunics. These white clothes show off the vibrant Holi colors and disguise differences in wealth and status. For one day, everyone is equal. Politicians, film stars, bosses, and children join the color-drenching fun. Mischievous behavior and pranks are excused by chanting *Bura na mano, Holi hai!* (Don't be offended, it's Holi!).

Holi bonfire

On the eve of Holi, communities light huge bonfires of dead leaves and branches, along with waste materials gathered from homes. The heat and flames symbolize the end of winter. Effigies of the demon princess Holika are burned to remember a Hindu legend about the triumph of good over evil.

The tourist economy

Tourism employs up to 7 percent of the world's workers, and contributes a massive $3 billion to the global economy every day. For remote tropical islands such as Curaçao in the south Caribbean, where tourists outnumber citizens almost three to one, tourism is the main source of income and employment.

Fragile planet

If tourism is not carefully managed, it can damage local culture and nature. Sustainable travel has a saying—take only memories and leave only footprints. But even footprints can harm the most fragile sites. The 2,000 pairs of tourist feet that explore Machu Picchu, Peru, daily are slowly eroding the 15th-century site.

Out of this world

Tourists with astronomical budgets can see the whole world in one trip—from a viewing point in space. Tour operators sell trips to the edge of Earth's atmosphere, where space tourists experience zero gravity for five minutes. For a longer vacation, you can spend 10 days on the International Space Station.

Extreme escapes

As travel becomes easier and more affordable, the demand for unique experiences increases. Today's thrill-seeking tourist is more likely to be found diving with sharks than relaxing on the beach. Adrenalin activities, such as bungee jumping, are the ultimate escape from everyday life.

Tourism

Since ancient times, people have enjoyed visiting new places, and today's tourists make almost one billion international trips every year. Tourism is big business. Every country wants a piece of the action, so tourist boards compete to offer unforgettable experiences from important historical sites to adrenalin-fueled adventure vacations.

Culture vultures
Interest in human lifestyles and customs inspires 40 percent of international tourist trips. Cultural events, such as India's colorful Holi festival, are advertised as once-in-a-lifetime adventures.

Green getaways
Ecotourism is a booming industry. The "eco" tag tells people that their safari or adventure vacation will protect the environment and help local communities. Many ecotourists carry out charity work.

Landmark figures
Paris, France, is the world's most visited city, with the Eiffel Tower's panoramic views as the biggest draw. A staggering 255,976,000 people have visited the iconic landmark since it opened in 1889.

Miniature marvels
Regions short on history and natural resources can become tourist destinations by building attractions. The mini landmarks at Legoland theme parks let visitors "travel the world" in minutes.

Religious tourism
Travel to religious sites is one of the oldest forms of tourism. Italy is a popular destination for Christian tourists. Its 30,000 holy sites include the beautifully painted Sistine Chapel in Rome.

Natural wonders
Awe-inspiring natural wonders, such as Uluru, are among the most famous tourist destinations. Most tourists avoid climbing the iconic Australian rock as it is sacred to the local Anangu community.

Historical draws
Heritage tourism is the UK's fifth largest industry. The popularity of historic sites and events, such as London's Changing of the Guard, means billions of dollars for hotels, restaurants, and shops.

The state

One of the key roles of the state—the governing authorities of a country—is making and enforcing laws, but states work in different ways. In the USA, the central government is split into three branches: executive, judicial, and legislative. They carry out their work from the government buildings in Washington D.C., seen here in miniature at Legoland California.

Washington Monument
In a democracy, individuals and groups are free to protest against the government's actions. The Washington Monument has been the site of many public protests, such as anti-war demonstrations.

The Constitution
The original Constitution, written in 1787, is kept in the National Archives building with the other founding documents. The Constitution sets out the role of each branch of the US government. This document also gives powers to the 50 individual US states and allows them to work together as one country, or federation. It also defines "checks and balances" that ensure no single branch has too much power.

Executive branch
The White House is the home and office of the US President, who heads the largest branch of government. The executive branch includes the Vice President, the armed forces, and many specialist departments and agencies. Their role is to enforce laws and run the process of government. The President also appoints members of the judicial branch, who ensure that the government's laws are fairly applied.

Lincoln Memorial
US presidents have great political power, both in the USA and abroad. When electing a new president, the entire country votes. Monuments like the Lincoln Memorial are built to remember former presidents.

Legislative branch
Congress and its supporting agencies make up the legislative branch of the US government. Congress is responsible for writing, debating, and passing new laws, and is made up of two parts—the House of Representatives and the Senate. It also has the power to declare war on other countries and controls the printing of money. Every US state elects its own members of Congress, who meet in the Capitol building.

Single-party rule
Most states are democracies run by elected officials, but some are run in other ways. China is a single-party state, which means that one political party rules the country and no other parties are allowed to run for election. The ruling party, the Communist Party of China, holds national parades celebrating the government's military power, with the aim of uniting Chinese citizens behind the party.

Constitutional monarchies
A monarchy is a government ruled by a single leader who inherited power from his or her family. In a constitutional monarchy, a king or queen remains the head of state but an elected government runs the country. The British monarch Queen Elizabeth II carries out ceremonial duties such as the State Opening of Parliament, but she has no political power. The Prime Minister is the head of the government.

State of change
Countries that are trying to adopt a new system of government are known as transitional states. Transition may take place after a new country is created, or after a war that gets rid of the old government. Before the current war, Iraq was a dictatorship—ruled by a dictator who gained power by using force. It is now trying to establish a democratic government, so residents can now support and vote for various candidates during elections.

Scaling up

Local and national economies operate on different scales but work in the same way. They involve people producing, selling, and buying goods. In small-scale economies, communities produce the things they use. The local economy in Barka, Oman, involves fishermen selling their catch directly to local customers.

The global economy

Countries have been selling raw materials and goods to each other for centuries, creating a global economy. Communications technology now makes it possible to sell many services at a distance too. A US company can have a call center in India that provides services to customers based in the UK.

Banks and money

In ancient times, people simply exchanged one type of goods or services for another. The invention of money and banks made more complex economies possible. In most countries, central banks print money and control the amount in circulation. This is one way that governments can regulate the economy.

The role of governments

Government influence on the economy varies from country to country. In the handful of command economies, the government controls everything from production of raw materials to the price that goods are sold for. Every Cuban has a ration book that lists certain foods they are allowed to buy at a low price.

Economy

Everything that we produce, sell, buy, exchange, and consume is part of the economy. This includes goods such as food, and the work of people who grow the ingredients, process them in factories, and sell the finished goods in supermarkets. Customers are also part of the economy, influencing what is sold and how much it costs.

The power of advertising
Branding, the identity of a product, has a big influence on customer choice. Creative advertisements on television or in magazines make people look out for memorable packaging in the store.

Eat & Drink

Pick me, please!
Different companies sell versions of the same product and compete for customers. This is good for the economy because it gives choice to customers, and makes companies increase quality and lower prices.

At your service
In many developed countries, such as the USA and UK, more people work in services than other parts of the economy like agriculture or manufacturing. Instead of being directly involved in producing raw materials or making products, they sell their services. Service industries include teaching and healthcare, giving legal or financial advice, cleaning, and serving customers in stores.

The customer knows best
A product's price depends on how much of it businesses produce, and how popular it is with customers. If a product sells out, the store might raise the price as the demand shows that buyers may pay more.

Poland Spring
NATURAL SPRING WATER

Poland Spring
NATURAL SPRING WATER

Bounty

0.0 lb

ITEMS   0
TAX   0.00
BALANCE 0.00

1,000 PIECE JIGSAW

Cashing in
Businesses make profits by selling products for more than the cost of the resources used to produce them. Profits can be invested – spent in a way that helps the business to grow bigger.

Creepy-crawly cuisine

Foods considered a delicacy in some places would be off the menu in others. Fried tarantulas are popular snacks in the Cambodian town of Skuon. Specially bred spiders are coated in sugar and salt then fried for a crispy coating. The high-protein body-meat is said to taste like raw potato, while the legs have the texture of shrimp.

Iconic diet

The traditional Mediterranean diet has been given world cultural heritage status, to recognize its famous cooking techniques and healthy ingredients, such as olive oil, fresh vegetables, and grilled fish. In Greece, Italy, and Spain, food is central to social and family life, and the focus of many songs and stories.

A fish a day keeps the doctor away

Japan has the world's longest life expectancy thanks to a diet rich in seafood. The average Japanese person eats 3 oz (85 g) of fish every day. Sushi favorites, such as this bluefin tuna, are packed with omega-3 fatty acids, which are thought to protect against heart disease—the world's biggest killer.

Unhealthiest diet

The Chilean appetite for fast food means that obesity rates there are soaring. Consumption of fruit and vegetables is falling in favor of highly processed snacks such as these *completos* (hot dogs), full of fat, sugar, and salt. More than half of Chileans are overweight and one in four adults is obese.

Food

Food shapes our lives, from the work we do to grow, buy, or prepare ingredients to the daily pattern of our meals. The way in which people eat reveals much about life in their part of the world. Street food is a central part of life in many countries, including Morocco. Traditional dishes are shaped by everything from local farming to religion.

Open-air feasting

Every evening, up to 100 street food vendors turn Marrakech's Jemaa el Fna square into a giant kitchen. Locals and tourists crowd onto the trestle tables that surround each stall and watch as their meal is cooked over charcoal burners. All Morocco's popular dishes are on offer, from spicy merguez sausages and ground meat kebabs, to boiled sheep's head scrapings served with bread.

National dish

Morocco's national dish is a spicy meat and tomato soup called *harira*. Traditionally it is the first dish eaten to break each day's fasting during the Muslim festival of Ramadan.

Cultural influences

Islam forbids eating pork meat, so the merguez sausages eaten across North Africa are made with lamb or beef. They are flavored with spicy red harissa paste, grilled, and eaten with couscous.

Tagine-cooked vegetables
Moroccan stews are named tagines after the conical pots they are cooked in. Meat and vegetables are piled in, and simmered for a long time over an open fire or bed of charcoal.

Global influences
Unlike some of the local dishes, soft drinks like these are available anywhere in the world. Coca-Cola is the world's leading brand, selling its products in almost 200 nations.

Staple foods
Couscous is a staple North African food that has spread around the world. It was invented in Morocco, when people found that the tiny balls of semolina flour stayed fresh for many months.

Flags

Flags are simple but powerful tools for communication. Most people will instantly recognize the shapes and colors on these hot-air balloons. National flags like these are used to represent countries. They are symbols of pride and identity, and are treated with great respect. Many countries even hold a national "flag day" celebration.

Rising sun
Japan's red sun disk symbol has a one-thousand-year history, having been used by traders and samurai warriors. It was used as a symbol of Japan long before becoming the country's official flag in 1999.

Child's play
A 14-year-old boy helped to design Australia's flag, along with four other winners of an international competition. Five small stars represent the Southern Cross constellation, celebrating Australia's location in the Southern Hemisphere. A seven-pointed star represents the original states and territories of Australia. The Union Jack remembers the country's history as a British settlement.

Three colors
Red, white, and blue is the most popular color combination for national flags. This trio of colors appears on 30 flags, including the French *tricolore*.

Iconic symbols
Most organizations worldwide—from the smallest scout group to the huge United Nations—have developed their own flags. One of the most recognizable is that of the International Red Cross, a symbol of hope and safety to refugees, disaster victims, and other people in need. Using the symbol on a flag makes it easy to spot in war zones, where it provides protection for medical staff and buildings.

Warning signals
In a hi-tech age of satellite telephones and radio beacons, simple fabric flags continue their 2,000-year run as a foolproof way to communicate at a distance. On beaches worldwide, flags instantly tell people if it is dangerous to swim. Ships use flags to signal anything from their identity to calls for help. Flags cut through language barriers, do not need a power supply, and can be operated by anyone.

Old Glory
Stars are the most popular flag symbol, appearing on more than 50 national flags. On America's "Stars and Stripes" they represent the 50 states of the USA. The 13 stripes remember the original US colonies. Blue stands for qualities such as loyalty and friendship, and red is a symbol of courage. Six US flags rest on the Moon as symbols of the country's achievements in space exploration.

Union of nations
The UK's "Union Jack" combines the three crosses of the patron saints of England, Scotland, and Ireland on a blue background. The design and colors have inspired many other national flags.

Who knows?
The meaning of flag colors is often lost in history. Some Italians say their flag's red, white, and green bands represent the country's landscape. Others link them to the traditional colors of Milan.

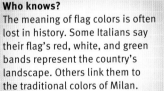

Controversial change
Malawi has one of the world's newest national flags, created in 2010 to represent the country's progress. Protest about the changed design showed that people become very attached to their national flag.

Harnessing the wind
Colorful prayer flags have fluttered outside the homes and temples of Tibetan Buddhists for many centuries. The flags are printed with prayers and mantras (holy words and phrases). Buddhists in Tibet, Nepal, and Northern India believe that these words are repeated every time the flags move in the wind, carrying blessings for happiness, peace, and wisdom to everyone.

Flagged down
The speed at which flags can be seen and understood makes them perfect for fast-paced sporting events. Officials at football games use them to communicate decisions at a distance to players of any nationality, without interrupting play. The black-and-white checkered flag used in Formula One is particularly easy to see when moving at speed, making it the perfect finishing-line sign.

Alliances

Countries often work together to improve the world. The United Nations (UN) is the largest international alliance. Its many different agencies, funds, and programs help millions of people toward better, healthier lives. This work takes many different forms. The UN Relief and Works Agency (UNRWA) is funding a project that provides laptops for refugee schoolchildren in the Middle East.

Training teachers
Local teachers are trained to use the new technology so it makes a real difference in the classroom. The UNRWA is developing digital textbooks and content to bring local curriculums to life.

One Laptop Per Child
The UNRWA is working with the One Laptop Per Child organization to provide every Palestinian refugee child with a laptop. The goal is to bring education up-to-date, connect children to the Internet, and allow them to access innovative learning tools. By providing a rich and inspiring education, the UNRWA hopes to improve the prospects of both individual children and the region as a whole.

Multitasking technology
A special hinge allows the screen to be rotated, tilted, and folded flat, so the laptop can be used as a video player, e-book or games console as well as a learning tool.

Keeping the peace
The UN was founded after World War II to "unite all nations." International peace and security is still its most important goal. The white tanks and blue helmets of UN peacekeeping forces, pictured here in Darfur, Sudan, are just one side of an operation that involves peace education and human rights.

Hope for the future
These children are the fourth generation of Palestinian refugees, people who have lost their homes as a result of conflict in the Middle East. The UNRWA works to build a better future for the refugees, and more than half of their budget is used for education. They build schools, train teachers, and invest in equipment to provide free primary education for refugees in various parts of the Middle East.

Disaster relief
A coordinated international response to disasters and emergencies brings huge benefits. After an earthquake devastated Haiti in 2010, the UN provided food distribution centers. It is now helping the Haitian government rebuild its institutions and resettle 1.5 million homeless people.

A healthier world
The world's poorest countries have the biggest burden of infectious disease and poor health, but lack the funds to tackle them. The UN's World Health Organization leads an international effort to improve health. Projects include this campaign in Chad to test for sleeping sickness, a disease caused by the tsetse fly.

The XO laptop
These robust "XO" laptops are specially designed for schools in developing countries. The screen is easy to read in bright sunlight, and a sealed keypad keeps dirt and water out. Built-in cameras and microphones mean that children don't need extra equipment. The laptop can be powered by solar panels, and the fold-up antennae pick up Internet signals in remote areas.

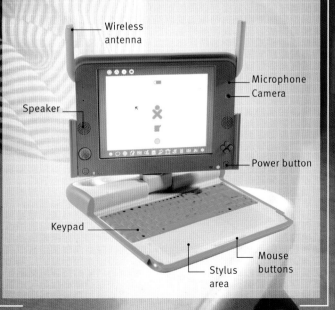

Wireless antenna

Microphone
Camera

Speaker

Power button

Keypad

Stylus area

Mouse buttons

UN member states
The work of the UN is funded by voluntary contributions from its 192 member nations, whose flags fly outside the UN headquarters in New York City, USA. These nations meet in the General Assembly to discuss new projects and policies. Contributions differ widely, but each country has an equal vote.

Marking life stages

All religions provide a way to mark important stages of life, including birth, coming of age, marriage, and death. Rituals and celebrations such as the Christian wedding ceremony bring families and communities together and are a chance for people to express their beliefs.

A code for living

Religions give their followers guidance on how to live a moral life. This code for living is often laid out in ancient holy texts and interpreted afresh by each generation. The Sikh holy text says that people should serve their community and help with the needy, guiding many Sikhs in their choice of career.

Pilgrimages

Religious people express their beliefs in many different ways. Some religions suggest things a follower should do to show their faith, such as a pilgrimage to a sacred site. Hundreds of thousands of Muslims journey to Mecca in Saudi Arabia every year to take part in the Hajj pilgrimage at Islam's holiest site.

After death

Beliefs about what happens after death are a part of all religions. Hindus believe that a person's spirit is reborn many times in a cycle of reincarnation. A person's ashes are often scattered into the sacred Ganges River in the hope of breaking the cycle and speeding their journey to heaven.

Religion

Religions offer people a way to explain the world and their place in it. The variety of beliefs is vast, from the major world faiths to newer religious cults. The Buddhists in this temple follow the way of life taught by Siddhartha Gautama (c.563–c.460 BCE), an Indian prince known as the Buddha. They believe that this will lead to peace, happiness, and wisdom.

The Laughing Buddha

A buddha is a person who, like Siddhartha Gautama, has attained "enlightenment," a state of spiritual self-awareness that is the goal of all Buddhists. Meditation is an important part of the journey toward enlightenment, and involves clearing the mind of unnecessary thoughts. This statue of the Laughing Buddha, a loving, friendly figure, greets people in the front hall of this Chinese Buddhist temple.

Prayer beads

Some Buddhists use prayer beads to count the number of times they have repeated mantras or prayers. These special words, sounds, and phrases are chanted to focus the mind during meditation.

Offering light

Candles are important symbols in many religions. In Buddhism, they are used as offerings of light to symbolize a worshipper's patience or the burning of vices such as greed and pride.

World religions

Most religious people follow one of six major world religions: Christianity, Sikhism, Judaism, Islam, Hinduism, and Buddhism. Each one is divided into different sects, denominations, or branches, with their own beliefs and customs. Christianity is currently the world's largest religion, but Islam is the fastest growing and is expected to take the top spot in around 2030.

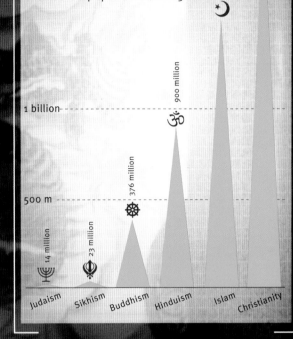

2.1 billion

1.5 billion

900 million

1 billion

376 million

500 m

14 million

23 million

Judaism   Sikhism   Buddhism   Hinduism   Islam   Christianity

Perfumed air
Incense is burned in Buddhist temples and homes as an offering. It produces a sweet smell that creates the right mood for meditation. In other religions, incense symbolizes prayers rising to heaven.

Gifts to Buddha
Buddhists worship by meditating and making offerings to statues or images of a Buddha figure. Many Chinese Buddhists bring gifts of food and flowers to the Laughing Buddha, in the hope that he will bring them wealth, luck, happiness, or children. Each offering has a special meaning. As in other religions, Chinese Buddhists mark holy days by visiting the temple to make offerings.

135

Layered with the vivid color
used to create art, this artist's
palette is a painting in itself.

ART AND CULTURE

For thousands of years people have been using art of all kinds to enhance their lives and communicate complex ideas. Over the centuries this has built up our rich cultural heritage of visual arts, music, drama, and sports.

Art

For many people, art is the creation of a beautiful painting, sculpture, or other object that the viewer will like to look at. For others, a work of art should stimulate the imagination, ask questions, or shock and disturb, leading whoever sees it to view the world with fresh eyes. Every work of art is a unique expression of the artist's ideas and feelings.

Giant sculpture
This sculpture of a giant spider, 30 ft (9 m) high, is by French-American sculptor Louise Bourgeois (1911–2010). Sculptures are three-dimensional works of art created from various materials, such as stone, wood, metal, plastics, and textiles. This is a piece of representational art: it is easily recognizable as a female spider. Much modern sculpture is abstract (non-representational).

Mother figure
The female spider is carrying eggs in a sac beneath her body. Bourgeois gave her work the name *Maman* (Mother) because it was inspired by her own mother who was a tapestry weaver.

Cast in bronze

The sculpture is molded, or cast, in bronze, a metal made from copper and tin. Bronze is a popular material for sculpture because it is strong, not prone to rust, and less brittle than marble and stone. It also expands when it cools to fill the intricate molds needed for detailed designs, like this one. Louise Bourgeois made several casts of the spider, and they have been exhibited all over the world.

Outside art

The spider towers over members of the public passing by. Large sculptures are often displayed in open urban spaces so they can be seen by everyone, bringing art to a wider audience.

Landscape painting

In this oil painting, "Wheatfield with cypresses," the Dutch artist Vincent van Gogh (1853–90) has combined vibrant color with free-flowing swirling brush strokes to capture the movement of the wind in the trees. Van Gogh was greatly influenced by the previous generation of French painters, especially Claude Monet (1840–1926). Although he sold only one painting in his lifetime, he rightly believed his work would have lasting value.

Art in the mind

With this exhibit, "The incredible journey" (2008), British conceptual artist Damien Hirst (1965–) shows the body of a zebra preserved in the chemical formaldehyde. In conceptual art, the idea behind the work is considered more important than the finished product, or even the name. Artists like Hirst deliberately intend to provoke a reaction from the viewer—even from those who believe they are not works of art at all.

Dreamtime

For the Aboriginal people of Australia, as for other indigenous and traditional societies, art is filled with spiritual meaning. In this acrylic dot painting by a modern Aboriginal artist, the dots, whorls, and circles represent "Dreamtime"—the era outside time when ancestral spirits dreamed the world into being. Dot artwork provides a much-needed source of income for Aboriginal communities across Australia.

Architecture

For centuries, the design and construction of buildings was influenced by the immediate concerns of where you lived in the world, what materials were to hand, and what the building was to be used for. Today, with developments in new materials and computer technology, architects have more freedom to create than ever before, resulting in amazing buildings that are works of art in their own right.

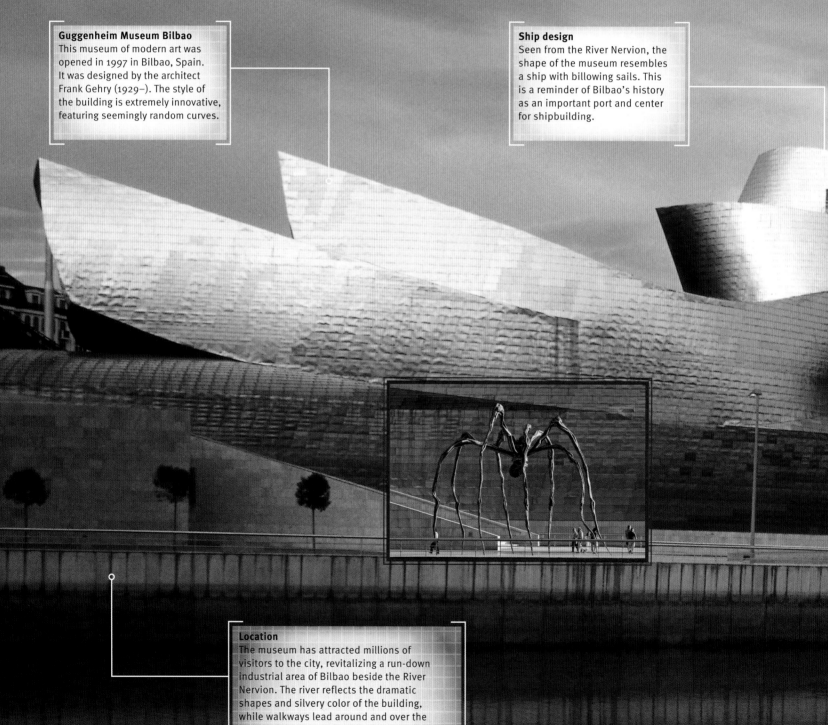

Guggenheim Museum Bilbao
This museum of modern art was opened in 1997 in Bilbao, Spain. It was designed by the architect Frank Gehry (1929–). The style of the building is extremely innovative, featuring seemingly random curves.

Ship design
Seen from the River Nervion, the shape of the museum resembles a ship with billowing sails. This is a reminder of Bilbao's history as an important port and center for shipbuilding.

Location
The museum has attracted millions of visitors to the city, revitalizing a run-down industrial area of Bilbao beside the River Nervion. The river reflects the dramatic shapes and silvery color of the building, while walkways lead around and over the water. It is an example of how buildings can be designed to blend successfully into their surrounding environment.

Architecture as sculpture

Gehry designed the museum as an urban sculpture to be viewed from all angles. The walls soar and bulge, making fantastical shapes, and the structure's steel skeleton is covered with paper-thin titanium panels that gleam and shimmer as they catch the light. To construct the fluid curves of the building, Gehry used a 3D computer program originally developed to build fighter jets.

Letting the light in

At the center of the musuem is the 164-ft (50-m) glass atrium. Gehry encased the central courtyard with glass to flood the inner space with natural light, which lessens the need for artificial lighting.

Strong stone

Many Ancient Greek buildings, such as the Parthenon in Athens, Greece (above), have survived the test of time because they were made with stone. The use of tall columns and the emphasis on balance and symmetry in Ancient Greek and Roman buildings has been a major influence on Western architecture.

Beautiful dome

The octagonal dome of Florence cathedral, completed in 1436, is regarded as one of the glories of the Renaissance (revival of Ancient Greek and Roman ideas). A miracle of engineering, it was designed by Filippo Brunelleschi (1377–1446) with a thin outer and inner shell to lighten the weight of the structure.

Combining styles

Completed in 1616, the Sultan Ahmed (Blue) Mosque in Istanbul, Turkey, combines elements of Islamic and late Roman design. Its six slender minarets (towers) are distinctive features of Islamic architecture, used in the call to prayer, but its dome is modeled on the Hagia Sofia, built in the 6th century by the Romans.

White Heron Castle

Built on top of a hill, and defended by three moats, the huge stone Himeji Castle in Himeji, Japan, was designed to withstand capture. It is sometimes called "White Heron Castle" because the curving eaves and gables, typical of Japanese and Chinese architecture, give it the appearance of a bird about to take flight.

Books

Authors write books to pass on useful information, to record important events, or simply to tell exciting stories to their readers. This would not be possible without the invention of writing, which allows us to read a book written in ancient times and still learn from it today. According to one estimate, worldwide there are 130 million different published books covering a huge array of topics.

Coffee table book
Big books on subjects such as art and architecture that have color illustrations and glossy photographs are sometimes called "coffee table books" because they are left out for casual reading.

Works of fiction
Novels are works of fiction, usually containing more than 50,000 words, created in the author's mind. Their stories focus on characters and events, and the way the story twists and turns is called the plot. There are many different kinds of novels, known as genres, including historical fiction, romances (love stories), crime thrillers, and science fiction. A short novel is known as a novella.

Biography
All books are either fact or fiction. A book written about the life and career of a person is called a biography. This is a work of fact, because the events described have really happened and are not made up. Biographies seek to define the main experiences in the subject's life, and how those events affected him or her. When someone writes the story of their own life, it is called an autobiography.

Reference
Dictionaries and encyclopedias are called reference books. People consult them to check the spelling or meaning of a word, or to find out the facts about a subject. Reference books are regularly updated.

GUGGENHEIM BILBAO
designed by Frank Gehry

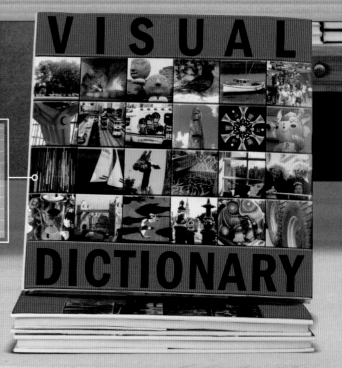

DEAD ON TIME

money power politics

ASSASSINATION

VISUAL DICTIONARY

A.N. AUTHOR

MANDELA
A BIOGRAPHY

20 children's stories for
bedtime

Children's fiction
Novels written especially for children and young people often focus on situations that many younger readers recognize in their own lives, or adventures they would love to experience themselves.

Poetry
Many writers choose to express their ideas and feelings creatively in poetry rather than prose (ordinary writing). Poets use rhythm and the sound of words to evoke feelings and convey ideas to the reader.

A TREASURY OF
poetry
500 POEMS TO INSPIRE YOU

NEW YORK
Travel Guide

FREE PULL-OUT MAP

Travel guide
Travel guides contain essential information for visitors to foreign countries and vacation destinations. They are usually published in a paperback format to make them easy to carry and use.

Code of law
The Sumerians of ancient Mesopotamia (modern Iraq) invented cuneiform writing more than 5,000 years ago by making shapes in wet clay with a wedge-shaped reed pen. This tablet records the deeds of King Hammurabi of Babylon (c. 1750 BCE) who left one of the earliest surviving written codes of law.

Mayan writing
The pages of this folding book from ancient Guatemala, called a codex, are made of bark cloth. Written by a scribe, it contains information about the Mayan calendar. The script, in the form of glyphs (symbols), appears ringed in black in the margin. The Maya were the only people of ancient America to use writing.

In print
This is an early printed version of the Bible, dating from the late 15th century. The words have been printed by a printing press, but the illuminated picture and colored letters have been added by hand. The Bible was the first book to be printed in Europe, by Johannes Gutenberg in about 1450.

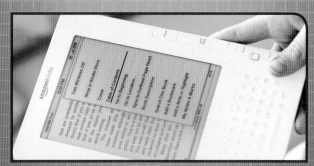

Electronic books
This portable electronic device, known as an electronic book (or e-book), downloads digital books and displays them on its screen in easy-to-read print. E-books can store thousands of books on their memory, and many people believe they threaten the long-term survival of printed books.

Language

There are some 6,800 languages in the world. Linguists divide them into "families," whose members descend from a common ancestral language. The largest family, Niger-Congo, contains more than 1,000 African languages. The Indo-European family includes most European languages as well as those of Iran, Central Asia, and northern India.

Mandarin
The world's most spoken language is Mandarin Chinese, with 1.4 billion speakers. It is the official language of China and Taiwan, and one of Singapore's four official languages.

Arabic
Used throughout the Middle East and North Africa, Arabic is the most widely spoken of the Semitic family of languages, which includes Hebrew. The *Qu'ran*, the holy book of Islam, is written in Arabic.

English
Due to the history of British colonial power and American economic dominance, English has 510 million speakers around the globe, with about 350 million of them being non-native speakers, using it as a second language. More than 110 countries list it as an official language, more than any other language. Because of this, it is the language of the Internet and international communications.

Spanish
Like French and Italian, Spanish descends from Latin, the language of the Roman Empire. It was taken to the Americas in the 1500s by the Spanish, which helped make it the second most spoken language.

Russian
With 254 million speakers, Russian is the most widely spoken of the Slavic subgroup of Indo-European languages. It is written in the Cyrillic script, which is based on the Greek alphabet.

Made-up languages
The alien Klingon warriors who appear in the *Star Trek* series speak a complete language of their own. Invented by American linguist Marc Okrand, Klingon even has its own dictionary. *Lord of the Rings* author J.R.R. Tolkien devised an entire family of elvish languages for his mythological land Middle Earth.

Lost languages
When a language dies out and is forgotten, an important part of human cultural history is lost. Hundreds of languages spoken by Native American, Siberian, and Aboriginal peoples today are threatened by extinction. Shawnawdithit (right), who died in 1829, was the last known speaker of the Beothuk language of Newfoundland, Canada.

Sign language
Many deaf people communicate by signing—a complex communication of gestures, hand shapes, facial expressions, and lip movements that convey meaning. People who work in places where speech is impossible, such as scuba divers, also use sign language.

Hindi
The main language of northern and central India, Hindi is only one of 445 languages spoken in the country. With English, it is the language of the government, but each state has its own languages.

Pidgin languages
Papua New Guinea has more than 800 languages. These children are being taught in Tok Pisin, a pidgin language made up of words from several languages, including English. Pidgin languages allow people who do not have a common language to talk with each other. Tok Pisin is now an official language.

Dance

People of all ages and cultures have a natural urge to dance—to carry out a series of movements, usually in time to music. There are many styles of dance. Some, such as ballet, are performed for audiences, and require many years of professional training. Other less formal styles are used to celebrate something special such as a wedding, to keep fit, or simply to let off some steam.

Street dance
This urban dance style began in the 1970s among young African-Americans in the Bronx area of New York City, USA. Meeting on street corners and in open spaces, they improvised complicated footwork routines to hip-hop music. There were no set steps, and groups of dancers (known as crews) competed against each other in inventing new moves, creating a style filled with poses, athletic leaps, and headspins.

B-girl
Another name for street dance is breakdancing, because the moves were originally performed during instrumental or percussion breaks between songs. Dancers are known informally as b-boys and b-girls.

Street style
Clothing is brightly colored and dancers like to wear name-brand jeans and jackets. Sneakers are also part of the look—essential for leaping, tumbling, and landing on hard concrete surfaces.

Sound system
Dancers perform to hip-hop music played through a radio or CD player. Hip-hop has its roots in African-American blues and jazz music, and includes rapping (speaking or chanting lyrics over a beat).

Ballroom

Popular as a social and competitive activity all around the world, ballroom dance is performed by couples in formal gowns and evening dress dancing together to music perfomed by a band. It originated with the waltz in Victorian times, but today it includes lively "Latin" steps such as the tango, samba, and jive.

Flamenco

This passionate style of dance comes from Andalusia, the southern region of Spain. No one knows its exact origins but it is probably influenced both by *gitano* (Gypsy) and Arab music. It is strongly rhythmic and the performers move their arms and stamp their feet to match the drama of the guitar music.

Limbo

Originating in the island of Trinidad in the Caribbean, limbo was traditionally performed at funerals. Dancers form a line and sway under a horizontal pole (not always set alight) without touching it or losing their balance. The pole is gradually lowered until it is only a few inches above the ground.

Bollywood

Developed in modern Indian "Bollywood" movies, this colorful dance style is a mixture of many different styles such as disco and bellydancing. It is also strongly influenced by Kathak, the classical dance tradition of northern India in which stories about the gods are told through facial expression and hand gestures.

Dance moves

Although street dance is less regimented than most other forms of dance, there are four basic moves. Freezes are dramatic poses held in mid-air, like this dancer's. Toprock refers to any string of steps performed while standing up. In downrock, hands and feet are on the floor while the dancer performs high-speed footwork combinations. Power moves are high-energy leaps and spins requiring athletic strength.

147

Film

A film is a way of bringing a story to life through moving images. Filmmakers capture individual images called frames, or create them using animation techniques. Movie "magic" happens when the frames are shown in rapid sequence, transforming them from frozen moments in time into a sequence of movement that can be played again and again. A large team of people—including actors, camera operators, and a director—is needed to make a film.

Boom microphone

The boom is a long pole with a microphone at one end. The boom operator is careful to keep the boom out of the shot, but must hold it steady and close to record the sound of the action.

Clapperboard

Before each take, the camera records the scene number written on the clapperboard. The loud clapping sound it makes is used to synchronize the audio track to the images when combined later on.

Silent comedy

The first films were shot in black and white, and, until the late 1920s, they were silent because the technology did not exist for adding sound. Actors told the story with clear movements and exaggerated facial expressions, with key moments in the plot explained with onscreen captions. Many silent films were slapstick comedies, with stars such as Charlie Chaplin, seen here with his trademark moustache, entertaining audiences with crazy stunts and visual gags.

Special effects

Many movies make the unbelievable look real, but to do this, they must use special effects. Make-up and costumes can do a lot, but CGI (computer-generated imagery) is perhaps the most important special effect. Here Superman prepares for a scene that will be shot against a green screen. With the help of computers the screen will be replaced afterward, showing him flying high above New York City, USA, in the final cut.

Camera

The camera records the images onto film. It has a stop-motion device, which operates a shutter in front of the lens to expose the film and capture the image for a fraction of a second— most cameras expose 24 frames per second. Today, digital technology is beginning to replace the use of camera film. Many Hollywood movies are now shot as digital images and stored on computer drives or other media.

Lights

The set is lit by powerful lights. This light is mounted behind the camera on a platform called a dolly, which moves backward and forward during filming for close-ups or more distant shots.

Creative control

The director is the film's creative boss. He is in charge of the screenplay and directs the actors, cameras, and sound, calling "action" and "cut" at the beginning and end of each take.

Animation

Traditionally, animated cartoon films were made by photographing hundreds of hand-drawings in sequence, and playing the series back at speed. Today, computer software makes the job easier, but it can still take many years and a great deal of money to make a feature-length animated movie using clay or plasticine models like this dog. Many of the biggest stars in film provide voice-overs for animated films, helping to flesh out the created characters further.

Another dimension

A 3D film projects two images at the same time in two different colors or at two different angles. When the viewer looks at the screen through special glasses, the images merge, giving the appearance of depth to go with the normal dimensions of length and width. 3D technology is not new, but several major blockbusters such as the science fiction film *Avatar* (left) released in the 3D format have renewed its popularity.

Media

For centuries, people had little idea about life beyond their own community. But thanks to the power of media—print, radio, television, and the Internet—we can now access information from all over the globe. Digital media, such as this news website, even allows users to broadcast their own views around the world.

Print media

The printed word was the first media revolution. Before print, very few people had access to information from outside their own experience. The earliest newspapers were printed in the 17th century in Europe, and began to change the world. We still rely heavily on the written word, but often it appears on an Internet-linked computer screen.

Radio

Broadcasting has transformed how we are entertained and learn about the world. Radio in particular is fast, responsive, and interactive, since it does not rely on high-quality imagery, and radio stations cater for a wide array of tastes. You can receive it in a car or on the beach, and take part in a broadcast discussion by simply dialling a phone number.

Television

Images such as these—of the first man to walk on the Moon—have captivated television viewers since the 1930s. Despite being initially in fuzzy black and white, television (TV) quickly became the most popular form of media. The latest technology enables viewers to play TV shows back whenever they want, to watch TV in high-definition, and to interact with live TV shows.

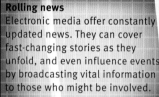

Rolling news
Electronic media offer constantly updated news. They can cover fast-changing stories as they unfold, and even influence events by broadcasting vital information to those who might be involved.

Staying in touch
Due to miniaturized electronics and wireless technology, people can carry Internet-linked computers in their pockets. These personal digital devices deliver all kinds of media content ranging from news, information and communication resources, to music and video. Many can be used to capture images and sound, and new applications related to all aspects of modern life are developed every day.

18 January 2012 | Last updated less than on

GLOBE new

NEWS **POLITICS SPORT S**

BREAKING NEWS Scientists unveil fossil t

Volcano continues to billow ash

Evacuations continue as the largest volcanic eruption in the last hundred years just keep on pumping

● Other volcanoes in the region are showing increased activity, raising fears that local ...

💬 Have your say: 28 comments

Music news

Festival highlights

Flaming Lip frontman V Coyne tak the stage true cult s

● Joining the line-up for this year's fest, "best small festival" last year, we chat

Watch the best moments h

nute ago

.com

ENCE ARTS SOCIETY FINANCE FEATURES EDUCATION

search **GO**

hrows new light on human origins ... READ MORE›

.000s stranded by floods

● **The devastating floods that have claimed at least 10 lives** and left 41 people missing have hit the capital city, where thousands of residents have been attempting to flee their homes ahead of the surging floodwaters.

Film news

Dynamic dance

Filming ends on the most highly awaited movie debut of the year

● Based on the biggest names in hip-hop, with urban dancers chosen ... ›

Weather

weather: sunny intervals
temperature: 64°F (18°C)
wind: SW, light 2–3
Outlook for next 5 days

Watch Sammy the waterskiing squirrel as he sends the crowds nuts!

Cultural heritage

Music has an important role in many traditional societies. The Aboriginal people of Australia play music together to pass on rituals and cultural knowledge about their history. The singing is accompanied by the didgeridoo (above), a long instrument that makes a deep drone when blown.

Indian sounds

This musician is playing a sitar, a plucked string instrument that is played all over India. A sitar can have more than 20 strings, some of which play the melody, while others provide a resonating sustained drone. The sitar is often accompanied by a player on the tabla, a two-piece drum sounded with the hands.

Mexican mariachi

Mariachi music is unique to Mexico. A typical mariachi band includes violins, trumpets, and guitars, and the players wear the traditional dress of Mexican cowboys. Mariachi's origins go back to the time of Mexico's struggle for independence from Spain, and many of the songs are revolutionary in flavor.

Classical orchestra

An orchestra is made up of many players performing together. There are four families of instruments: percussion, woodwind (blown instruments, such as flutes and clarinets), brass (blown metal instruments), and stringed instruments. They are directed by a conductor, who waves a baton to the beat of the music.

Music

The instinct to make music by singing or playing instruments is age-old. There are only 12 notes in the musical scale, but countless ways these can be played to produce a staggering array of musical styles. Music can be listened to through recorded media, but the most exciting way is to enjoy it live, as at this rock gig.

Electronic keys
Keyboards are able to replicate an array of different instruments and sounds, which are heard when the keys are pushed down. Each key is a note in the musical scale, and form chords when combined.

Back beat
The drummer provides the beat—the steady rhythmic pulse that drives the music forward. Drums and cymbals are percussion instruments, producing sounds by being struck with the hand or sticks.

Concert venues
Big rock shows are usually staged in an arena on a specially built set with lighting effects and backdrops. Other types of live music may be performed in concert halls in front of a seated audience.

At the front
The lead singer fronts the band, moving around the stage as he or she sings the lyrics of the songs. In many rock bands, the lead singer also plays guitar, providing the melody lines for the song, and adding instrumental fills and guitar solos. The lead singer often writes the songs, and may wear costumes, dance, or interact with the audience in order to make the performance more exciting.

Enjoying the show
Fans at a rock gig show their enjoyment by shouting, clapping, and dancing to the music. Audiences at classical concerts, however, save their applause for the end of the performance.

Bassist
The bass guitarist is part of the rhythm section of the band, laying down the beat with the drummer. His guitar has four strings instead of the six on the lead guitar, and has a much deeper sound.

Raising the roof
Amplifiers placed at the front and sides of the stage take the barely audible signals from the instruments and the microphones and boosts their sound by playing them through loudspeakers.

Field of view

Reflex cameras can be fitted with various lenses to provide different fields of view. Telephoto lenses with a long focal length magnify distant objects, and are great for sports and wildlife. Short wide-angle lenses give a broader view and exaggerated perspective, creating dramatic images of buildings. Zoom lenses like this one have variable focal length—some go all the way from wide-angle to telephoto.

Steady now

Holding the camera steady is a vital part of taking a photograph, especially in low light when the camera takes longer to record an image. Many modern cameras have stabilization systems that help.

Photography

At the press of a button, a photographer can capture a piece of history, a glorious landscape, or a complex emotion. All it takes is a camera and an eye for the critical moment. That split-second of creativity may record a personal insight into what is beautiful or meaningful, but it can sometimes create an image that becomes world-famous.

Moving image

Many people use compact video cameras to shoot their own movies. Digital technology makes it easy to edit the results on a computer, and turn a mass of material into a professional-looking narrative.

Tool for the job

Professional photographers like to use big reflex cameras like this one. They give a much better view of moving subjects than compact cameras, and they offer more control options. Big digital cameras also have larger electronic sensors that improve image quality. But many people prefer small, light pocket cameras. These are also better for taking portraits of friends without making them self-conscious.

Point and click

Anyone could be a photographer. The skill lies in knowing where to point the camera, and when to squeeze the shutter button. In the right hands, the cheapest camera can generate a masterpiece.

A photographic history

Photography dates from the early 1800s, when it was found that a metal plate coated with silver iodide and placed in a box would record an image focused on it by a lens. This image of a street in Paris was one of the first photographs, taken in 1838 by French physicist Louis Daguerre (1789–1851). The first color film for ordinary cameras was marketed in 1935 by Kodak, and soon became hugely popular. But most users now prefer digital cameras, which can also record video and sound, and some can record 3D images too.

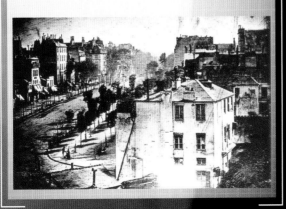

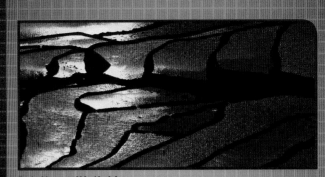

Painting with light

Although photography has practical uses, it is also an art. This picture resembles an abstract painting, but it is actually a photograph of flooded Chinese rice paddy fields. Turning a real scene into a satisfying graphic pattern is a basic photographic skill, but here it is the whole point of the image.

Making the news

As soon as photographic equipment became small enough to carry around, people started using it to report on current events. Newspapers were transformed by the inclusion of photographs, such as this image of Lyndon B. Johnson being sworn in as US President after the assassination of John F. Kennedy in 1963.

Paparazzi

The public appetite for photographs of celebrities has created a profitable market for the "paparazzi" who take them. Using long telephoto lenses, they try to snatch images that show their targets in unguarded moments. But they are often accused of invading their subjects' privacy and even breaking the law.

Star nursery

Our understanding of the world and even the Universe has been transformed by photography. This awe-inspiring view of immense clouds of heated hydrogen gas in the Omega Nebula was captured by the Hubble Space Telescope in 1999, using a system that vividly depicts this hotbed of star formation.

Sports

A sport is any form of physical activity that has a set of rules and involves an element of competition. Some sports are played at professional level by sportsmen and women who are paid for taking part. Big occasions, such as the Olympic Games, bring the greatest sportspeople from around the world together to compete in an array of events. But many people play sports just for fun, and many more also like to watch the drama from the sidelines.

True colors
Teams play in distinctive uniforms (team colors), which make it easier for players on the same team to see each other. In soccer, each player's name and number is shown on the back of his or her shirt.

Teaming up
Soccer is the world's most popular team sport, played and watched by millions of people. Two teams of 11 players each try to kick or head a ball into the opposing team's goal over the course of two 45-minute halves. Each player in the team has his or her own role. Here, the players in navy blue are defending their goal, while the player in red is attacking it. The defending team's goalkeeper is in green.

Hands off!
In soccer, only the goalkeeper can handle the ball. Originally made of leather pumped with air, the ball's design and structure has changed over the years to make it lighter and more aerodynamic.

Playing area

The rules governing different team sports usually stipulate the size and markings of the playing area, or field, and always spell out how a victory is earned. Soccer fields are marked with white paint, and feature a net attached to white goalposts. A goal is scored when the ball completely crosses the line between the posts, and play is then restarted from the center circle by the other team.

Making waves

A large number of sports take place on or in water and require very different skills to land-based sports. Swimming and diving are for single competitors, but synchronized swimming (above) is a team sport. It combines swimming with dance and gymnastic moves performed in the water, with scores awarded by judges.

Snow and ice

Snowboarding, where competitors navigate downhill and pull off tricks while strapped to a single board, has grown in popularity since it first emerged as a winter sport in the 1970s. It has joined snow events such as tobogganing, skiing, and ski jumping. Popular ice sports include skating, ice hockey, and curling.

Gymnastics and athletics

Gymnasts and athletes need great physical and mental strength, coordination, and agility but, above all, determination and self-discipline. Gymnasts competing in the uneven bars (above) are marked for their dramatic somersaults, twists, and landings as they vault from one bar to another.

Wheel it

Wheeled sports include cycling, skateboarding, and rollerblading. Although all have federations that organize competitions, only cycling is a mainstream sport. The Beijing 2008 Olympic Games featured 18 cycling events in four disciplines: track, road, mountain bike, and BMX.

Design

The work of designers is all around us: in the furniture we use, the clothes we wear, and the products on supermarket shelves. Designs evolve as new materials become available and tastes change. Dark, heavy wooden furniture was popular at the end of the 1900s. Simple shapes and bold colors were the hallmarks of the 1920s. Modern designs mix styles and are often made of materials such as plastic. Some items become so popular they become design classics.

Star time
American designer George Nelson (1908–86) stripped the wall clock back to its bare essentials. His Asterisk Clock of the 1950s proved to be extremely popular, and sold in huge numbers.

Egg-shaped
Though he used cutting-edge materials such as steel, the work of Danish designer Arne Jacobsen (1902–71) was often inspired by the natural world. This can be seen in his Egg Chair from the 1950s.

Beetling about
Car designers take many things into account when designing new models: safety, looks, engine power, cost, and passenger comfort. Some car designs are so successful they come to be regarded as classics. The Volkswagen Beetle, originally produced as a cheap family car in 1930s Germany, later became popular worldwide thanks to its price, reliability, and iconic shape.

Funky phone
Created in 1954 by the Swedish Ericsson company, when telephones were clunky, black, and had a separate dial and handset, this all-in-one plastic model came in a revolutionary choice of 18 colors.

Elegant artichoke

Designers aim to find elegant solutions to tricky problems. Danish architect Poul Henningsen (1894–1967) created an overhead lamp that would eliminate blinding glare from the bulb. His answer was to arrange 72 overlapping leaves of metal that shield the bulb from direct view and redirect the light downward. Made in 1958 for a Copenhagen restaurant, Henningsen's Artichoke Lamp is now a design classic.

Shelf life

This steel map of the United States made by Israeli designer Ron Arad (1951–) blurs the boundaries between art and design. Though it's a very striking wall feature, it can also be used as shelving.

Fantastic plastic

This table is made of plastic that was injected into a reusable mold. Mass production of plastics in this way began in the 1930s, bringing stylish-looking but low-cost interior design into many homes.

On the catwalk

Clothes design can be studied in fashion schools and art colleges. Many designers work for large fashion houses, mass producing clothes for the ready-to-wear market. Some also create haute couture items, made for a specific customer and featuring expensive materials and extravagant designs. Catwalk models show off the latest collections in fashion shows held twice a year in major cities such as Paris, New York, and London.

Food favorites

Creating the right package for a consumer product is a very important aspect of design. Food companies want their products to stand out and be instantly recognizable to customers searching the supermarket shelves. The famous Heinz tomato ketchup bottle, with its distinctive shape and label, has been in existence for more than a century, and is the same everywhere in the world.

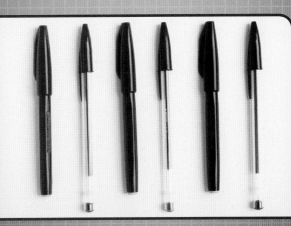

Pen picked

Sometimes luck plays a part in creating a design classic. Hungarian journalist László Bíró (1899–1985) developed a smudge-free pen with a ball-bearing nib in 1935. His invention made little headway until World War II, when the British government, looking for a pen that their pilots could use at altitude, started using Bíró's pen. Other manufacturers took up the idea after the war, and the ballpoint pen was born.

Music all the way

Audiences all over the world love the colorful and brilliantly staged extravaganza of modern musicals like *The Lion King*, which brings together music, singing, and dance to tell an emotion-packed story. Many of the most popular shows in London's West End and on New York's Broadway are musicals.

Shadow puppets

Puppets have been used since ancient times to act out stories. *Wayang* is a traditional form of puppet theater from Indonesia. Tall puppets are mounted on bamboo sticks and lit from behind. A puppeteer uses the sticks to move their arms and legs, and the audience sees shadows thrown onto a white sheet.

Spoken drama

Dramas that tell a story through spoken dialogue are called plays. Actors make the audience believe in what is happening on the stage not only with their tone of voice, but also through their facial expressions and gestures. Costumes, make-up, and scenery all help to bring the realistic performance to life.

Opera

An opera is a drama set to music. Opera originated in Italy in the early 17th century. It belongs to the western tradition of classical music, and is performed in large custom-built opera houses. The singers on stage, who are accompanied by a full orchestra, must project their voices to every part of the theater.

Theater

The ancient Greeks were the first people to write stories as plays, and the word "theater" comes from a Greek word *theatron*, meaning "the seeing place." Around the world, many different traditions have developed, including the classical Noh theater of Japan—a form of musical drama that features masked actors.

Mysterious pine tree
A pine tree is always painted on the back wall of the Noh theater. It is said to symbolize the ladder by which the gods descended to earth in Shinto ritual (the traditional religion of Japan).

Playing the tune
Four musicians, called *hayashi*, accompany the dancing and singing. From left to right, they play the *taiko* (stick drum), *otsuzumi* (hip drum), *kotsuzami* (shoulder drum), and *fue* (flute).

Simple stage
The Noh theater is simpler in design than most western theaters. The stage is raised about 3 ft (1 m) above the audience and the stage floor is polished so that actors can move in a gliding manner.

Masked performer

Instead of applying heavy stage make-up, Noh performers wear painted wooden masks. There are different styles of mask for men and women, old people, demons, and ghosts. This one is an *otoko*, or young man's mask. The actor can adjust the mask to display different emotions with slight movements of the head. Tilted up, the mask appears to be smiling; tilted down, it seems to frown.

Stage setting

Noh theater was originally performed outside or at temples and shrines. Modern Noh stages are based on the design of Shinto shrines—complete with a roof even when built indoors. A bridge leads backstage, and three real pine trees give a sense of distance, with the tallest tree closest to the main playing area.

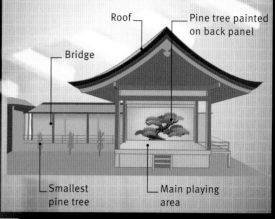

Roof

Pine tree painted on back panel

Bridge

Smallest pine tree

Main playing area

Acting the part

Music, dance, singing, and chanting form the slow, graceful drama of Noh theater. The main performer is called the *shite* and actors playing secondary roles are called *waki*. Traditionally, male actors played both men or women. In this play, by the Noh master Zeami (1363–1443), the *shite* is playing a god and wearing a wig. He uses his folding fan (*ogi*) to communicate with the audience as he sings and dances.

Costume

When Noh theater first emerged in the 14th century, the actors wore realistic clothing. But since the late 16th century, they have worn symbolic costumes of beautifully embroidered silk brocade.

Ancient hand-prints on a rock
in Guyana, South America, are
traces of prehistoric people.

HISTORY

Human history has been a saga of discovery and political innovation. Great civilizations have come and gone, scarred by war and plagued by disease, but leaving behind a rich heritage of ideas and practical achievements. From the world-changing inventions of the Industrial Revolution to the devastation of World War II, history weaves a colorful tapestry of humanity's triumphs and failures.

Border motifs
Exotic beasts decorate the border, but nobody is totally sure what they signify. Some of the creatures are mythological in nature, like this griffon, which has the head of an eagle and the hind legs of a lion.

Battle charge
A Norman knight steadies his spear as he charges at the English. For body protection, both armies wore armor made of flexible rings of steel called mail. Their iron helmets had projecting nosepieces.

Invasion!
In 1066 William, Duke of Normandy in France (c.1028–87), invaded England and defeated King Harold II (c.1022–66) at the battle of Hastings. The story of the battle is told on the Bayeux tapestry, seen here. It was completed a few years after William, now king of England, had conquered the country. It is a work of propaganda, with the aim of portraying the Normans as the rightful conquerers of England.

War

Wars have been fought throughout history—over land, access to resources, or to prove who is the most powerful tribe or nation. Methods of fighting changed as weapons became more accurate and able to travel further. Until the Middle Ages, wars were fought with spears, swords, and bows and arrows. The use of guns only became widespread in Europe after 1400.

Under siege
Sieges were a common form of warfare in ancient and medieval times. An invading army would surround a city or castle and attack its walls while those inside could retaliate by throwing boiling oil, arrows, or fire onto them. Attacking armies often used siege machines such as battering rams and stone-throwing catapults to try to topple the walls. This picture from the 1800s shows Roman soldiers catapulting Carthage during the Third Punic War of 146 BCE.

Largest empire
In the 13th century, the Mongol leader Genghis Khan (1162–1227) led an army of mounted warriors out of eastern Siberia to conquer the largest land empire in history, stretching at its height from China to Russia and into the Middle East. Their success lay in their swift horses, their terrorizing tactics, and their short, powerful bows, which they would fire at full gallop, turning in the saddle to aim a stream of arrows at the enemy.

War casualties
Losses were high on both sides. The bodies of soldiers killed in the fighting are shown sprawled in the bottom border of the tapestry, a chilling reminder of the human cost of war.

On the waves
The history of naval warfare was transformed in the 16th century by the introduction of cannons—guns mounted on wooden carriages that could fire heavy iron shot (balls) at enemy ships. European ships armed with cannons came to control global sea routes. Huge battles took place at sea, such as the battle of Trafalgar in 1805, (left), when the British admiral Lord Nelson (1758–1805) defeated the French and Spanish fleets, but was killed in the action.

Bombing raids
Warfare first took to the air during World War I (1914–18), when airplanes mounted with machine guns fought dogfights (close combats) in the sky. By World War II (1939–45) bombers capable of flying long distances had brought a new, terrifying element to war—the mass death and injury of civilian populations and the destruction of entire cities. This image shows the German capital of Berlin lying in ruins in 1945, flattened by Allied bombs.

Early farmers

Catalhöyük in southern Turkey is the site of a 9,000-year-old village. Its mud-brick dwellings were closely crammed together, with their entrances in their roofs. The inhabitants were farmers, who grew wheat and barley and kept animals such as chickens and cattle. Most people at that time were still hunter-gatherers.

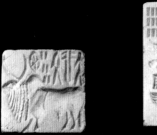

Indus city dwellers

These stone seals belong to a civilization that flourished in the Indus Valley (Pakistan and northwest India) more than 4,000 years ago. The Indus people built large cities of mud-brick houses and even had indoor sanitation. The seals—which are carved with an unknown script—may have been identity tags.

Babylonian splendor

The Ishtar Gate, decorated with dragons and bulls, once guarded the entrance to the city of Babylon—the center of a powerful Mesopotamian empire that conquered the city of Jerusalem in the 1st millennium BCE. Babylon's famous Hanging Gardens were one of the seven wonders of the ancient world.

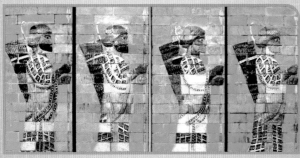

The power of Persia

In 539 BCE, the armies of the Persian king Cyrus the Great (559–530 BCE) overran Babylon. Cyrus ruled the largest empire that the ancient world had seen so far, stretching from the Mediterranean Sea to Afghanistan. These archers, from a palace at Susa (modern-day Iran), proudly display Persia's might.

First cities

Many of the first cities arose in Sumer (in modern-day Iraq), about 5,500 years ago. Each was ruled by a king on behalf of the local god. These cities were the birthplaces of some of the earliest civilizations, complex societies with a ruling elite, technology, writing, and laws. This scene shows a procession bringing food for the king of Ur.

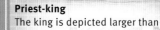

Priest-king
The king is depicted larger than any other figure to emphasize his divine status. In many early civilizations, rulers performed religious duties, assuming the character of gods themselves.

Entertainment
This musician is playing a stringed instrument called a lyre, which has been decorated with the head of a bull. The figure next to him may be a singer; she is the only woman shown on the Standard.

Living off the land
The Sumerian city-states grew up on the fertile floodplain between the Tigris and Euphrates Rivers. Although relatively little rain falls in this area, canals were dug to divert water from the rivers to irrigate the land. Farmers grew more food than they needed for themselves. They took their surplus crops to the city temples, which served as storehouses from where food was distributed to non-farming workers.

The Standard of Ur

Once believed to be a royal standard, scholars now think that this magnificent object may have been part of a musical instrument. It was discovered in the grave of a king of Ur who died c. 2,500 BCE. A mosaic of lapis lazuli, sandstone, and shell, this side depicts food being brought in procession for a royal banquet, while the other shows scenes of war. Its actual size is 8.5 in by 19.5 in (21.5 cm by 50 cm).

The Fertile Crescent

The Fertile Crescent is a strip of land that runs in an arc from the Mediterranean coast through the Middle East. It was here that farming first developed. Hunter-gatherers began to harvest wild grains, and then to purposefully cultivate them as crops. Over time they moved from a nomadic (wandering) lifestyle to living in settled communities, and the first cities were born.

Fringed skirts

Most of the people are wearing kilt-like woolen skirts that tie at the waist, while the king's is made from a whole sheepskin—a high-status garment that is often seen on statues of gods and kings.

Domesticated animals

Sheep, goats, and cattle were domesticated in the Middle East between 10,000 and 8,000 years ago. They provided meat and cheese, and their wool and hides were used to make clothes and leather. They were also used to haul heavy loads—oxen often pulled plows—while a scene on the other side of the Standard shows onagers (domesticated wild asses) pulling war chariots with solid wooden wheels.

Ardipithecus ramidus
This chimpanzee-like hominin lived about 4.4 million years ago in Africa. Although it walked on the ground on two feet, it used its big toes to grasp branches when traveling through trees.

Australopithecus afarensis
The name of this small-brained hominin means "southern ape of Afar." Afar was the region of Ethiopia, Africa, where the first skeleton was found in 1974. It lived between 4 and 3 million years ago.

Walking tall
Homo erectus ("upright man") lived from about 1.8 to 1 million years ago. They hunted animals in groups with stone tools and may have used fire to cook. Fossil remains of *Homo erectus* have been found in Africa, Europe (Spain), and Asia (Indonesia and China). One theory is that *Homo erectus* migrated out of Africa and into Asia. Other experts believe that the Asian fossils are a distinct species.

Human origins

The story of human evolution began more than 5 million years ago in Africa. It was then that early hominins—the primate family that includes modern humans and their ancestors—started to leave their homes in the trees to walk on two feet. The process of change took millions of years, and can be traced by studying the fossilized bones of our human ancestors.

Homo habilis
This African species is about 2.5 million years old. Its name means "handy man" as it was the first ancestor to make simple pebble tools. Its brain was less than half the size of a modern human's brain.

Homo neanderthalensis
Named for the Neander valley in Germany where their fossils were first identified, Neanderthals lived between 300,000 and 30,000 years ago in Europe and western Asia, for some of this time living alongside modern humans. They foraged for plants as well as hunting animals for food. They were about 5 ft 6 in (1.6 m) tall, and very stocky, with a large nose and projecting brow.

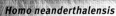

Modern man
Anatomically, modern humans—*Homo sapiens* ("knowing man")—evolved about 200,000 years ago in Africa. By about 50,000 years ago they had developed a wide range of tool-making skills, the ability to communicate through language and art, and the practice of burying their dead. They began to migrate out of Africa about 100,000 years ago and had spread around the world by 15,000 years ago.

Out of Africa
Olduvai Gorge, a canyon in the Great Rift Valley of Tanzania, holds many clues to human evolution. It was here in the 1950s and 1960s that archaeologists Louis and Mary Leakey discovered a collection of hominin fossils that proved that Africa had been the birthplace of humanity.

Prehistoric art
Prehistoric hunters from about 31,000 years ago in southern France and Spain made the first artworks by humans—caves covered with lifelike figures of bulls, horses, and deer, and matchstick humans, in reds, oranges, and blacks. They give an insight into the things that concerned these early humans.

Tool kit
Useful hand axes made by chipping away at flint were developed from about 700,000 years ago. Sharpened flints were attached to wooden handles with leather bindings, and used as digging or scraping tools, or as spears. By 30,000 years ago, harpoons and needles were being made from bone and antler.

Ice-age hunters
During the last Ice Age, between 30,000 and 10,000 years ago, great ice sheets covered much of northern Europe and Asia. Humans had to develop new skills to survive. They hunted mammoths (large hairy animals related to elephants, now extinct) for their meat and used their skins to keep warm.

Early America

Many complex civilizations blossomed and fell in the Americas before the arrival of European invaders in the 1500s. The warlike Aztecs—who dominated from the 1300s onward—were the last in a line of remarkable cultures that had flourished in Mexico for more than 2,000 years. They shared many aspects of their society with the peoples who had gone before them.

City of the gods
Teotihuacán in Mexico was the largest city of ancient America. Little is known about the people who built the city, but by 1000 CE it covered an area of 12 sq miles (31 sq km) and was home to up to 250,000 people. The Aztecs found its ruin and named it Teotihuacán—"city of the gods." This image shows the Pyramid of the Moon with the Pyramid of the Sun. The Aztecs adopted a similar building style for their own cities.

The last of the Aztecs
The arrival of Europeans spelt the end of the American civilizations. When Spanish conqueror Hernán Cortés (1485–1547) landed in Mexico in 1519, the Aztecs mistook him for the god Quetzalcoatl. The last Aztec king, Moctezuma II, welcomed Cortés to Tenochtitlán, the Aztec capital. Cortés responded by taking Moctezuma prisoner. His soldiers laid waste to the city and by 1521 the whole of Mexico was in Spanish hands.

Giant heads
The Olmecs (c. 1500–400 BCE) were the earliest civilization of Mexico. Although little is known about them, later civilizations are believed to have adopted aspects of Olmec culture, including the ritual calendar, bloodletting, the making of jade masks, and the playing of a ceremonial ball game. This colossal stone head carved from volcanic rock portrays an Olmec ruler and is one of several that have been found around La Venta on the Gulf of Mexico.

Recorded in stone
The Maya (250–900 CE) of modern-day Guatemala and Mexico were the only ancient American people to develop writing. They recorded the deeds of their rulers on carved tablets (steles) like this one, and built cities with tall pyramid temples where victims were sacrificed and their hearts offered to the gods. The Maya also performed painful bloodletting ceremonies, piercing their own tongues with sting-ray spines to enter a trance-like state.

Ancient American game

Versions of a ritual ball game were found throughout ancient Central America. It was played on a court between teams of men using only their hips to strike a hard rubber ball through a hoop.

Aztec gods

This mask represents Tezcatlipoca, the god of the night, sorcery, and war, whose name in the Aztec language means "smoking mirror." He was the twin brother (and enemy) of Quetzalcoatl, the feathered serpent god. The Aztecs worshipped hundreds of gods. They believed the gods made the Sun rise, the rain fall, and the crops grow. Some of the gods were kind, but others, like Tezcatlipoca, were terrifying.

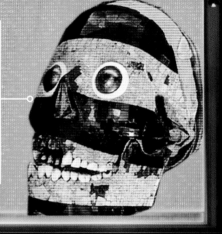

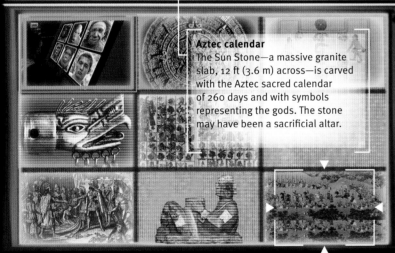

Aztec calendar

The Sun Stone—a massive granite slab, 12 ft (3.6 m) across—is carved with the Aztec sacred calendar of 260 days and with symbols representing the gods. The stone may have been a sacrificial altar.

Sacrificial knife

The Aztecs believed that the gods demanded human sacrifice. The hearts of victims were cut out by priests using quartz blades, such as this one. The crouching figure on the handle is an Aztec eagle warrior.

Toltec warriors

Tall columns of carved stone warriors guard all that remains of the former Toltec capital of Tula. The Toltecs were a warrior people who controlled much of central Mexico from about 950 CE to 1200 CE. They seem to have made themselves rulers of the Mayan city of Chichén Itzá on the tip of the Yucatán peninsula. The Aztecs who came after them adopted the Toltec cult of the feathered serpent god Quetzalcoatl, the creator and protector of humans.

Machu Picchu

There were people in every part of the Americas. In the 15th century, the vast Inca empire stretched 3,000 miles (4,800 km) along the Pacific coast of South America. The Incas did not have wheeled transportation but used llamas and alpacas to carry goods along the network of roads that united their empire. The Inca city of Machu Picchu is nestled high in the Andes mountains. The Spanish failed to discover it when they conquered Peru in 1532.

Imperial China

The Shang Dynasty (c. 1766–1122 BCE) was the first in a long line of Chinese imperial dynasties that lasted until 1911. China grew powerful through trade and war, and introduced new inventions such as gunpowder, paper, and porcelain to the world. Art and culture flourished under the Ming Dynasty (1368–1644), as this detail from a 85-ft- (26-m-) long painted silk scroll known as "Herald Departure" shows.

Imperial progress
These riders are part of an imperial procession from the capital, Beijing, China, to the tombs of the previous emperors nearby. The emperor's visit is to pay his respects and pray to his predecessors.

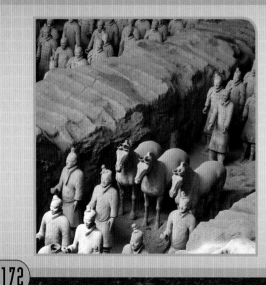

Terra-cotta Army
This army of 8,000 life-size clay soldiers, 520 horses, and 130 wooden war chariots, arranged in battle order, was discovered buried in a pit near the tomb of Qin Shi Huang (259–210 BCE), placed there to protect him in the afterlife. Each of the soldiers is unique, with distinct facial features, expressions, and hairstyles. Qin Shi Huang came to power at 21, and unified China, imposing uniform laws, a writing system, measures, and coinage.

Giant Buddha
Carved from the face of a cliff in Leshan, China, this seated Buddha is 233 ft (71 m) high. It was made during the Tang Dynasty (618–907 CE), one of the most successful dynasties ever to rule China. Art and trade flourished under the Tang emperors. They were great patrons of Buddhism, which had entered China from India some centuries earlier, and thousands of Buddhist monasteries were founded at this time.

Ming Emperor

The Jiajing Emperor (1507–67) rides at the center of the procession, surrounded by his officials and soldiers. Founded after the overthrow of the Mongol emperors, the Ming Dynasty brought unrivaled prosperity to China. Its frontiers expanded and trade in luxury goods such as porcelain and silk soared. Chinese ships explored the world's sea routes, returning laden with treasure.

Military might

Soldiers guarding the emperor are wearing ceremonial armor. Under the Ming emperors, the army had nearly two million men, many of whom used gunpowder weapons (a 9th-century Chinese invention).

Court officials

The empire's system of government was large and complex. Officials were recruited by week-long written examinations that tested knowledge of Chinese history and the classics of Chinese literature.

Great Wall of China

The open flat land in the north of China made it vulnerable to invasions, a fact that worried the emperors. Earth and stone ramparts were first constructed along its northern borders to keep out raiders in the 6th century BCE, and were extended by Qin Shi Huang. The Ming emperors rebuilt the wall in stone, adding watchtowers and gun platforms. The wall ran for 5,500 miles (8,850 km), some of which can still be seen today.

Beginning of the end

The Qianlong Emperor (1711–99) was the sixth emperor of the Qing Dynasty (1644–1911), the last dynasty to rule imperial China. His six-decade reign was the longest in Chinese history. By this time, China was exporting quantities of porcelain, cotton, silk, and tea to Europe, and was paid in silver, making it the richest country in the world. However, the last years of Qianlong's reign were marked by corruption, and after his death, Chinese power went into decline.

The New World

Christopher Columbus (1451–1506) set foot in the Americas in 1492 after sailing across the Atlantic on a voyage to find a sea route to China. His discovery resulted in the Spanish conquest of South America, but he was not the first European to reach America—Vikings had done so 500 years before.

Round-the-world trip

Portuguese explorer Ferdinand Magellan (1480–1521) was one of many explorers to meet a tragic fate. He led the first round-the-world voyage in 1519, sailing from the Atlantic into the Pacific Ocean, but was murdered by islanders in the Philippines. Just 18 of the 237 crew members returned home in 1522.

South Pacific

By the 1700s a race was on among European mariners to explore the South Pacific. British sailor James Cook (1729–79) led an expedition to the Polynesian island of Tahiti with instructions from King George III to claim any new land he found for Britain. In August 1770, he landed in Australia and claimed the coast.

Scientific exploration

Charles Darwin (1809–82) was a naturalist on the British survey ship *HMS Beagle* from 1831 to 1836, as it voyaged around the coast of South America. The observations he made of the natural life of the region led later to his writing *On the Origin of Species* (1859), his famous work on evolution.

Surrounded by ice
In June 1910, Scott's ship *Terra Nova* sailed from England. In Australia, Scott heard that Amundsen was also racing south, from Norway. Both men reached Antarctica in January 1911. Amundsen sailed as far south as he could, anchoring 60 miles (96 km) closer to the Pole than Scott, who set up base on Ross Island. Here, 25 of Scott's party spent the dark Antarctic winter of 1911 on the *Terra Nova* surrounded by pack ice (left).

Rival progress
Amundsen's team had set off with four sleds, each pulled by 13 dogs. They shot six dogs when the animals became exhausted and transferred to skis, taking just 55 days to reach the South Pole.

Exploration

The urge to explore is fundamental to human nature. As transportation and navigation skills improved, people made long journeys of exploration. By 1900, only Antarctica remained unexplored. In 1911–12, British explorer Robert Falcon Scott (1868–1912) and Norwegian Roald Amundsen (1872–1928) raced to be first to the South Pole.

Man power
Scott's decision not to use dogs to pull the sleds may have been a mistake. His ponies died, and the engines on his motorized sleds broke down, so his men had to haul the supplies themselves.

Protection against the cold
Fur boots—which Scott called *finneskos*— worn with an inner pair of felt boots helped keep the explorers' feet warm and dry. But compared with the lightweight insulated polar clothing of today, their heavy woolen garments were cumbersome and feeble. Many of the men got frostbite and suffered from snow blindness because they did not wear goggles. Their diet lacked vitamins, adding to their problems.

Ancient Greece

Dotted around the eastern Mediterranean Sea in more than 300 city-states, the Ancient Greeks spent much of their time fighting each other. What united them was a common language and a love of ideas. They invented democracy and recorded their ideas. Many of their immense achievements in literature, science, and philosophy have survived and still influence how we think today.

Doctor's orders
A great physician, Hippocrates (c. 460–370 BCE) believed that illnesses had physical causes, rather than being sent by the gods. He also valued the benefits of rest and diet in bringing about a cure.

First historian
The first person to write what we now call history, Herodotus (c. 484–c. 425 BCE) set out to discover from eyewitnesses the truth about the war between the Greeks and Persians (499–449 BCE).

Alexander the Great
Alexander (356–323 BCE) became king of Macedon, in northeastern Greece, at the age of 20. A great general, he subdued the Greek city-states and the Persians, before going on to conquer a vast empire stretching across Asia to northwest India. He founded many cities named after himself. One of these, Alexandria in Egypt, replaced Athens as the center of the Greek-speaking (Hellenistic) world after his death.

Gods and goddesses
The Greeks believed in many gods and goddesses. The 12 most important (the Olympians) lived at the top of Mount Olympus, a tall mountain in northern Greece, and were ruled over by Zeus, the king of the gods (left). Zeus had many children, including the other Olympians, Apollo, a lover of music and the lyre, and Hermes, the messenger of the gods and guide to the underworld. A quarrelsome group, the gods made trouble by intervening in human affairs.

Good sports
Sports were a favorite pastime of the Greeks. Starting in 776 BCE, athletes in Greece traveled to Olympia to take part in games held in honor of Zeus every four years. Only Greek-speaking males could enter, and there were separate contests for men and for boys. Events included running, discus, horse and chariot racing, javelin, wrestling, and boxing. Athletes competed for an olive crown and to win lasting fame for themselves and their city-state.

The poet

Nobody knows for sure when Homer lived, or even if he really lived at all, but he is credited as the author of two great epic poems, the *Iliad* and the *Odyssey*, which recount the deeds of the Greeks in their legendary war against the city of Troy. The poems date from about the 8th century BCE, and came to be so well known, loved, and recited throughout the Greek world that he was simply called "the poet."

Sappho

One of the few known female poets of the ancient world, Sappho (c. 610–c. 550 BCE) wrote about love, family, and friends. She was admired for her lyrical style, but only fragments of her work remain.

Great philosophers

The Greeks were passionate about philosophy (a Greek word meaning "love of wisdom"). Plato (427–347 BCE) was one of three significant thinkers who lived and taught in Athens, and who constantly questioned the world and how people should live. The other two were Socrates (469–399 BCE), Plato's teacher, and Aristotle (384–322 BCE), famous for his studies of the natural world.

Warfare

Greece was a male-dominated society. Only men were considered to be citizens, and had to be ready at all times to fight for their city-state. The finest soldiers came from Sparta where boys began 13 years of military training at the age of seven. Greek armies included heavily armed foot soldiers called hoplites, and the phalanx, a unit of soldiers with overlapping shields for protection. At sea, the Greeks used wooden battleships called triremes (like the replica on the left).

Eureka!

Science flourished during the Hellenistic age. One of the greats was the mathematician Archimedes (c. 287–212 BCE). Struggling to find a method of calculating the volume of oddly shaped objects (such as himself), he noticed the water rise as he stepped into his bathtub. He quickly realized that he could measure the volume of the water displaced by the object instead. He rushed naked into the street shouting "*Eureka!*" ("I've got it!").

American Revolution

The Boston Tea Party of 1773 (above) was an early act of defiance against British rule by colonists in North America. The rising swell of protests led to the Declaration of Independence (1776), with its radical statement that "all men are created equal," and to the war that saw the birth of the USA.

The Year of Revolutions

In 1848, revolutions broke out across Europe. This print depicts events in Berlin, then the capital of Prussia. The demands of the protestors varied from country to country but included fair voting systems, elected parliaments, freedom of the press, and the right to self-government. Despite promises of reform, nothing was won.

Workers' party

The political theory of communism called for workers to seize control of production and establish their own governments. The world's first communist country, the Soviet Union, emerged from the October Revolution of 1917 in Russia. It was led by Vladimir Lenin (1870–1924), here seen speaking to the crowds in Moscow.

Peaceful revolution

In November 1989, protestors started smashing sections of the hated Berlin Wall that divided communist East Germany, then a separate country and an ally of the Soviet Union, from capitalist West Germany. The East German government collapsed, leading to the peaceful reunification of the country.

End of the French monarchy
The execution of King Louis XVI (1754–93) brought an end to the monarchy. The Revolution began in July 1789, when rioters, angered by food shortages and high taxes, turned against the king's government. He attempted to flee, but he was caught and returned to Paris. France became a republic, but, as happens after many revolutions, the country was unstable, with violence and lawlessness rife.

On the streets
The main events of the Revolution took place on Paris's streets. The most fervent revolutionaries were the poor of the city, called the *sans-culottes*, because they did not wear expensive breeches (*culottes*).

MORT

Political revolutions

A political revolution occurs when the people act together to overthrow an unpopular government, as happened during the French Revolution of 1789–99 (above). The revolutionaries often aim to create a fairer society, to win political freedom for themselves, or to get rid of a bad or unpopular ruler.

The guillotine

Revolutions often require the elimination of their perceived enemies. In France, the favored way of disposing of such enemies was the guillotine, a machine that dropped a steel blade on the victim's neck, quickly severing the head from the body. Thousands of people from all walks of life in France were killed on the guillotine during the Terror, a period of extreme violence that followed the king's execution.

Rise of Napoleon

Corsican-born Napoleon Bonaparte (1769–1821), a general in the French army, shot to fame after successful campaigns in Italy and Egypt. He restored order at home by 1799, and crowned himself Emperor in 1805, then set about building his empire through a series of European wars. This cartoon shows him (on the right) dividing up the world with the British, the agents of his final defeat and downfall in 1815.

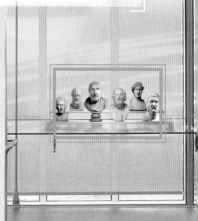

Revolutionary guard

National Guards were citizen armies set up in every French city with the job of protecting the interests of the Revolution, and administering law and order in the vacuum that followed the end of the monarchy.

UIS CAPET, 16ᵐᵉ DU NOM, LE 21 JANVIER 1793. (A))

Industrial Revolution

The Industrial Revolution was a period, roughly between 1750 and 1900, of rapid technological advances that brought dramatic changes in the way people lived and worked. It began in Britain and spread around the world. At the start, most people worked on the land; by the end, most people were living and working in cities. The railways played a key role in bringing about these changes.

People and goods

In 1825 British engineer George Stephenson (1781–1848) opened the first public railway to carry coal between towns in northeast England. Its open wagons were soon carrying passengers as well, transported at a leisurely 8 mph (13 kph). As the railways expanded rapidly, more and more people began to use them, traveling to their destinations in long trains of passenger-coaches. Goods wagons were hauled separately.

Spread of the railways

Railways spread quickly around the world. This picture shows the opening of the first railway line in Russia in 1837. The first coast-to-coast railroad across the USA was completed in 1869. In Britain, the process of industrialization had started before the railways, but in other parts of the world the railways encouraged industrial growth by making it possible to distribute materials and consumer goods to distant markets cheaply and quickly.

Keeping on track

The railways massively increased demand for coal and iron. Mile after mile of iron tracks, resting on wooden railroad ties, were laid to carry the heavy locomotives and trains, transforming the countryside for ever. The engine boilers had to be made strong enough to withstand the steam pressure (many exploded). Methods of making and casting iron improved steadily to meet this demand.

Spinning success

The Spinning Jenny (left), invented in 1764, allowed one person to spin several spools of yarn or thread at a time. It was the first of several new machines that revolutionized the making of cloth at the start of the Industrial Revolution. Previously wool had been spun at home. Now it was done on water-powered or steam-powered machines in mills and factories owned by wealthy manufacturers who employed cheap labor, mostly women and children.

Crowded cities

Many people left the countryside to work in the new textile mills and factories. Over-crowded towns grew up around these industrial centers, made filthy by smoke and pollution. By 1851, more than half the population of Britain was living in towns—the first time this had happened anywhere in the world. There was dreadful poverty in the city centers, as this London slum, pictured in 1872, shows.

Up to speed

In 1904 this locomotive, the *City of Truro*, became the first to reach a speed of more than 100 mph (160 kph). Restored to working order, it repeated its record-breaking run 100 years later in 2004.

The power of steam

Steam engines had been used to power machines such as weaving looms in British factories since the 1770s. In 1805 Richard Trevithick (1771–1833) built the first steam-powered locomotive (moving) engine designed to run on rails. Coal was burned to heat water in the large round iron boiler at the front of the engine. This created steam, which pushed the pistons to turn the wheels.

News travels fast

The 19th century saw great advances in the use of electricity. In 1837, American inventor Samuel Morse (1791–1872) devised a method of sending electric signals along wires using Morse code—a system of dots and dashes to stand for letters. Called the electric telegraph, it transformed communications. In 1861 the first submarine telegraph cable was laid beneath the Atlantic, bringing the world closer together than ever.

Victorian engineer

British engineer Isambard Kingdom Brunel (1805–59) was the greatest engineer of the railway age. He designed tunnels, bridges, and viaducts that are still impressive working structures today, including the Clifton Suspension Bridge (left) in Bristol, England. Brunel also designed a number of famous steamships, including the SS *Great Britain* (1843), the first propeller-driven ocean-going iron ship.

Philosophical thinker
French philosopher René Descartes (1596–1650) believed that science and mathematics can be used to explain everything in nature. His works became very influential during the 18th-century Enlightenment, an era that placed reason and logic above all other concerns in fields such as philosophy, science, and culture.

Sky gazing
The first astronomical telescope was invented in 1605 by Italian astronomer Galileo Galilei. He used it to observe the craters on the Moon and four of Jupiter's moons. He proved the earlier theory of Polish astronomer Nicolaus Copernicus (1473–1543) that the Earth travels around the Sun, and not the other way round.

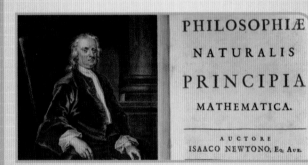

What goes up
English mathematician Sir Isaac Newton (1642–1727) published his most important work, the *Principia Mathematica*, in 1687. In it, he showed that gravity keeps the Earth and planets in orbit around the Sun, and causes objects to fall to the ground. This proved to be one of the most significant discoveries ever made.

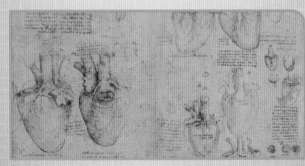

Renaissance man
Best known as a Renaissance painter, Italian Leonardo da Vinci (1452–1519) was also an inventor, scientist, architect, and mathematician, filling his notebooks with careful studies of nature, anatomy (above), and designs for ingenious machines. His thirst for knowledge helped to inform and shape the times.

New ideas

Between the 14th and 17th centuries, new ideas and discoveries transformed the way Europeans thought about the world. Known as the knowledge revolution, it was helped by the new technology of the printing press, which, like the Internet today, allowed these exciting breakthroughs to reach a wider audience than ever before.

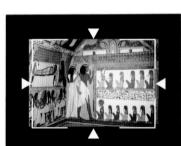

Setting the type
Reading from a copy of written text, this workman is placing type—pieces of metal bearing a single raised letter—inside a wooden frame (called a forme) to make up a page of text ready for printing.

Books old and new
Before printing, books were copied laboriously by hand. This restricted book learning to the Church, which included most literate people, and to a few wealthy families who could afford these expensive luxuries.

Printed propaganda

The printing press soon made an impact. In 1517, German monk Martin Luther (1483–1546) hung a list of complaints against the Roman Catholic Church on a church door in Wittenberg, Germany. Within days, printed copies of his statement (known as the *Ninety-Five Theses*) had circulated far and wide, and his ideas sparked the period of religious upheaval in Europe known as the Reformation. Opponents of Luther's views used the printing press, too—in this caricature, Luther is playing the Devil's tune.

The first press

Gutenberg modeled his press on ones used since Roman times to press olives or grapes. The large screw exerted force onto a wooden board, impressing the inked letters on the paper beneath. The first completed book printed on Gutenberg's press was the Bible. It took a year to produce the first edition of about 180 copies. It seems slow by today's standards, but was faster and more accurate than copying by hand.

Inking the letters

As one sheet is printed, another workman prepares the next one. He spreads black ink evenly over the pieces of type within the forme and lays a sheet of paper on top. It is then ready to go under the press.

Gutenberg

This 19th-century painting shows the German Johannes Gutenberg (1398–1468), the man who started the printing revolution, in his workshop in about 1455. The Chinese had already discovered printing, but Gutenberg's invention was moveable type: using small separate letters to form the words to be printed. The beauty of his invention was that the letters could be used over and over again, in any order.

Ancient Egypt

More than 5,000 years ago, a unique civilization arose among farmers living along the banks of the River Nile in Egypt. It lasted for 3,000 years, longer than any other civilization in history. Its spectacular monuments and elaborate tombs still amaze us today. This is the burial chamber of the skilled artisan Sennedjem and his wife Iineferti, built in 1298 BCE at Thebes (Luxor), Egypt.

Jackal guides
Two jackals recline, beneath eyes of the god Horus. The jackals represent Anubis, the god of mummification, and guide the spirits of the dead through the many parts of the underworld.

Journey into the afterlife
The Egyptians believed that after death they would enter the afterlife, a farming paradise where food was plentiful. A deceased body was mummified (preserved by embalming) so the soul could return to the body after death. Here we see Sennedjem's mummy, protected by the funeral goddess Nephthys (in the form of a falcon), as his soul prepares to make the dangerous journey to the afterlife.

Well-dressed couple
Iineferti and Sennedjem are shown in fine linen robes. They are both wearing make-up and wigs, and have scented cones of animal fat on their heads. Their tomb was filled with the things the couple wanted to have in the afterlife, such as food, drink, furniture, and jewelry, and reflected their wealthy status. Poor people sometimes buried their dead near the tombs of the rich in the hope of joining their feasts.

Family reunion
This special kind of priest, called a *sem*, awakens the couple from the dead, and pours them a drink. The other people are friends, family, and children (shown smaller) the couple wish to see in the next life.

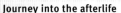

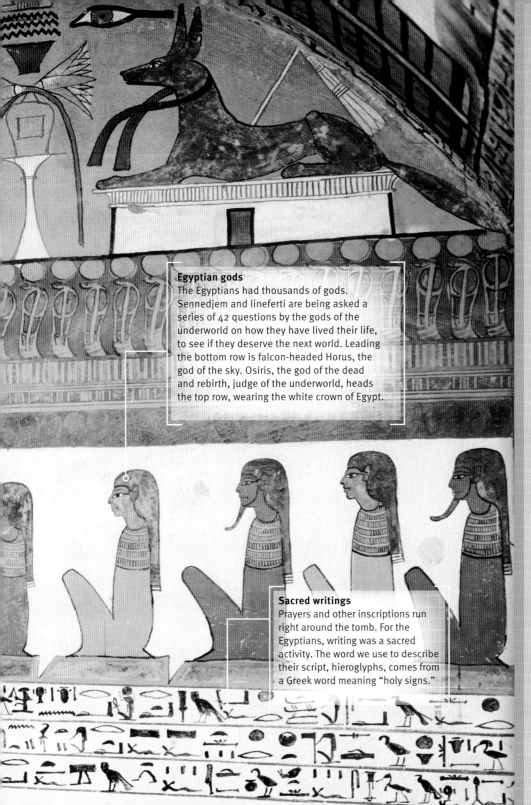

Egyptian gods
The Egyptians had thousands of gods. Sennedjem and Iineferti are being asked a series of 42 questions by the gods of the underworld on how they have lived their life, to see if they deserve the next world. Leading the bottom row is falcon-headed Horus, the god of the sky. Osiris, the god of the dead and rebirth, judge of the underworld, heads the top row, wearing the white crown of Egypt.

Sacred writings
Prayers and other inscriptions run right around the tomb. For the Egyptians, writing was a sacred activity. The word we use to describe their script, hieroglyphs, comes from a Greek word meaning "holy signs."

Life-giving river
The civilization of Ancient Egypt owed everything to the River Nile. On either side of the narrow Nile valley is barren desert. Every year the Nile flooded, watering the land and leaving behind deposits of fertile silt to renew the fields. If the Nile failed to flood, as sometimes happened, the Egyptians starved.

Pharaoh's mummy
For 3,000 years Egypt was ruled by dynasties of powerful god-kings called pharaohs. In 1922, archaeologists stumbled upon the treasure-filled burial chamber of a young pharaoh, Tutankhamun (reigned 1336–27 BCE). His mummy was found intact inside a golden coffin, wearing a mask of solid gold.

Pyramid tombs
The pyramids, built some 4,500 years ago as tombs for the pharaohs, are the earliest stone buildings in the world. The tallest, the Great Pyramid of Giza, is some 480 ft (146 m) high and contains about 1.3 million quarried limestone blocks. It was originally capped with gold to catch the rays of the rising Sun.

Cracking the code
The ability to read ancient Egyptian hieroglyphs was lost until 1822. The French linguist Jean-François Champollion (1790–1832) used the Rosetta Stone—a carved tablet with inscriptions in Egyptian hieroglyphs and ancient Greek (above)—to decipher them, greatly increasing our knowledge of Ancient Egypt.

Africa

In past centuries a series of civilizations rose and fell in Africa. Little about these diverse cultures was known in the outside world, except what was told in the tales of travelers—men such as the Islamic scholar Ibn Battuta (1304–69) who crossed the vast wastes of the Sahara to visit Timbuktu and other distant places.

Tomb of Askia

The Songhai empire controlled all trade in gold and salt across the Sahara in the 1500s. One of the rulers of this Muslim state, Askia Mohammad I (c. 1442–1538), is buried in this tomb in Gao, Mali.

Great Zimbabwe

The massive stone walls of the ancient city of Great Zimbabwe (c. 1250–1450) have given their name to the modern country of Zimbabwe in southern Africa. The walls are all that remain of the fortified city built by the Mwenemutapa, a cattle-herding people. They grew rich through their control of the gold and ivory trade, and established a military empire in the area of the Zambezi River.

Fabled Timbuktu

The medieval city of Timbuktu, on the Niger River, Mali, West Africa, was a bustling center of trade. Also the site of an Islamic university noted for its scholarship, travelers carried its fame far and wide.

African slaves

Slaves were exported from Africa from ancient times. "Memory for the Slaves," in Zanzibar, Tanzania, is a memorial to the millions sold in the market there from the 10th to the 19th centuries, destined for slavery in the Middle East. From the 1500s, up to 12 million Africans were taken from West Africa to plantations in the Americas. Crammed below deck, many died on the Atlantic crossing. This well-organized trade took place on European ships until the abolition of the slave trade in 1807.

Explorers in Africa

Few Europeans had set foot in Africa's interior before the 1800s when scientific bodies such as Britain's Royal Geographical Society sponsored expeditions into the heart of the continent. When the Scottish missionary and explorer David Livingstone (1813–73, on right), disappeared on a journey to the source of the Nile River, Henry Morton Stanley (1841–1904) set out to find him. News of their meeting in 1871 was telegraphed around the world.

Rock-cut church
This 12th-century church in Ethiopia, East Africa, was carved from a single block of granite. Ethiopia (previously the kingdom of Aksum) has been Christian since the 4th century.

Kingdom of Kush
Also known as Nubia, the kingdom of Kush was founded on the Upper Nile River (now in northern Sudan). Its rulers were influenced by the Egyptian civilization to the north, and continued to be buried in pyramids long after the custom ceased in Egypt. For a time, the Kushites even ruled Egypt as the 25th Dynasty (760–656 BCE). One of the Kush capitals was at Meroë, but little remains of this once great city.

Africa's early kingdoms
The first African kingdoms rose in Egypt (c.3000 BCE) and in Kush (c.1000 BCE). Trading kingdoms, such as those in Mali and Songhai, began to emerge in west and central Africa south of the Sahara, before 1000 CE. Later, kingdoms such as Aksum and Great Zimbabwe formed among cattle-farmers on the grasslands south and east of the Congo basin.

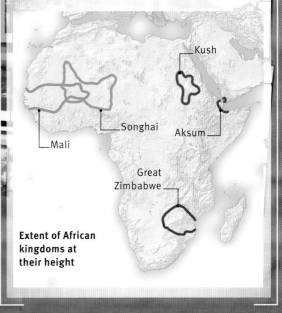

Kush

Songhai

Aksum

Mali

Great Zimbabwe

Extent of African kingdoms at their height

Africa divided
Between 1870 and 1900, Europe's colonial powers—Britain, France, Belgium, Germany, Portugal, Spain, and Italy—scrambled to gain possession of Africa's vast mineral wealth: gold, diamonds, copper, and coal. The map of Africa was redrawn with new boundaries that cut through existing tribal areas. This cartoon shows the ambitions of British imperialist Cecil Rhodes (1853–1902) who dreamed of building a railway to run from Cairo, Egypt, to Cape Town, South Africa.

New freedoms
Before 1950, there were only four independent nations in Africa; today there are 54. The struggle of these countries to win their independence from Europe's colonial powers was often bitter, with years of conflict. Despite being imprisoned for 27 years, Nelson Mandela led a fight against South Africa's harsh apartheid (segregation) laws that deprived black people of all civil rights. In 1994, he became the first president of a multiracial South Africa.

India

The Indian subcontinent, birthplace of two world religions—Hinduism and Buddhism—has a long history of invasion and settlement from Central Asia. In the 16th century, the Mughals—Muslim warriors from Afghanistan who claimed descent from the Mongols—conquered an area of northern India. They established a powerful empire and built many fine buildings, including the Taj Mahal.

Perfect symmetry
Standing on a raised platform and surrounded by four minarets, the Taj Mahal is perfectly symmetrical (balanced) in design. The taxes from 30 villages were used to pay for its construction and upkeep.

Token of eternal love
Mumtaz Mahal (1592–1631), the second and favorite wife of the Mughal emperor Shah Jahan (reigned 1628–58), died giving birth to their 14th child. Overcome by grief, the emperor built the Taj Mahal as a magnificent tomb in her honor. More than 20,000 workmen were employed in the tomb's construction, and 1,000 elephants were used to haul the blocks of white marble to the site.

Great builder
The Taj Mahal stands just outside the old Mughal capital of Agra. In 1639, Shah Jahan decided Agra was too crowded and moved the capital to Delhi, where he built himself a magnificent palace, the Red Fort. His life ended tragically. His youngest son Aurangzeb seized the throne by force. Aurangzeb had his brothers executed, and kept his father a prisoner for eight years until his death.

Extent of the empire

Founded by Babur (1483–1530) in 1526, the original heartland of the Mughal empire lay in Kabul, now in Afghanistan. By 1605, Mughal rule extended across northern India. The empire was at its height during the reign of Aurangzeb, when it stretched far into south India, but declined after his death in 1707. Weakened by the revival of Hindu military strength in the west and north, the empire had all but ended by 1803.

•Kabul
•Delhi
•Agra

The Mughal empire at its height

Religious divide

Mughal architecture mixes Persian, Hindu, and Islamic influences—minarets are a traditional feature of mosques. The Mughal emperors were Muslims, but their subjects were mostly Hindus. Rather than risk rebellion, the Mughals gave Hindus important positions. Akbar the Great (reigned 1556–1605) was noted for religious tolerance, but Shah Jahan promoted Islam. Aurangzeb's reign (1658–1707) was harsher still.

Garden of paradise

In Islamic tradition, gardens should contain water as a reminder of the rivers of paradise. The Mughal emperors were great lovers of gardens and patrons of the arts, especially miniature painting.

Ancient origins

The origins of Hinduism stretch back at least 3,000 years, where it emerged among farmers living on the Ganges plain of north India. Hindus believe in a supreme spirit, Brahma, who reveals himself through hundreds of gods and goddesses. This carving shows Shiva the Destroyer, one of the oldest Hindu gods.

Kingdoms and dynasties

For much of history India was divided into a patchwork of small Hindu and Buddhist kingdoms and short-lived dynasties. The temple of Mukteswar in the modern state of Orissa in eastern India dates from the 11th century when the region was enjoying a golden age of prosperity under the Ganga dynasty.

British rule

European traders first began visiting India in the 15th century. By the mid-19th century Britain had taken direct control of the government of India. In 1877, Queen Victoria (1819–1901), seen here at Windsor Castle, UK, with an Indian servant, became Empress of India even though she never visited the country.

Path to freedom

Mohandas Gandhi (1869–1948) led the struggle for India's independence from British rule, which was won in 1947. Gandhi believed that political change should be brought about by non-violence, and organized mass protests against British laws. He boycotted British-made cotton and spun his own thread.

Bubonic plague

In the 1340s, the Black Death, an outbreak of bubonic plague, killed about a third of the population in Europe and millions more in Asia. Fleas are responsible for the spreading of bubonic plague, but people then blamed bad air. This doctor is wearing a birdlike mask to ward off poisonous fumes.

Deadly cholera

The victims of cholera, caused by drinking water polluted with human waste, die in great pain. Cholera epidemics occurred regularly in the overcrowded, unsanitary cities of 19th-century Europe until checked by the provision of proper sewers and a clean water supply. It is still a threat in many parts of the world.

Spanish flu

The Spanish flu pandemic (widespread outbreak of disease) of 1918–19 was the deadliest in history. It started among soldiers on an army base in Kansas, USA. Human carriers of the virus spread it along rail and shipping routes to infect one-fifth of the world's population, and 50–100 million people died.

The fight against AIDS

AIDS (Acquired Immunodeficiency Syndrome) affects an estimated 33 million people, mostly in Africa. Until the 1980s, the HIV virus that causes AIDS was unknown. The ribbon symbol, shown in this sculpture in Durban, SA, raises awareness of AIDS. Drugs can slow the virus's progress, but the search for a cure continues.

Smallpox gets the needle

Infectious and deadly smallpox devastated whole populations for centuries. British doctor Edward Jenner (1749–1823) found his patients would not catch it if he injected them first with cowpox, a weaker form of the disease. He called this a vaccine. Though people did not yet understand how it worked (by producing antibodies to resist the smallpox virus), it was a major breakthrough in the fight against disease.

Hole in the head

A surgeon has removed these disks, probably to relieve pressure on the brain. This procedure, called trepanning, has been carried out since prehistoric times and similar, safer operations are still in use.

Medicine

Disease has always been part of life, but when people settled as farmers, living together and with their animals, infectious diseases spread, often with devastating effect. For thousands of years, people were at the mercy of doctors who had little understanding of disease. Improved knowledge and hygiene has made life safer for us all.

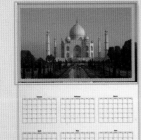

Through the microscope
When microscopes were invented in the 1600s, scientists discovered animalcules—tiny organisms living in air and water. Today we know them to be disease-producing germs such as bacteria and viruses.

Life-saving mold
When Scottish scientist Alexander Fleming (1881–1955) went on vacation in 1928 he left a dish containing bacteria in his laboratory. On his return, he found a blue mold had grown on the dish—and had killed all the bacteria. In 1940, doctors in Oxford, UK, used his discovery to develop penicillin, the world's first antibiotic drug (one that destroys harmful bacteria). Before this, a simple infection could be fatal.

Blood suckers
In the past, doctors believed bloodletting—removing "bad" blood from the body—would cure most diseases, but it more often killed the patient. Leeches (small, blood-sucking worms) were a safe way to draw out the blood. When a leech attaches to a human or animal host, it releases a chemical that stops the blood from clotting. Surgeons today may use leeches to clean wounds and restore blood flow.

First emperor

Octavian (63 BCE–14 CE) brought an end to civil war and made himself sole ruler of Rome. In 27 BCE he took the titles of Augustus ("honored one") and Imperator ("commander", from which the word emperor is derived) to become the first Roman emperor. Before this, Rome had been a republic.

Buried under ash

On August 24, 79 CE, Pompeii, a city on the Bay of Naples in Italy, was destroyed when Mount Vesuvius erupted without warning. For centuries it lay buried under a thick layer of volcanic ash. Excavations of this once-thriving city have provided rare insights into the daily life of the Roman empire.

Blood sports

Emperors and wealthy patrons won favor with the people of Rome by providing lavish public entertainments. Most popular of all were the gladiators—trained killers who fought in hand-to-hand combat in front of crowds. Another favorite display was the mass slaughter of lions, tigers, and other exotic wild beasts.

Engineering feat

The Romans were skilled structural engineers, building great monuments in stone, brick, and concrete. The Pont du Gard, in southern France, is part of a Roman aqueduct constructed in the 1st century CE to carry fresh water supplies a distance

Other duties

All Roman legionaries carried pickaxes and spades in their heavy packs. They dug ditches, built forts and bridges, and constructed the roads that allowed the army to travel quickly around the empire.

From citizen to soldier

The Roman army originally consisted of land-owning citizens who left their farms when called upon to fight. Once Rome became involved in lengthy overseas wars, a better system was needed. Reforms in the 2nd century BCE meant that any Roman citizen could enlist as a soldier for 25 years. They were fully trained and paid a salary, and normally given a plot of land to farm when they retired.

Ancient Rome

From a small settlement on the banks of the River Tiber in Italy, Rome grew into a mighty military empire. At its height, it stretched across Europe and into the Middle East and Africa, and its people enjoyed several centuries of stability and prosperity before the empire collapsed in the 5th century CE.

Chain of command

The centurion, marching at the head of his men, commanded a century (unit) of 80 soldiers. The century was part of a cohort, a fighting force of 480 men. There were 10 cohorts in a legion.

Keeping up standards

Each century had its own standard (*signum*)—a long pole mounted with disk emblems—to act as a rallying point in battle. The standard bearer (*signifer*) wore a wolfskin over his armor.

Fighting order

Half of the army was divided into legions of about 5,000 soldiers, called legionaries, who were provided with armor and weapons and given a tough training on joining up. Soldiers fought in line about 4 ft (1.2 m) apart. They attacked with swords and javelins and protected themselves behind a wall of shields. The rest of the army consisted of the auxiliaries, which included men from tribes allied to or conquered by Rome.

Rome at its height

The Roman Empire was at its greatest extent in 117 CE, under the emperor Trajan. Its territories stretched all around the Mediterranean Sea (called *Mare Nostrum*, "our sea", by the Romans) and beyond. Plunder from defeated territories was sent back to Rome and helped pay the troops, and many slaves were captured, too. The Romans took their systems of government and law, engineering, and coinage wherever they conquered, leading to people from Britain to Egypt and from Spain to Syria sharing a single state and a similar way of life.

Britain · German tribes · Gaul · Rome · Spain · Asia · Mediterranean sea · Syria · Egypt

Ionized gas in a plasma globe
glows with electricity emitted
by a charged metal ball.

SCIENCE AND TECHNOLOGY

We have an insatiable curiosity about the world around us. What is it made of, and how does it work? Questions like these inspired the critical discoveries that are the basis of modern science. In the process, scientists and inventors devised the amazing technologies that have become part of our daily lives.

Falling fuel tank

Eight minutes after launch the orbiter reaches its intended altitude and the main fuel tank is jettisoned. The higher up an object is, the more gravitational potential energy it has. Once the tank starts falling back to Earth, its potential (stored) energy gradually decreases as it gains more kinetic energy, falling faster and faster. When it hits the sea, its kinetic energy becomes heat, sound, and the movement of the water.

Solid Rocket Boosters

The fuel contained in the Solid Rocket Boosters (SRBs) is burned in a very short time. Two minutes after launch the SRBs are jettisoned—they fall back to Earth, where they are retrieved and reused. During the launch, the orbiter's three main engines are also firing. They burn the liquid fuel stored in the huge main fuel tank. After the SRBs are discarded these engines take the orbiter the rest of the distance into space.

Blasting off

The force needed to get the Shuttle off the ground is provided by two Solid Rocket Boosters that burn solid fuel. When the fuel burns, its stored chemical energy is converted to heat. Gases in the fuel heat up and expand rapidly, pushing their way out of the rocket's exhaust pipes in billowing clouds. The force of the gas pushing down propels the rocket in the opposite direction. The moving rocket is said to have kinetic energy.

Energy

Energy is needed for anything in the Universe to happen, from blinking an eye to blasting off into space, and it is all around us in many forms. Energy cannot be destroyed but it can change from one kind to another. Here, the US Space Shuttle is being launched: the chemical energy of its rocket fuel is changing to kinetic (movement) energy, and to sound, light, and heat.

Orbiter

At its intended altitude, up to 300 miles (500 km) above the Earth, the orbiter fires two side engines to change its direction and go into a circular orbit. In order to do this the orbiter must carry its own fuel supply. Heavier objects need more kinetic energy to make them move at a given speed or change direction. By discarding the SRBs and main fuel tank, the orbiter has less mass and needs to carry less fuel.

Light and heat

When the chemical energy in the fuel changes to kinetic energy and propels the rocket upward, it is doing useful work. However, some of the energy is wasted in the process, turning to the light, heat, and sound of the exhausts. Whenever we use energy, some is always wasted as excess heat. The smaller the fraction of energy wasted, the more efficient a process is said to be.

Life-giving Sun

Solar panels convert sunlight into electricity. Almost all of the energy we use comes from the Sun. Nuclear reactions in its core release energy that travels to Earth as light. Plants use it to make food, stored as chemical energy. Fossil fuels are formed from ancient plants. Burning them releases the energy they contain.

Static charge

During a thunderstorm, clouds build up a store of electrical energy in the form of static electricity. Eventually, some of the energy is released in a flash of light. Some is converted to heat energy, which expands the air rapidly, producing the sound energy we hear as a clap of thunder.

Energy from atoms

German-born physicist Albert Einstein (1879–1955) showed that mass is a form of energy. In a nuclear explosion like this one, atoms change from one type to another, and the new type has slightly less mass. This tiny loss of mass produces vast amounts of heat, light, and sound.

Energy for us

Human beings need energy to live, and we obtain it from the chemical energy in food. The energy is used in many ways—to build and repair our cells, to move around, and to keep the body's systems functioning. Our food is like a fuel that we burn in order to stay alive.

Dynamics

The science of motion is called dynamics. It involves the study of forces (pushes and pulls) that make objects move. An airplane traveling through the air has four forces acting upon it: thrust, lift, drag, and gravity. The thrust from the engines moves the plane forward and creates the lift that raises it up. These forces must overcome gravity, which is pulling the plane down, and drag, which is pulling it backward.

Thrust
The thrust that keeps the plane moving is provided by the engines, which draw air in at the front and force it out at the back at high speed propelling it forward. The bigger the engine, the more thrust.

Lift
The shape of the wings provides the lifting force that keeps the plane in the air (see boxed text, right). Thrust provided by the engines pushes the plane forward, forcing air over and under the wings. Air applies a pressure to whatever it touches, as its molecules knock against it. It is this pressure of the air on the wings that keeps the plane aloft. The faster the plane is moving the more airflow and the greater the lift.

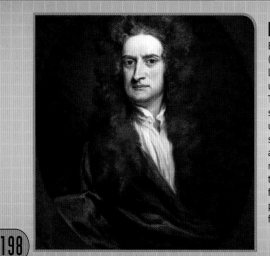

Laws of motion

English physicist Isaac Newton (1642–1727) formulated three laws of motion that allow us to understand how objects move. The first law says an object will stay still or move at a steady pace unless a force acts on it. The second law says that when a force acts on an object, the object will move or change direction. The third law explains that when a force acts on an object, the object pulls or pushes back with equal force in the opposite direction.

Inertia

Newton's first law of motion says that objects stay where they are or move at a steady speed unless a force acts on them. This is called inertia. The heavier an object is, the more inertia is has. The people in this picture must pull much harder to start the plane moving than they will to keep it going. Similarly, once a heavy object starts moving, its inertia makes it difficult to stop or change its direction.

Drag

The air resists being pushed aside, producing a force called drag that pulls back on the plane, slowing it down. Drag can be reduced by streamlining—giving something a smooth, rounded shape.

The science of flight

There are two effects that provide the plane's lift. The first is supplied by the angle of the wings. Because they cut into the air at an angle, the air that hits the underside of the wing is deflected downward, which pushes the wing upward. This is an example of Newton's third law of motion (see panel below).

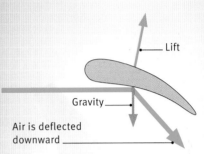

Lift

Gravity

Air is deflected downward

The second effect is called Bernouilli's Principle. The wings' shape means that their upper surface is longer than their underside. Air traveling over the upper surface has further to go and must move faster. Its higher speed makes it press down less hard than the slower air traveling underneath pushes the wing upward. There is more pressure pushing up on the wing than there is pushing down, helping to keep the wing aloft.

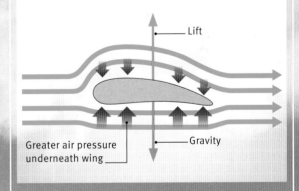

Lift

Gravity

Greater air pressure underneath wing

Weight

The mass of an object is how much matter it contains. The force we call weight is really the Earth's gravitational pull on an object's mass. The lifting force must be at least equal to the plane's weight.

Velocity and acceleration

Velocity is speed in a particular direction. In physics, acceleration is the rate at which something changes velocity—speeds up, slows down, or changes direction. (In common speech acceleration only means speeding up.) Newton's second law of motion says that in order to accelerate, force is needed—skiers at the top of a hill push off with the force they need to speed up, and the pull of Earth's gravity accelerates them further as they race downhill.

Falling objects

If it were not for the air it moves through, the plane would not be able to fly. Air has an effect on falling objects, too. It produces resistance that holds some objects back more than others. When a hammer and feather are dropped together, air resistance makes the feather fall much more slowly. But with no air to slow them down, both would hit the ground at exactly the same time, because the pull of gravity would be working on them equally.

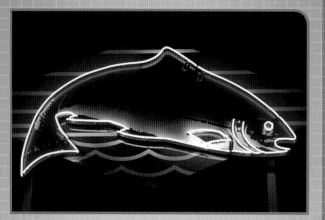

Atoms

Atoms are the building blocks of matter. They can join together to make larger particles called molecules. Although a great deal is known about atoms, they are much too small to see without a special kind of microscope: about six million of them could fit on a pinhead.

Elementary

An element is a pure substance that cannot be broken down into anything more simple. An element's atoms are all exactly the same. There are 92 elements that occur in nature and 26 more that have been produced in laboratories. Everything on Earth is made up of one or more different elements. This sign is filled with a gaseous element called neon, which glows when electricity passes through it.

Molecular you
Everything you can see around you is made of atoms—and that includes your own body. Human flesh is made up of carbon-based molecules called proteins. All living organisms found on Earth contain carbon, which is why the study of carbon is called organic chemistry. The most common molecule in a human is water, which makes up more than 95 percent of our bodies.

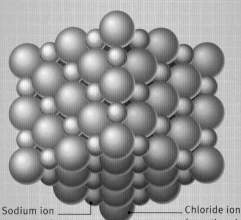

Sodium ion (positive charge)   Chloride ion (negative charge)

Ions

Some atoms gain or lose their electrons easily. If this happens the atom becomes an electrically charged ion. An atom that loses an electron is a postively charged ion; one that gains an electron is negatively charged. Some molecules are made by joining oppositely charged ions together in what is known as an ionic bond. When sodium ions and chloride ions join together they form molecules of sodium chloride—common salt.

Diamond

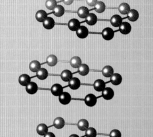

Graphite

Allotropes

The atoms of some elements can join together in different ways to create allotropes. Allotropes of the same element can produce substances with very different properties. Diamond and graphite are both allotropes of carbon. In diamond, the atoms are bound very tightly together, creating one of the hardest known substances. In graphite, a very soft substance, layers of carbon atoms slide over one another.

Molecule model

Molecules are made of atoms joined together with chemical bonds. Substances that contain atoms of the same type are elements—the oxygen in the air is made of molecules of two oxygen atoms. Substances whose molecules contain different types of atom are called compounds. This is a model of acetic acid. It is a compound because it contains atoms of three different types.

Atomic structure

Atoms are made of subatomic particles. At the center of an atom is the nucleus. In all atoms except hydrogen, there are two types of particle in the nucleus—positively charged protons and neutrons, which have no charge. One or more negatively charged particles called electrons orbits the nucleus. Most of the mass of an atom is contained in its nucleus, which occupies less than one millionth of a billionth of the space the whole atom takes up. Most of the atom's volume is the area in which the electrons orbit.

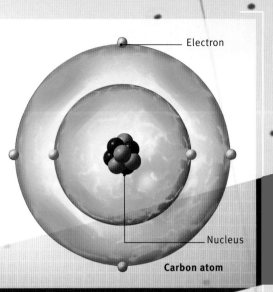

Electron

Nucleus

Carbon atom

Carbon atoms

Acetic acid molecules contain two carbon atoms, represented here in black. Carbon can join with many other types of atoms and with other carbon atoms too, so it can make a vast number of compounds.

Oxygen atoms

The red atoms in the model are oxygen. There is more oxygen in the Earth's crust than any other element. Oxygen atoms bond easily to other atoms—this happens, for instance, when things burn.

Hydrogen atoms

Hydrogen, shown here in white, is the simplest atom, containing just one proton and one electron. It is the most common element in the Universe and fuels the nuclear reactions that make the Sun shine.

Chemical bonds

Atoms in a molecule are held together by chemical bonds. In acetic acid, atoms are joined by covalent bonds, where they share some of their outermost electrons. Two atoms can share two pairs of electrons (shown here as a double bar), or they can share a single pair of electrons (shown here by a single bar). Double bonds are stronger and shorter than single bonds.

Lightspeed

Nothing in the Universe travels faster than light. It moves at an incredible 983,571,056 ft (299,792,458 m) per second. This means that it takes just over eight minutes for light from the Sun to travel the 93 million miles (150 million km) to Earth. In a light year, light can travel about 6 trillion miles (10 trillion km).

Path of light

Light only travels in straight lines, which is why we can't see around corners. A beam of light, like that emitted by a lighthouse, spreads out a little as it travels because although the light rays are traveling in perfectly straight lines, they start off pointing in slightly different directions.

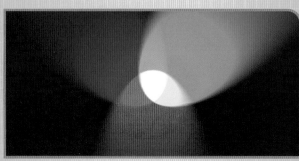

Mixing light

A rainbow shows that white light contains light of lots of different colors. In fact, white light can be made by mixing light of just three colors: red, blue, and green. Mixing these three colors of light together in different combinations will make almost any other color.

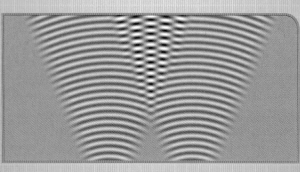

Waves or particles?

Sometimes electromagnetic radiation behaves like waves: when light rays mix, the patterns look just like water ripples. At other times it acts like a stream of particles: gamma rays appear on detectors as patterns of dots. Scientists know a lot about electromagnetic radiation, but what it really is is still a mystery.

Light

Light is one example of a type of energy called electromagnetic radiation. It allows us to see the world in a glorious array of colors. Together all these colors make up white light. When light hits an object some colors are absorbed and others reflected. The color of the object depends on the color of light it reflects.

Scattering sunlight

The color of light depends on its wavelength. Sunlight is white and contains all the colors of the spectrum. Short-wavelength light—which we see as blue or violet—is deflected or scattered by air molecules, spreading through the sky and making it look blue. Violet light is scattered most of all, but the sky does not look violet because our eyes are less sensitive to violet light and there is less of it in the sunlight in the first place.

Mirror image

Objects that do not produce their own light are visible because light bounces off them. Those with rough surfaces bounce the light off in all directions. But materials with surfaces that are very smooth reflect the light—the light bounces off in one direction only. Here, the chrome surface of the aircraft's engine is acting as a mirror and reflecting the sunlight.

Electromagnetic spectrum

Light is the only type of electromagnetic radiation visible to the human eye. The others types are invisible, but they differ from light only in their wavelengths. Radio waves, microwaves, and infrared have longer wavelengths than visible light and carry less energy. Ultraviolet (UV) waves, X-rays, and gamma rays have shorter wavelengths than light, and carry more energy. Together, they form the electromagnetic spectrum.

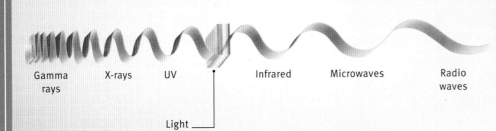

Gamma rays   X-rays   UV   Infrared   Microwaves   Radio waves

Light

Trick of the light
Rainbows are caused by sunlight shining through raindrops suspended in the air. Each raindrop bends the light that passes through it. The shorter the wavelength of the light the more it is bent. This makes the different colors contained in sunlight spread out and appear in different parts of the sky, arranged in order of wavelength, from violet, the shortest, to red, the longest.

Passing through
Most gases and liquids are transparent (light can pass through them), but very few solid materials are. Glass is transparent to visible light, which is why you can see through windows. However, it is opaque (not transparent) to UV rays, which is why you can't get a suntan through a window—although you can feel the warmth of the sunlight because infrared rays pass through glass.

Seeing red
Objects look colored because they reflect some wavelengths of light while absorbing others. This strip looks red because it reflects only the longest wavelengths—those that we see as red.

Solid frame
Some metals are very strong, and when heated they are easily bent or molded into different shapes. Cars are made in this way from steel—an alloy of iron that has been strengthened with carbon.

Natural finish
Wood is a very adaptable natural material. It is strong, fairly lightweight, and can be flexible too. It is often stained or painted to make it last longer. Here it is being used as a decorative trim.

Let the light through
Glass is a synthetic material made from melted sand. It is transparent—ideal for windows. Being unreactive it is often used to make containers because it will not damage or be damaged by its contents.

Materials

All objects are made out of some sort of material. Some, such as wood or stone, are found in nature. Others, such as steel or plastic, are created artificially—these are called synthetic materials. Each material has its own physical properties—hard or soft, heavy or light, brittle or flexible—that make it suitable for manufacturing certain products.

Fit for purpose

Often, materials are selected for very specific purposes. The fuselage (main body) of this airplane must be both very light and very strong. Special alloys of aluminum fulfil both these criteria. The plane's windows are made of specially toughened glass, while the parts of the engine that need to withstand great pressure are made from the extremely strong, light, and unreactive metal titanium.

Flexible friend

This car's steering wheel is made from plastic, one of the most useful artificial materials. Created from chemicals extracted from oil, plastics have atoms that are linked in long-chain molecules called polymers. They can be given almost any property and consequently can make objects as diverse as plastic bags, heat-resistant food containers, building materials, and nylon fabrics.

Alloys

Metals can be mixed together, or with some non-metals such as carbon, to make alloys. Alloys often have much more useful properties than their components. Steel is an alloy of iron with carbon and other substances. It is the most widely used metal in the world, thanks to its great strength and resistance to corrosion.

Fabrics

Fabrics are materials that are used to make clothing, bedding, and other coverings. They are usually woven or knitted from fibers—either natural fibers like wool or cotton, or artificial ones like nylon. Clothing fabrics are designed to allow air to pass through them, which makes them comfortable to wear.

Colorants

Materials are colored using dyes or pigments. Dyes are colored liquids, while pigments are powdered solids mixed with liquids. Some materials, like glass or plastic, are colored while they are being made. Others, like the metal frames of these cars, are sprayed at the end of the manufacturing process.

Adhesives

Glues (also called adhesives) are used to stick materials together. They are often made from polymers, and there are types designed for all sorts of uses. Contact adhesives stick as soon as they are pressed together, silicones provide a flexible seal, and epoxy resins can glue almost anything to anything else.

Organic chemistry

Organic chemistry is the study of chemicals that include carbon. There are vastly more carbon compounds than any other type and their molecules are often huge and complicated. All living things, from this bird to the tree it is perching in, contain organic compounds.

Inorganic chemistry

Inorganic chemistry is the study of those compounds, such as minerals and metal oxides, that do not include carbon. Rust is an inorganic compound. It is created when iron reacts with oxygen in the air (oxidizes) to form iron oxide. Oxidation is also involved in breathing and burning.

Chemical industry

Chemists understand which elements every substance is made of, and how and why their atoms join together. With this knowledge, they can make chemicals for specific purposes. Industrial chemistry involves the large-scale production of chemicals such as fertilizers, plastics, medicines, and cleaning products.

Lighting the fuse

Reactions will only take place if conditions of heat and pressure are right. Firework manufacturers take advantage of this fact when they make their products. The iron and magnesium in fireworks react with oxygen to produce spectacular displays, but only when they are set alight.

Chemistry

Chemistry is the study of the ways in which substances react and change. Unlike a physical change—for example ice melting—or mixing substances together, a chemical reaction involves the making or breaking of the bonds between atoms to make new substances. Chemical reactions are occurring around us all the time.

Tricky mixtures

In a mixture, molecules of different substances are jumbled together but not chemically combined. Some liquids, like the oil and vinegar in mayonnaise, do not easily mix. By adding an emulsifier—in this case egg yolk—they can be made to form an emulsion, where tiny droplets of one liquid are suspended in the other. The emulsifier's molecules are attracted to both substances and help them stick together.

Edible enzymes

A catalyst is something that speeds up a chemical reaction. The yeast in bread contains natural catalysts called enzymes. The yeast reacts with sugar to produce carbon dioxide, making the dough rise.

Acids and bases
Many chemicals are either acids or bases. Vinegar is a weak acid that gives food a sharp taste. It is useful to know whether a substance is an acid or a base because it helps predict how they will react with other substances: strong acids and bases can cause skin burns and dissolve some materials. Many acids are found in living things. Our stomachs produce hydrochloric acid to help us digest food.

Compounds
A compound has very different properties to its elements: sodium is a soft metal and chlorine is a yellowish poisonous gas, but together they form the salt we use to season food.

Flaming fuel
Creating bonds between atoms requires energy, while breaking bonds releases energy. If a chemical reaction produces energy overall some of the energy appears as heat, and the reaction is called exothermic. Reactions that require more energy than they release are called endothermic. Combustion (burning) is an exothermic reaction. Fuel combines with oxygen to produce new chemicals and a great deal of heat.

Basic baking soda
Bases that dissolve in water, such as baking soda, are called alkalis. When bases and alkalis meet acids the result is a "neutralization" reaction, where the products of the reaction are neither acidic nor basic.

Irreversible reactions
Chemical changes can be reversible or irreversible. Most chemical changes are irreversible. Raw eggs become hard and opaque when they are heated, and once cooked they can't be made raw again.

Organic oil
Oil is an organic compound—it is derived from living organisms and so contains carbon atoms. Olive oil comes from plants, but oils can also be made from animal or fossil sources.

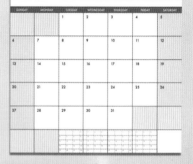

Heat and cold

Heat is a form of energy—the energy something has because its molecules are moving. Heat always moves from a hotter object or area to a cooler one, and it can be transferred in three different ways. In solids it is transferred by conduction, in liquids and gases it can travel by convection, and it can move through air or empty space by radiation.

Insulation

A warm body on a cold day will lose heat and have to work harder to keep its internal temperature constant. Clothing reduces the loss of heat by trapping a layer of air, a very poor conductor of heat. Materials that do not conduct heat well are insulators. Saucepans are often made out of metal, a good conductor, but their handles may be made from an insulator—plastic or wood—so they don't get hot to the touch.

Ice cold

What we think of as cold is simply an absence of heat. Snow feels cold to the touch, but even at low temperatures objects retain some heat energy. Their molecules are vibrating ever so slightly.

Convection

When a gas or liquid is heated from below, the part near the heat source becomes hot and expands. This makes it less dense and therefore lighter, so it moves upward and is replaced by cooler material. This is then heated and rises in its turn. This process, known as convection, can sometimes be seen as swirling motions over flames. It continues until all of the liquid or gas is the same temperature.

Radiation

Heat travels through air or empty space by a type of electromagnetic radiation called infrared. Anyone standing next to the fire would feel on their skin the infrared radiation coming from the flames.

Conduction

Heat moves through solids by conduction. The molecules in a heated part of a solid knock against their neighbors, passing their heat energy on. This fire pit is conducting heat from the burning fuel inside it.

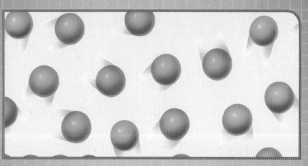

Moving molecules

Heat is really motion—the motion of molecules. In liquids and gases, molecules constantly move around, crashing into each other and bouncing off again. In solids, the molecules are not free to move around but they continually wobble from side to side. The more heat something has the more its molecules are moving.

Measuring heat

Temperature is a measure of how hot something is. There are three main scales of temperature—Celsius, Fahrenheit, and Kelvin. This is a thermogram, a picture that shows the temperatures of different objects. The freezing cold ice pop is black while the warmest parts of the child's skin are red.

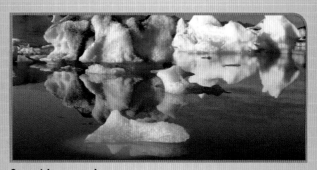

As cold as can be

On Earth, temperatures can fall to around -130°F (-90°C) in extreme conditions. But icebergs like this still contain some heat energy. The lowest possible temperature is -459.67°F (-273.15°C), known as absolute zero. At this temperature molecules would have no heat energy at all; they would stop moving altogether.

Heat and cooling

As the fast-moving molecules of a hot object collide with the slower-moving molecules of something cooler, the slow molecules slow down the faster ones and are speeded up in the process. This hot cup of tea will lose heat, and warm the air around it, until the tea and the air are the same temperature.

Telecommunications

Throughout history, people have constantly sought new ways to communicate, and this urge has lead to many of the greatest inventions, from writing to the Internet. Telecommunications are methods people use to communicate over a long distance—from telephone calls to television broadcasts to email and chatrooms. The way we communicate has changed dramatically, fueled by the cheapness and variety of new telecoms devices.

The world in your pocket
A few decades ago, most households had one television set, one landline telephone, and some radios. All were fragile and expensive—and only the radios were portable. Now, many of us have our own personal telecommunication systems in the form of Internet-linked computers and handheld devices, each combining many functions within one small, tough, and portable device.

All-in-one
Early cell phones were simply portable telephones, but modern cell phones are more like media centers. The user can browse the Internet, edit documents, and play music and video.

Broadcast bonanza
Originally, television programs were all broadcast in the same way: by radio waves sent from huge TV transmitter aerials. Now things are very different: broadcasts are sent by satellite signal or cable, and can also be accessed via computers over the Internet. Some systems even allow people to order the programs they like, whenever they wish to watch them.

Better broadcasts
Digital radio is much clearer than the analog version it is replacing. It also means that text information can be transmitted along with the audio signals, and displayed on the radio's screen.

Clearer chatting
Although they are gradually being replaced by cell phones, landline telephones often provide clearer calls. This is because their signals travel down cables. Cell phones rely on radio signals, which can vary in strength with weather conditions and with distance from the nearest transmitter. Landline handsets like this one use short-range radio signals so that the receiver can be used wirelessly.

Analog and digital
Early telecommunication signals were analog: messages were sent as electrical currents or radio waves that had the same shapes as the sound waves they reproduced. Digital signals, rather than varying gradually in level like sound waves do, are either "off" or "on," usually represented as Os and 1s.

Optical fibers
For long-distance communication of all kinds, from Internet links to phone calls and TV broadcasts, optical fibers are far superior to metal wires. These transparent glass-like strands transmit signals by pulses of light rather than electrical signals. The signals can carry a great deal of data at very high speeds.

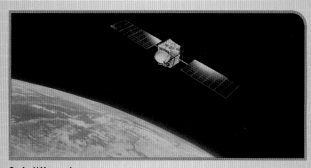

Satellite relays
High above Earth, a network of satellites relays telephone conversations, Internet links, and TV and radio programs, connecting distant parts of the Earth by means of radio waves. Today there are about 2,000 working communication satellites, about one-third of which are for military use.

Networks of networks
The Internet is a vast telecommunication system spanning the entire world, allowing users to exchange emails, view video content, and even make telephone calls. Computers are linked with one another in local networks, which are in turn connected to each other by cable, radio, and satellite links.

All sound is produced by vibrations. When we speak or sing, air is blown out of our lungs and passes between our vocal cords (two folds of flesh in the throat). The folds vibrate, making a sound. We vary the quality of this sound by changing the tension of our vocal cords and the speed of the air rushing through them. The shape of the inside of the mouth, and the position of our lips, tongue, and teeth, refine the sound further.

Capturing sound

A microphone contains a thin plate called a diaphragm, which vibrates when sound waves strike it. The microphone turns these vibrations into a changing pattern of electricity. Increasing the strength of this electrical pattern and turning it back into sound waves amplifies the sound (makes it louder). The electrical patterns can also be stored on CD or computer to be played back later.

Sound

A type of energy produced by vibrating objects, sound travels as waves at different speeds through different materials. The shape of sound waves determines how we hear them—loud or soft, high- or low-pitched, a musical trill or a deafening din. Any unwanted sound, whether made by a jet engine or a dripping faucet, is called noise.

Bang the drum

When a drum is struck, its skin moves up and down rapidly. Each upward movement produces a pulse of pressure in the air above it—the air molecules there start to vibrate. They make the air molecules next to them vibrate, which in turn pass the vibrations on to the molecules next to them. In this way the sound travels as a series of compressions (high-pressure pulses) separated by rarefactions (low-pressure regions).

Loud and clear

A loudspeaker turns electricity into sound waves. It uses an electrical signal to make a diaphragm vibrate, which vibrates the air around it. Boosting the signal amplifies the sound.

Longer wavelength: compressions are further apart

Shorter wavelength: compressions are closer together

Pitch and frequency

The pitch of a sound is determined by its frequency. If a sound wave has many compressions per second, it is said to have a short wavelength and a high frequency. We hear sounds like this as high-pitched. Low-pitched sounds have fewer compressions per second—they have a long wavelength and a low frequency.

Playing in harmony

Music relies on harmony—combinations of sounds that are pleasing when heard together. A pair of sound waves sound harmonious if their wavelengths fit simply together—if one is exactly twice the length of the other, for example. When waves don't fit, the result is dissonance—sounds that seem to clash.

Amplitude

The larger the changes in pressure in a sound wave the greater its amplitude—the louder the sound is. Amplitude is a description of how much energy a sound wave carries. The sound of a nearby racing car carries many billion times as much energy as the quietest sound a person can hear.

Speed of sound

Sound travels more quickly through liquids and solids than it does through air. This is because the molecules are closer together, so they transfer the sound vibrations more quickly. Whales communicate underwater using low-pitched moans, which can travel many hundreds of miles.

Sonic boom

Sound waves travel through air at about 1,080 ft (330 m) per second. When the object that makes them goes faster than this, it overtakes some of the sound waves. They pile up into a shock wave and make a sudden loud bang called a sonic boom. The shock wave can also condense water vapor to form a cloud.

Machines

The modern world is full of machines. Machines make jobs easier to do by magnifying the force that is put in or by changing its direction. Most machinery contains hundreds of moving parts, but many complex mechanisms are based on just six simple machines: the lever, pulley, wheel and axle, wedge, screw, and inclined plane.

Mechanical muscles
The moving parts of heavy-duty machinery are often controlled by hydraulic systems that use a liquid to transmit forces through pipes. The pipes contain close-fitting disks called pistons. When the driver opens a valve, oil is forced into the pipe, pushing the piston along. The part of the machine the piston is attached to moves when the piston does. Pneumatic systems work in the same way, but gas takes the place of oil.

Wedge
The tip of the digger is a wedge. As it is pushed down by the mechanical arm, the shape of its sloping sides converts the downward force into a greater sideways force, splitting the concrete apart.

Energy supply
An engine inside the digger converts energy from fuel—usually diesel or gas—into movement. This allows the vehicle to move around and also powers its moving parts.

Pulley system

A pulley is a cable looped over a wheel. It changes the direction of a force, so that pulling downward on one end of the cable results in a lifting force at the other. Using several pulleys together—like this crane—means less force is required, because the weight of the load is shared between all the pulleys. But the cable must be pulled through a greater distance than the distance the load is lifted.

Inclined plane

A plank propped up at one end forms an inclined (sloping) plane. Pushing a wheelbarrow diagonally up the plank takes less force than lifting it vertically, but the barrow moves over a greater distance.

Two-in-one

A wheelbarrow's handles work as a lever. Lifting them requires less force than would be needed to lift the load in the barrow directly. The wheelbarrow also has a wheel and axle, making it much easier to move the load than dragging it along. As a wheel turns, only a tiny part of it is in contact with the ground, and that part is constantly lifted away, so there is very little friction.

Screw

A screw must be turned many times to move a short distance into wood, but it needs much less force to penetrate the wood than would be needed simply to press it in. This is because the screw turns around and around through a much greater distance than it advances into the wood.

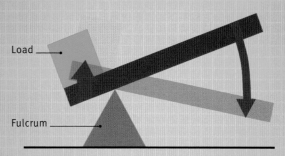

Load

Fulcrum

Levers

In this lever, the part of the rod on the right of the fulcrum is four times longer than the part on the left. When the right end is pushed down, the left end moves up only a quarter of the distance but it presses up with four times the force with which the right end is pushed down. This makes it easier to lift the load.

Turbine

Some machines use motion to produce useful energy. A turbine is an engine that changes the flow of air or water into electricity by using a rotor (rotating part). In a wind turbine, the sails catch the wind and move the rotor, which turns a dynamo (a machine that turns motion into electricity).

Friction

All machines waste some energy, mostly as heat, because not all the effort put in is used for the job in hand. Some has to be used to overcome friction—a force that makes it hard for surfaces to slide past each other. Early steam engines wasted almost all the energy of the coal they burned.

States of matter

Every object and material in the Universe is made of matter, and matter exists in four states: solid, liquid, gas, or plasma. Many materials can exist in any of these states, changing from one state to another. Often, a material will be found in several states together: ice is usually covered with a water layer and surrounded by water vapor.

Solids
Solid matter, like ice, is made up of particles that are tightly packed together. Solids have a definite shape and are usually denser than their liquid versions, because there are more particles packed into a smaller space. Ice is unusual: it is less dense than water, which is why it floats. This is because when water freezes its molecules arrange themselves into a lattice structure that takes up more space.

Solutions
Gases can dissolve in liquids—the fizziness of carbonated drinks is caused by bubbles of carbon dioxide gas, which comes out of solution when the pressure on the liquid is reduced by opening the bottle. There are many types of solution, including solid-in-liquid and gas-in-solid ones. The substance that is dissolved is called the solute, the substance it is dissolved in is the solvent.

Gases

The particles in a gas move around freely and very fast. Nothing holds them back except the walls of their container, which the gas molecules will spread out to fill, or gravity, which holds Earth's atmospheric gases close to Earth's surface. Water vapor (water in its gas state) is invisible—we can only see steam because it contains many tiny droplets of liquid too.

Liquids

In liquids, the particles are not as tightly packed as in solids. They slip past each other easily, which is why liquids flow. A liquid does not have a definite shape—it will take on the shape of its container.

Fourth state of matter

Solids, liquids, and gases are the first three states of matter; plasma is the fourth. On Earth, it is rarer than the others. A plasma is like a gas, but its atoms have been broken down so that it is made of positively charged ions and negatively charged electrons. This means that plasmas can conduct electricity. The Sun, stars, and the upper atmosphere of the Earth are made of plasma, and it causes effects like the Northern Lights (above).

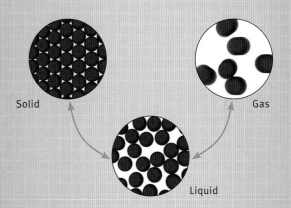

Solid

Gas

Liquid

Changes of state

If a solid is heated, its particles start to vibrate. Eventually, the solid structure breaks down and the solid melts into a liquid. Heating a liquid has a similar effect. The particles in the liquid move around more until at a certain temperature they break free of one another and become a gas. Cooling a substance has the opposite effect: a gas will condense into a liquid and then freeze solid. Changing the air pressure changes the temperature at which changes of state occur.

Skipping a step

Usually, substances change from a solid to a liquid to a gas, but sometimes the liquid stage is missed out. At room temperature, frozen carbon dioxide (also known as dry ice) turns directly into carbon dioxide gas in a process called sublimation. This happens because the normal air pressure on Earth is not enough to stop molecules in the dry ice from flying apart above temperatures of -108°F (-78°C).

217

Robots

Robots are machines that can carry out mechanical tasks by themselves—
"robot" comes from the Czech word *robota*, meaning "work." Not all robots
are used for work, though. This tiny hexbug® is a toy that imitates an
insect, sensing and reacting to its surroundings and scuttling around for
the amusement of its owner.

Bug board
Visible beneath the blue cover is the
hexbug's printed circuit board. This board
contains electronic devices, including the
microprocessor that controls the robot. There
is also a microphone, which picks up sound
waves and converts them to electrical signals.
If the signals are strong enough—generated by
a loud enough sound—the microprocessor
instructs the hexbug to change direction.

Electric antenna
The hexbug detects obstacles with its antennae
or feelers. The base of each feeler is made from
a coiled spring with a metal rod inside. Usually
there is a gap between the rod and the spring, but
when the feeler presses against an object, the
spring bends and touches the rod. Electricity can
then flow between them, informing the robot's
circuits that an obstacle has been encountered.
In response, the bug backs up and steers away.

Cool cover
The translucent (partially see-
through) cover protects the robot's
circuitry and makes it look
insect-like too. The hexbug is less
than 2.7 in (7 cm) long—its simple
circuits take up little room.

Battery-powered

Like almost all robots, the hexbug is powered by electricity. There are two tiny 1.5-volt button cell batteries in a compartment on the underside, and a switch at the rear.

Simple scuttler

The robot's legs are cleverly designed so that a single motor moves all six of them at once. The motor turns one small gear, which is connected by a series of other gears to the central pair of legs. These legs are joined to the front and rear pairs by rods, so that the movements of the middle pair make the others move too. The bug's feet are made of rubber so that they can grip smooth surfaces.

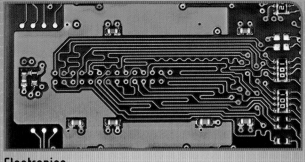

Electronics

Electronic circuits are usually built up in layers on printed circuit boards. Tiny components control the flow of electricity, sending it to motors to move the machines. Circuit boards use materials called semiconductors, whose properties can be adjusted to allow different amounts of electricity to pass through them.

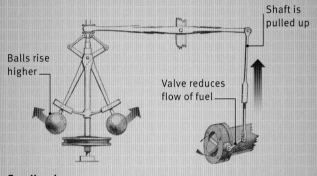

Shaft is pulled up

Balls rise higher

Valve reduces flow of fuel

Feedback

Robots modify their behavior according to feedback. One of the first feedback devices was the governor, used to maintain the speeds of steam engines. The faster the engine, the faster the governor spun and the higher the balls rose. This gradually closed off the engine's fuel supply, so that its speed was reduced.

Industrial robots

Almost all the robots in existence today are used in industry: many cars are made almost entirely on robotic production lines. Robots have many advantages over human workers for jobs like these: they are accurate, strong, tireless, they function in dangerous or unpleasant environments, and never get bored.

Explorer robots

Some robots are used to explore places humans cannot visit, like the deep ocean. At just 0.6 miles (1 km) depth, the pressure is 100 times the air pressure on Earth's suface, enough to crush a person's lungs. This submersible can be a scientist's eyes and ears while he or she remains in the safety of the lab.

Computers

It's hard to imagine a world without computers—more than a billion of us have a laptop or other personal computer. And many of the world's computers are connected to the Internet, a vast network of computers that has transformed all our lives. Many more computers are at work behind the scenes in systems and devices that we all use every day, such as car SatNavs.

Compact computers
Portable computers like laptops run on batteries and must be lightweight, so their screens are designed to be very thin and to use as little power as possible. This is a Liquid Crystal Display (LCD) screen. It uses patterns of electricity to change the properties of liquid crystals, allowing light to shine through colored filters to form images.

Output devices
Screens, headphones, printers, and other devices output information to the user in whatever form they require. Video images like this one require a great deal of memory and processing power.

Wireless world

The Internet is a worldwide network of computers, connected together by wires, optical cables, and radio waves. When radio waves are used, the connection is referred to as "wireless." Wireless laptops like this one contain radio receivers and transmitters that communicate with a nearby router. This device connects to the rest of the Internet via cables.

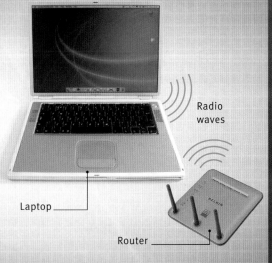

Radio waves

Laptop

Router

Input devices

A webcam, like a keyboard, is an input device: it feeds data into the computer for storage, transfer, or processing. This webcam sends images of the user to whoever they are talking to.

Memory on a stick

Computers store information that they are working on in electronic circuits called RAM (Random Access Memory), while other data is stored on a hard disk drive. RAM can only store a few gigabytes of data, whereas hard disk drives can store several hundred. To copy data between computers, it can be sent over the Internet or saved to memory sticks like this one.

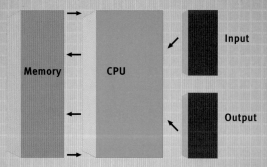

Memory | CPU | Input

Output

How computers work

Computers work by transferring information—in the form of text, numbers, sounds, or images—from an input device to a Central Processing Unit (CPU). The CPU processes the data, holding only what it needs and saving the rest in memory. The processed data is returned to the user through an output device.

Early computers

The first computers used electronic devices called vacuum tubes, which switch current flows and store data. The large panel above, part of the Pilot Ace computer from the 1950s, is full of vacuum tubes. Computers filled whole rooms and frequently broke down when the tubes burned out.

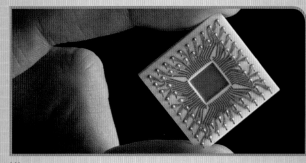

Microprocessor

In today's computers, tiny microprocessors do the work that it took thousands of vacuum tubes to do—and far more besides. A microprocessor is like a miniature circuit board. It is made of several layers of silicon and other materials, with electronic circuits built into them in the form of printed patterns.

Embedded computers

A great many gadgets, vehicles, and household appliances have computers built into them. Unlike those on laptops, the software on these embedded computers is designed to carry out specific tasks and cannot be changed. The computer in this SatNav links up with a satellite network to guide the driver.

Electricity and magnetism

Electricity is a form of energy caused by the behavior of electrically charged particles called electrons. A magnet is an object that attracts (pulls) or repels (pushes) other magnets, and which also attracts some metals. Under some circumstances, electricity can cause magnetic effects and magnets can cause electrical ones. Maglev (magnetic levitation) trains use this to provide smooth fast transportation.

City of lights
Electricity not only lights up buildings, it also heats them, powers their computer and security systems, and runs their escalators and elevators. It is supplied though a national network of power cables called a grid. Electricity is usually produced by power stations, which burn fuels such as oil, coal, or gas, or by nuclear reactors. Greener sources of electricity include wind and wave power.

Speedy and silent
A maglev train is moved along the track by a system of changing magnetic fields. Because it has no engine on board, it is very much quieter than other forms of public transportation.

Floating on air
Magnets in the track and the sides of the train repel each other, creating a cushion of air between the train and the track. This results in little friction, meaning the train can reach higher speeds.

Electromagnetism

When electricity flows along a wire, it creates a weak magnetic field. If the current is turned off, the magnetic field disappears. This effect is called electromagnetism. Winding the conductor around an iron core turns the iron into a temporary magnet, greatly increasing the electromagnet's strength. Changing the direction of the current makes the north and south poles swap places.

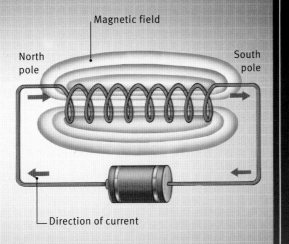

Magnetic field

North pole

South pole

Direction of current

Fields of force

Electrical power is supplied to the maglev by means of a conductor that runs along the inside of the track. The magnets in the track and the train are electromagnets—they only become magnetic when an electric current passes through them. Alternating the direction of the current reverses the poles of the magnets so they rapidly repel and then attract each other, pushing the train forward.

Conductors and insulators

Metals are conductors—they contain electrons that can move around easily. This allows electricity to pass through a conductor. Most non-metals resist the flow of electricity and are called insulators. Wires and cables have conductive metal cores surrounded by insulating plastic coatings.

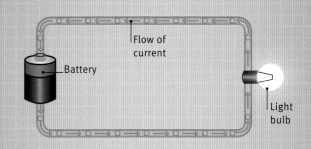

Flow of current

Battery

Light bulb

Electric currents

Electricity flowing in a circuit is an electric current. When a conducting wire is hooked up to a battery, negatively charged electrons flow toward the battery's positive terminal. In the circuit above, the bulb resists the current and the electrical energy changes to heat and light.

Static electricity

Not all electricity flows along conductors. When electrons build up on an object and cannot flow away, they charge the object with static electricity. When hair becomes charged with static electricity it stands up on end. Clouds also become charged with static, and then discharge it in the form of lightning.

North   South

North   North

North and south poles

Every magnet has a north pole and a south pole. Opposite poles attract each other, and like poles repel each other. The area around a magnet where these magnetic forces act is called a magnetic field. In the picture above, sprinkling tiny iron filings between two magnets shows these forces at work.

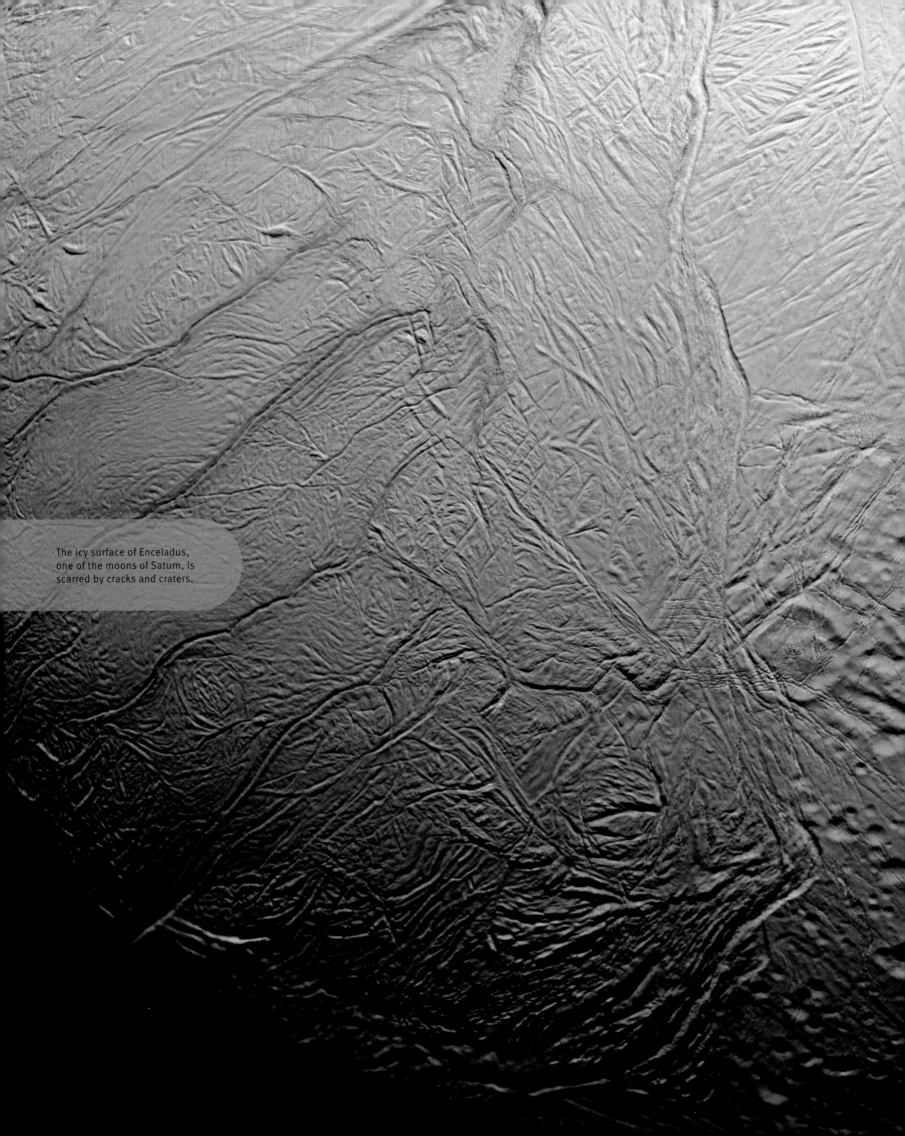

The icy surface of Enceladus, one of the moons of Saturn, is scarred by cracks and craters.

SPACE

Our fascination with astronomy dates back to the stone age, but our understanding of the cosmos has been hugely advanced by space exploration. Images and data gathered by space probes have revolutionized our ideas about the Solar System, while details of distant stars captured by space telescopes have given us a new window on the Universe.

Looking into space

Look up and into Earth's sky and you are looking into space. Early skywatchers used their eyes alone to explore space. Today, powerful telescopes give us the best view of space objects. Telescopes based on Earth and in space collect light and other forms of energy, such as X-rays and radio waves. Together they give us a more complete view of the Universe.

Eye on the sky

Telescopes collect and focus light from distant objects. A telescope such as this one uses mirrors and is called a reflecting telescope. Telescopes that use lenses instead are called refracting telescopes. The larger the main lens or mirror, the more light it can collect, so the astronomers who use it can see fainter or more distant objects. The largest reflecting telescopes have many small mirrors working as one big one.

Finder telescope

Smaller finder telescopes are attached to the main telescope. They show a larger area of sky. The astronomer locates an object with a finder then uses the bigger telescope for a detailed view.

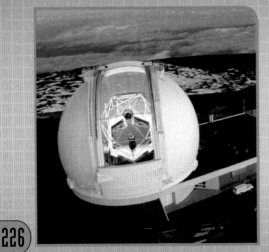

Optical telescope

Telescopes that collect visible light are called optical telescopes. They are often built at mountain-top locations where they are above the clouds and the air is dry and still. Inside this dome is one of the two identical Keck telescopes, which are located on the summit of the Mauna Kea volcano, Hawaii. They are among Earth's largest telescopes and collect light in their 33-ft- (10-m-) wide mirrors.

Radio waves

Radio waves are collected by huge dish antennae. The dish reflects the waves to a receiver positioned above its center. The Very Large Array (left) is a collection of 27 dishes laid out in a Y-shape on the plains of New Mexico, USA. Each dish is 82 ft (25 m) across but together they work like one giant antenna 22 miles (36 km) wide. Whole galaxies have been discovered because of the radio waves they emit.

Inside a reflecting telescope

The light from a space object is collected and focused by the telescope's main mirror. A secondary mirror intercepts the light and directs it to someone's eye or an instrument such as a camera. In this telescope, known as a Cassegrain, the light is sent through a hole in the center of the main mirror.

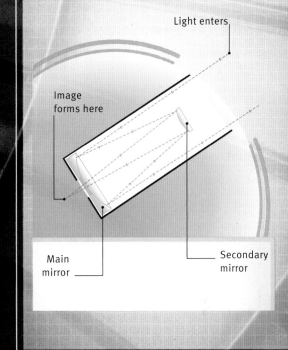

Light enters

Image forms here

Main mirror

Secondary mirror

Open dome
The telescope is protected by a dome, which opens to reveal the sky above. An object being observed soon moves out of view because the Earth spins. Computer controls move both the telescope and the dome in the opposite direction to the Earth's spin to keep the object in view through the dome's opening. A dome-shaped building that houses a telescope is called an observatory.

X-ray vision

X-rays are emitted by material that has a temperature of about 1.8 million°F (1 million°C), such as the remnants of exploded stars. They cannot penetrate Earth's atmosphere and have to be collected in space. The Chandra X-ray Observatory is a space telescope that follows an elliptical orbit around Earth. Its mirrors have been collecting X-rays from space objects for more than 10 years.

In the infrared

The James Webb Space Telescope will be launched into space in 2014. It will work at a distance of 900,000 miles (1.5 million km) from Earth, collecting infrared energy from relatively cool objects, such as star-forming regions. The telescope's mirror, which is 21 ft (6.5 m) wide, is so large it will be folded up for launch and opened out once in space. Its sunshade (blue in this picture) is the size of a tennis court.

The Moon

The Moon is the closest space object to Earth and the brightest thing in our sky after the Sun. It is a lifeless ball of rock that orbits our planet and travels with us as we follow our yearly path around the Sun. About a quarter the size of Earth, its cratered and mountainous surface is covered by a blanket of dusty lunar soil. The Moon is the only place that humans have been to beyond Earth.

Mare Imbrium

The Moon's dark, flat areas looked like seas to early astronomers, so they called them *maria* (singular *mare*), Latin for seas, and the name has stuck. Mare Imbrium is a huge dark circular plain that took shape about 3.8 billion years ago when a large asteroid crashed into the Moon. The impact formed a crater that then filled with volcanic lava that oozed up through crack's in the Moon's crust and solidified.

Apennine Mountains

A 370-mile (600-km) long range of mountains called the Apennines forms part of Mare Imbrium's rim. The mountains were pushed up by the same asteroid impact that formed the mare.

Covered with craters

The surface of the Moon is covered with circular-shaped craters created by asteroids. They range in size from tiny bowl-shaped hollows to those more than 90 miles (150 km) wide. Many of them formed during the first 750 million years of the Moon's life when it was heavily bombarded by asteroids. At 800 million years old, the 57-mile (93-km) wide Copernicus Crater is relatively young.

Tycho Crater

Tycho, only 100 million years old, looks much as it did when first formed. It is still surrounded by bright rays of ejected material. Older craters change in appearance as more recent ones form on top.

Lunar phases

The Moon keeps the same face pointing toward the Earth at all times. This is because the Moon takes exactly the same amount of time to rotate on its axis as it does to make one orbit around the Earth. The face seen from Earth seems to change shape, because the amount of it that is bathed in sunlight changes as the Moon orbits Earth. The different shapes are the Moon's phases; one cycle of phases lasts 29.5 days.

New Moon

Waxing crescent

First quarter

Waxing gibbous

Full Moon

Waning gibbous

Last quarter

Waning crescent

Line of light
The boundary between the sunlit and dark parts of the Moon is called the terminator. It moves across the Moon's face from day to day as the phase of the Moon changes. Craters and mountains cast long shadows when close to this boundary, making them more distinct and easier to see. Anyone standing on the terminator would see the Sun set in the Moon's sky.

Earthrise

In December 1968, Apollo 8 became the first manned mission to orbit the Moon. On the fourth of 10 orbits, the craft emerged from the Moon's far side and its crew took this photograph. It was the first time the Earth had been seen from another world and people were amazed to see it appear so small and fragile.

Origins

The Moon formed about 4.5 billion years ago when a Mars-sized asteroid gave Earth a glancing blow. Material from the two bodies formed a ring of rock and dust around Earth. Over tens of millions of years, the ring pieces bumped into each other and eventually came together to form a large single body, the Moon.

Man on the Moon

A total of 12 men have been on the Moon. Neil Armstrong of *Apollo 11* became the first person to step onto the lunar surface on July 20, 1969, while Gene Cernan of *Apollo 17* was the last to leave on December 14, 1972. Cernan (above) used a battery-powered rover to explore the lunar surface.

Callisto   Titan   Ganymede

Io

Moon

Planetary moons

Earth's Moon is just one of more than 160 moons that orbit Solar System planets. It is the fifth largest of all these moons. Three moons of Jupiter—icy Ganymede and Callisto, and volcanic Io—are all bigger. Saturn's Titan—the only moon with a substantial atmosphere—is the second largest Solar System moon.

International Space Station

The International Space Station (ISS) is a football-field-sized home and workplace for astronauts. It orbits around Earth almost 16 times a day about 240 miles (390 km) above the ground. The ISS was built and is run by the space agencies of the USA, Russia, Europe, Japan, and Canada. Up to six astronauts stay here for weeks or months at a time.

Central support
The truss is the backbone of the ISS. It supports the habitation and work modules and the solar arrays. The truss was launched in parts over eight and a half years and fitted together in space.

Largest lab
Kibo is one of three laboratories. The largest single unit, it is about the size of a large bus and consists of two cylindrical modules and an outside deck for exposing experiments to space.

Supplying the station
The Russian unmanned craft *Progress* brings supplies to the ISS. Astronauts unload it and then fill it with waste. The craft and cargo burn up as it re-enters Earth's atmosphere.

New crew
Three astronauts inside a Russian Soyuz-TMA capsule head for the ISS. The capsule, which was launched by a Soyuz rocket, is delivering a new crew. It will later undock from the ISS with a returning crew on board. The returning craft will split into three and the central part, slowed by parachute, will deliver the astronauts to the ground. The US Shuttle orbiters are the only other craft to have carried astronauts to the ISS.

Room with a view

From the ISS, views of Earth can be spectacular. This photograph shows sunrise over the cloud-covered Pacific Ocean. Such shots are taken through special windows fitted with panes that do not distort the light passing through. Astronauts spend about 30 minutes each day taking photographs requested by scientists on the ground of geographical features, or events such as floods, fires, and volcanic eruptions.

Working in space

Astronauts spend some part of every day working on experiments. Here, cosmonaut Yuri Malenchenko tends to pea plants growing in the controlled environment of a small greenhouse. Plant growth experiments are important in establishing how astronauts can feed themselves on future long-duration trips to the Moon and Mars. Experiments on the astronauts themselves reveal how the human body is affected by space travel.

Weightless environment

Astronaut Naoko Yamazaki squeezes a water bubble out of her drink container during her stay on the ISS in April 2010. The water and astronaut are both affected by the sensation of weightlessness. Earth's gravity pulls on them but along with the ISS they are also traveling horizontally around Earth. This means they are constantly falling through space, which makes them weightless.

Power supply
The ISS's power is supplied by its huge solar arrays that produce electricity from sunlight. The arrays consist of 16 wings, which rotate as the ISS orbits so they always face the Sun.

Building the ISS

The station is made of about 20 major parts as well as many smaller ones. The parts were transported into space individually and then fitted together by astronauts during more than 150 spacewalks. The first to be joined were Zarya (pictured here on the left), which provided power in the early stages, and Unity (on the right) a connecting module, in December 1988.

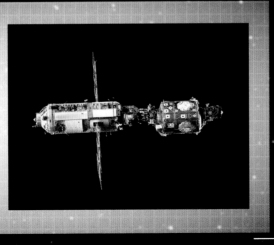

Space travelers

More than 500 men and women from 40 different nations have traveled into space. Most have journeyed only as far as near-Earth space, a few hundred miles above the Earth's surface. The only people to go further were the 24 Americans who made the 238,900-mile (384,400-km) trip to the Moon in the 1960s and 1970s. Until recently, only professional astronauts went into space. But today it is possible to buy a ticket to space from a commercial organization, albeit for a hefty sum.

Life support suit
The sealed spacesuit supplies oxygen for breathing and maintains the correct temperature and pressure, without which the blood would boil and the body would quickly blow apart. The suit also provides protection from the Sun: in space there is no atmosphere to absorb the Sun's rays, making it bright and scorching in the glare of the Sun, and freezing cold and pitch black in the shade.

Spacewalking
This is astronaut Piers Sellers spacewalking outside the ISS. A spacewalk is activity an astronaut does outside their spacecraft—building or repairing craft, and working on experiments.

Gripping gloves
An astronaut's gloves have two main purposes. They need to protect an astronaut's hands but also be comfortable and flexible enough that he or she can perform tasks. The finger and thumb tips are made of molded silicone rubber for sensitivity. Heaters in the fingertips prevent fingers from getting cold. But the thick and inflated glove fingers are difficult to bend and astronauts can suffer injuries.

Embroidered emblem
Each space mission has its own unique mission badge, with a graphic design and the names of the mission and its crew. This one depicts the shuttle docked with the International Space Station.

Lighting the void
Lights mounted at either side of the helmet illuminate the area in front of the astronaut so he or she can see when working in shadow. A camera mounted in the upper helmet records the view.

Golden shield
The astronaut's face is shielded by a clear plastic screen with a gold-coated visor on top. The visor can be pushed up and down as necessary to protect the eyes from the glare and heat from the Sun.

Non-human travelers
The Russian dog Laika was the first animal to orbit Earth. She was launched in *Sputnik 2* in 1957. Laika and other early animal astronauts, such as monkeys and chimpanzees, helped prepare the way for human space travel.

We have lift off!
In October 2003, this *Long March 2F* rocket launched the first Chinese astronaut into space. Yang Liwei's flight meant that China had become the third nation, along with America and Russia, to launch humans into space.

First to space
The first human into space was Russian Yuri Gagarin. On April 12, 1961 he orbited once around Earth in his *Vostok 1* spacecraft. Toward the end of his 108-minute trip he ejected from his craft and parachuted back to Earth.

Spaceport America
The world's first spaceport is being built in New Mexico, USA. Space tourists will take a two and a half hour trip to just beyond an altitude of 62 miles (100 km), the official start of space. Six passengers at a time will travel inside the *SpaceShipTwo* craft.

Rocky planets

Mercury, Venus, Earth, and Mars are the four closest planets to the Sun. Commonly known as the rocky planets, they are made of mainly rock and metal. A slice through any one of them would reveal a metal core surrounded by a rocky mantle and crust. Yet, their surfaces are very different. Mercury is covered by craters, Venus by volcanic lava, Earth has oceans of water, and much of Mars is frozen desert.

Red planet
Mars's distinctive rust-red color is due to iron oxide in the dusty soil covering its surface. Winds sweep up the dust and transport it around the planet producing temporarily dark areas where it has blown away.

Surface of extremes
Mars's surface is marked by tens of thousands of impact craters that formed when asteroids hit the planet more than 3.5 billion years ago. It also features giant, extinct volcanoes, such as Olympus Mons—at 15 miles (24 km) high, the largest volcano on any planet or moon. In contrast, Valles Marineris is a huge system of canyons up to 5 miles (8 km) deep that formed as the surface split when Mars was young.

Northern ice cap
Most of the little water there is on Mars is permanently locked up as ice in the planet's polar regions. A white cap permanently covers the North Pole, seen here in summer when the region is bathed in continuous sunlight. In the winter, the same area is in permanent darkness and the temperature drops to about -193°F (-125°C). Carbon dioxide in the atmosphere turns to frost and snow, and covers the water in ice.

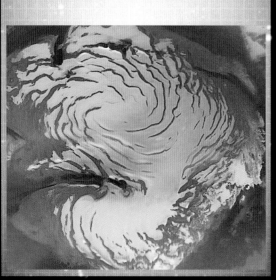

Hellas Planitia
Carbon dioxide frost covers this low-lying plain. The region took shape 4 billion years ago when an impacting asteroid formed a 1,350-mile (2,200-km) crater, which later filled with volcanic lava.

Schiaparelli Crater
The 293-mile- (471-km-) wide Schiaparelli Crater straddles Mars's equator. Martian winds have eroded much of it and created sand dunes on its floor. Smaller craters have formed within it.

Telltale signs
Today Mars is a cold, dry planet, but areas such as this crater floor were once covered by water. Dried-up riverbeds add further evidence that Mars was once warmer and water flowed across its surface.

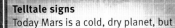

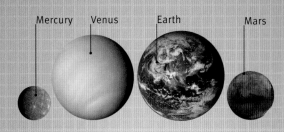

Mercury   Venus   Earth   Mars

Terrestrial planets
Earth is the largest of the rocky planets and for this reason the four are also known as the terrestrial planets (from the Latin for Earth, *terra*). The smallest, Mercury is about one and a half times the size of Earth's Moon. The four formed at the same time and from the same material about 4.6 billion years ago.

Gray globe
Gray, dry Mercury is covered by impact craters and has changed little since it was young. The largest crater in this image is about 83 miles (133 km) across and named Polygnotus. Mercury's craters range from small bowl-shaped ones to Caloris Basin, which covers a quarter of the planet.

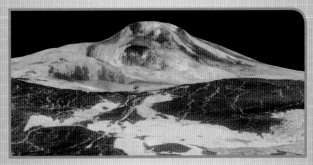

Hidden from view
Venus's surface is hidden from view by the planet's dense atmosphere, but radar observations have revealed what it is like. This is Maat Mons, the largest of hundreds of Venusian volcanoes. Lava that erupted hundreds of millions of years ago solidified and now covers most of the planet.

Water world
Water and life are unique features of planet Earth. Oceans cover more than 70 percent of its surface and water moves constantly between the land and the air. Life forms have existed on Earth for three-quarters of the planet's history. It is the only place where life is known to exist.

New Horizons

After a nine-year journey, *New Horizons* will arrive at Pluto in 2015. Its camera will take images of Pluto and show us for the first time what this dwarf planet is like. Other instruments will collect data to produce maps and analyze the thin atmosphere. It will then head to the Kuiper Belt to look at its icy-rock objects.

Rosetta

The *Rosetta* spacecraft is currently on its way to Comet Churyumov-Gerasimenko. When it arrives in 2014 it will release a small craft called *Philae* that will land on the comet. *Rosetta* will then travel with the comet around the Sun observing the comet as it changes and develops a huge head and tails.

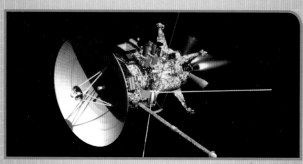

Cassini

At 22 ft (6.7 m) long, *Cassini* is one of the largest craft to be sent to a planet. It has been traveling around Saturn and some of its moons since 2004. *Cassini* has discovered huge storms on Saturn, small moons orbiting the planet, and enormous lakes of liquid methane on Saturn's largest moon, Titan.

Messenger

After flying by Mercury three times, *Messenger* started to orbit the planet in early 2011. The craft's cameras are photographing Mercury's entire surface, including areas never seen before. Information collected by detectors will help to identify the planet's surface material.

Exploring space

Robotic spacecraft have been sent across the Solar System, exploring planets and their moons, asteroids, comets, and the Sun. Each craft is designed and built for its particular job, but they all have common features: a central computer, a power source, instruments to investigate the target, and communications equipment to send results home.

Roving around
This is the sloping edge of 2,625-ft- (800-m-) wide Victoria Crater. For two years from 2006, the rover *Opportunity* explored in and around the crater, guided by controllers on Earth. It rolled along at about 0.5 in (1 cm) a second, stopping now and again to study its surroundings. *Opportunity* is one of two robotic craft that landed on different sides of Mars in January 2004.

Robotic arm

Opportunity took this view of its own arm extending out and away from its body. Like a human arm it has three joints. Its shoulder (left) moves side to side and up and down, its elbow (top) folds the arm in or out, and its wrist twists the hand sideways and up and down to get close to the rock.

Surveying the view
This panoramic camera is one of a pair mounted on the top of *Opportunity*'s mast. The cameras are like the rover's eyes, picking out likely spots to travel to and investigate.

Talking to base
This antenna is the rover's ears and voice. It receives commands from Earth and sends information back. The antenna can turn to communicate with Earth while the rover stays still.

Kitted out
The RAT (Rock Abrasion Tool) is one of four instruments in the rover's hand. It grinds away the surface to expose fresh rock. Two other tools analyze the rock, and a microscopic camera takes pictures.

The Sun

Our local star is a huge spinning ball of hot, luminous gas, made up mainly of hydrogen and helium and kept together by gravity. Energy produced deep inside the Sun constantly erupts through its surface and is released into space. Some of this energy reaches Earth, which orbits the Sun along with a host of other objects that make up the Solar System.

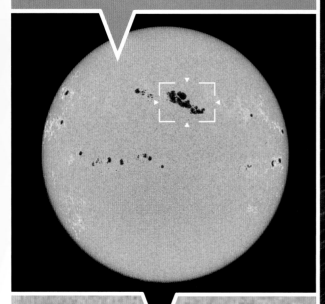

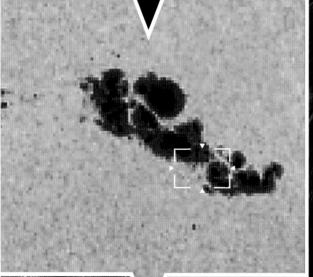

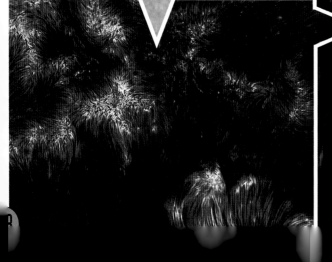

Bubbling gas

The photosphere is the Sun's visible surface. It has an average temperature of 9,900°F (5,500°C) and appears smooth from a distance, but this infrared image shows bubbles of hot gas up to 600 miles (1,000 km) wide, which rise up, cool, and sink back down. Occasionally, some cool gas is blown up from the surface and forms a huge loop in the Sun's atmosphere. This prominence is held in place by the Sun's magnetic field.

Fiery surface

Short-lived spicules (jets) of hot gas, a few thousand miles long, shoot up across the entire surface. They last for about five minutes each and look like red-hot blades of grass moving in a breeze.

Inside the Sun

The Sun's core is 27 million°F (15 million°C) and is the Sun's hottest and densest part. Here, nuclear fusion reactions convert hydrogen to helium, producing energy in the process. Over about 100,000 years this energy moves upward, through, and out of the Sun: first it travels by radiation, then by convection as it bubbles upward, until it finally escapes through the Sun's inner atmosphere—the photosphere and the chromosphere.

Prominence

Photosphere

Chromosphere

Convection zone

Radiation zone

Core

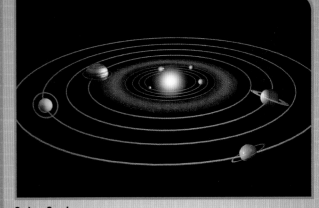

Solar System

The Sun and all the bodies that orbit it make up the Solar System. These orbiting bodies include eight planets and their moons, asteroids, dwarf planets, Kuiper Belt objects, and comets. They were all born together from the same cloud of gas and dust about 4.6 billion years ago. The Sun is by far the biggest object of the Solar System, consisting of 99 percent of all the System's material, and it is the Sun's gravity that keeps the System together.

Asteroid Eros

Billions of small bodies made of rock and metal orbit the Sun. These are the asteroids. More than 90 percent of them make up a doughnut-shaped belt between Mars and Jupiter. Nearly all, such as Eros (above) are irregular-shaped lumps with cratered surfaces. Only eight are larger than 186 miles (300 km). Eros is 19 miles (31 km) long and was the first to have a spacecraft land on it— the *NEAR* (Near Earth Asteroid Rendezvous) *Shoemaker* in 2001.

Pluto and its moons

Extending out beyond the most distant planet, Neptune, is a flattened belt of objects known as the Kuiper Belt. The objects are irregular-shaped lumps of ice and rock that are less than 600 miles (1,000 km) wide. The belt also includes a small number of larger and rounder dwarf planets. One of these, Pluto (seen here), has three moons and was considered to be a planet until the other similar-sized objects in this region were found.

Sunspot

Dark patches called sunspots appear periodically on the photosphere, varying over an 11-year cycle. These cooler regions are caused by the effect of the Sun's magnetic field and last for weeks at a time. They look small on the Sun's face but are often bigger than Earth. The dark patch is the central region of the spot. It is called the umbra and is the spot's darkest and coolest part.

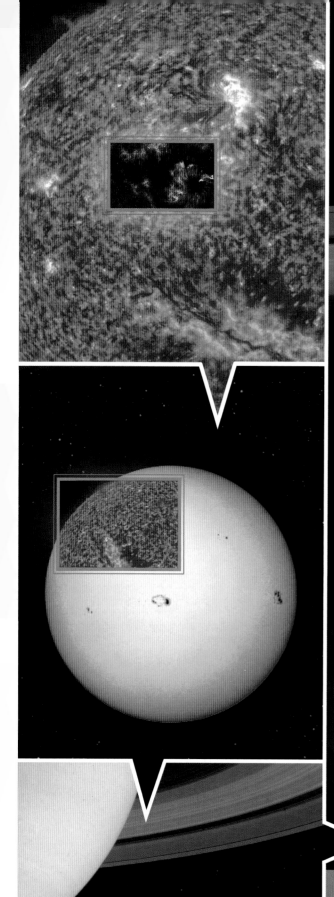

Gas giant
Saturn is the second largest planet in the Solar System and the sixth furthest from the Sun. High-altitude haze in its outer layer of gaseous hydrogen and helium gives it a soft, calm appearance but masks a world of fierce winds and huge storms. Saturn's material changes with depth. The gaseous layer merges into a liquid-like layer and deeper still behaves like molten metal. At the very center is a core of rock and ice.

Giant planets

The four most distant planets—Jupiter, Saturn, Uranus, and Neptune—are by far the biggest objects in the Solar System after the Sun. None of them has a solid surface; they are made mostly of gas and liquid, with colorful hydrogen and helium gas atmospheres, and each has a ring system and a large family of moons.

Jupiter

Saturn

Uranus

Neptune

Big, distant, and cold

Jupiter is the biggest of all eight planets that are orbiting the Sun. It is made up of about 2.5 times more material than is in the other seven planets combined, and it is about 11 times Earth's size. Jupiter is a cold world, and the giants get colder with distance: the smallest and coldest of the four is Neptune, which is 30 times further from the Sun than Earth and has a chilling temperature of -330°F (-201°C) in its upper atmosphere.

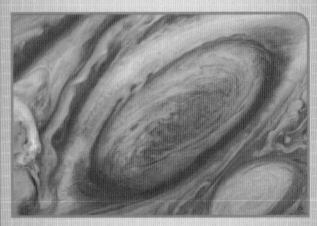

Great Red Spot

All four of the giant planets have stormy weather in their upper atmospheres. Jupiter's is the most noticeable: its visible surface consists of clouds in alternating red and white stripes, and the red and white spots in those stripes are huge weather storms. The biggest is the Great Red Spot, which is about twice the size of Earth. It is the largest storm in the Solar System and has been raging for more than 300 years.

Ringed world

Of all the planets, Saturn has the most extensive ring system. It is made up of hundreds of ringlets consisting of pieces of dirty water-ice. The pieces range in size from specks of icy dust to car-sized boulders, and each follows its own orbit around the planet. The rings shown here are those most easily seen. They extend to about 50,000 miles (80,000 km) beyond Saturn and are 33 ft (10 m) thick at their deepest.

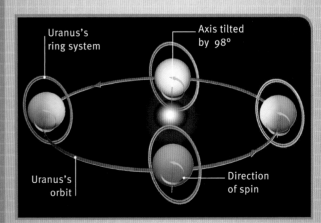

Uranus's ring system

Axis tilted by 98°

Uranus's orbit

Direction of spin

Sideways planet

Compared to the other planets, Uranus seems to roll along its 84-year orbit around the Sun. This is because the planet tilts 98° to one side. As a result, its rings and moons, which orbit Uranus's equator, appear to circle it from top to bottom, and its north and south poles appear to lie where other planets have their equators. Its tilt could be due to a collision with a large asteroid when Uranus was a young planet.

Comets

At least a trillion comets exist far beyond the planets in the freezing outer reaches of the Solar System. Each comet is a city-wide dirty snowball, called a nucleus, that follows its own path around the Sun. Occasionally one travels through the planetary part of the Solar System and close to the Sun, increasing in size as it develops a vast head and two tails.

Spectacular comet
The comet Hale-Bopp was one of the brightest comets of the 20th century. It is seen here in 1997, just after passing around the Sun when it was easily visible to the naked eye. The comet was discovered independently by Alan Hale and Thomas Bopp and took the name of its discoverers. Its previous visit to Earth's skies took place 4,200 years ago, and it is predicted to return in another 2,530 years.

Path around the Sun

We know of about 2,500 comets that have traveled through the inner Solar System. Some make return trips at relatively short and regular intervals; these are called periodic comets. Others, like Hale-Bopp, take thousands of years between trips. A new coma and new tails form each time a comet rounds the Sun. Formation stops as it moves away and the material dissipates into space.

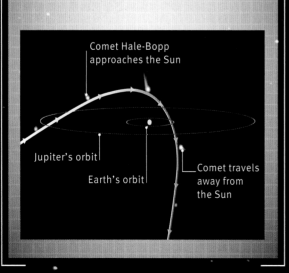

Comet Hale-Bopp approaches the Sun

Jupiter's orbit

Earth's orbit

Comet travels away from the Sun

Coma
As a comet approaches the Sun, a huge head of gas and dust called a coma forms around the comet's nucleus. It forms as the Sun's heat turns the nucleus's surface snow to gas, releasing dust in the process. A coma is typically 62,000 miles (100,000 km) wide. Hale-Bopp's was unusually large at approximately 1.6 million miles (2.5 million km), about 200 times the size of Earth.

Gas tail
As the comet travels, coma material is pushed away by the solar wind and solar radiation, and separates to form a gas tail and a dust tail. The gas tail is straight and blue, and both tails are longest just after the comet has rounded the Sun. A comet's tails always point away from the Sun: they are behind the nucleus as it moves toward the Sun and in front as it moves away.

Dust tail
The dust tail is predominantly white and curves away from the nucleus. Dust lost on each path around the Sun slowly reduces the size of the nucleus until eventually there will be nothing left.

Snowball nucleus
The 4.7-mile- (7.6-km-) long nucleus of Comet Tempel 1 was imaged by the spacecraft *Deep Space* in July 2005. A comet's nucleus is an approximate mix of two-thirds snow and one-third rock dust. Comet Tempel 1 completes an orbit around the Sun every 5.5 years and cannot be seen by the human eye.

Meteor shower
Streaks of light seen in Earth's night sky are meteors, also known as shooting stars. Showers of meteors are produced when Earth travels through a stream of dust lost by a comet traveling near the Sun. Each trail of light is produced by a single fragment that speeds through Earth's atmosphere.

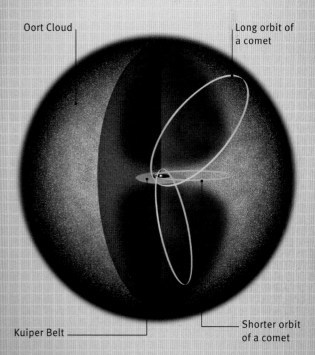

Oort Cloud

Long orbit of a comet

Kuiper Belt

Shorter orbit of a comet

Oort Cloud
The huge sphere of comets that surrounds the disk-shaped planetary part of the Solar System is called the Oort Cloud. The cloud's inner edge starts beyond the Kuiper Belt and consists of comets with relatively short orbits. The cloud's outer edge is made up of comets with the longest orbits, reaching up to 1.6 light years away—halfway to the nearest stars. The comets follow individual elongated orbits that take them around the Sun at all angles.

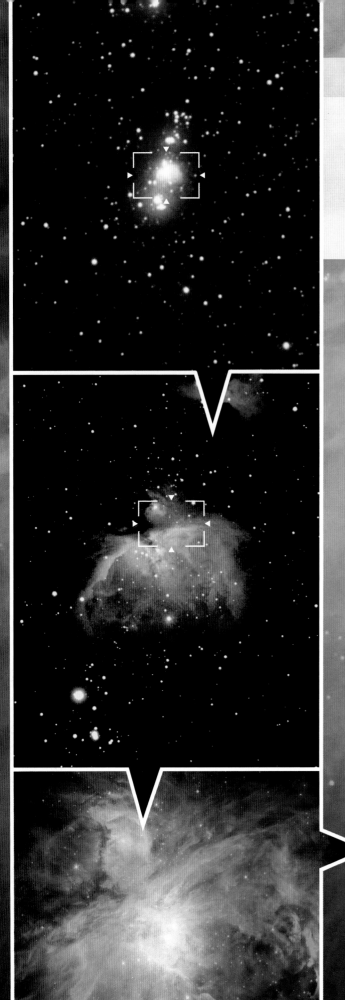

Stars

The trillions of stars that exist in the Universe are all globes of hot, glowing gas. Each one of them is unique, differing in size, temperature, color, luminosity, age, and mass. Each star follows a life cycle, and its characteristics change as it ages. New stars are being born all over the Universe, such as here in the Orion Nebula.

Trapezium cluster

The center of the Orion Nebula is lit up by a handful of hot newborn stars called the Trapezium cluster. They were produced out of the nebula's material. The nebula is predominantly hydrogen gas, which appears pinkish-red from a distance. In this enhanced close-up, swirls of green reveal hydrogen and sulphur gas affected by radiation from the Trapezium stars, and wisps of red and orange are carbon-rich molecules.

Planetary formation

Some of the newly born stars in the nebula are surrounded by disks of material. The disks, which are made of 99 percent gas and 1 percent dust, will go on to form planets that will orbit the star.

Stellar nursery

Interstellar space is filled with clouds of gas and dust. A trigger event, such as a shockwave from a nearby supernova (exploding star) can cause a cloud to start to collapse and form new stars. All of the colorful gas and dust in this image is part of the Orion Nebula—one of the nearest star-forming regions to Earth. The nebula is about 30 light years across and part of a larger cloud system.

Star sculpture

Radiation emitted by the Trapezium stars affects the material around them. The pressure of the radiation, along with stellar winds, press and shape the nebula while ultraviolet radiation makes it glow.

Star birth

A star starts to take shape when a piece of nebula slowly forms a spinning sphere of gas. The central material is compressed and heats up, and nuclear reactions produce energy, making the star shine.

Living together

Stars are produced in clusters; each star in the cluster forms from the same nebula material and at the same time. The 80 or so stars in this Butterfly Cluster were born less than 100 million years ago and are loosely grouped in an open cluster, meaning they will move apart over hundreds of millions of years. The Sun was once in a cluster but it is now alone. But some stars exist in much denser, globular clusters that stay together.

Bright and beautiful

Sirius is the brightest star in Earth's sky. Like the Sun, it is in the middle of its life, shining brightly and steadily. But Sirius is a truly brilliant star: if placed next to the Sun it would be twice as big and about 25 times as bright. Sirius has a tiny, dim companion (lower left), which is 10,000 times fainter than Sirius. The two stars revolve around each other and complete a revolution every 50 years.

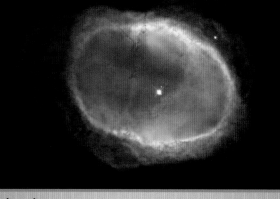

Dying star

Stars made of about the same amount of material as the Sun evolve into giant, red stars. They then move into the last major stage of their life. The giant star pushes off its outer region, which becomes a colorful shell of gas speeding off into space. This shell is known as a planetary nebula. In the center is a white dwarf—the remains of the dying star.

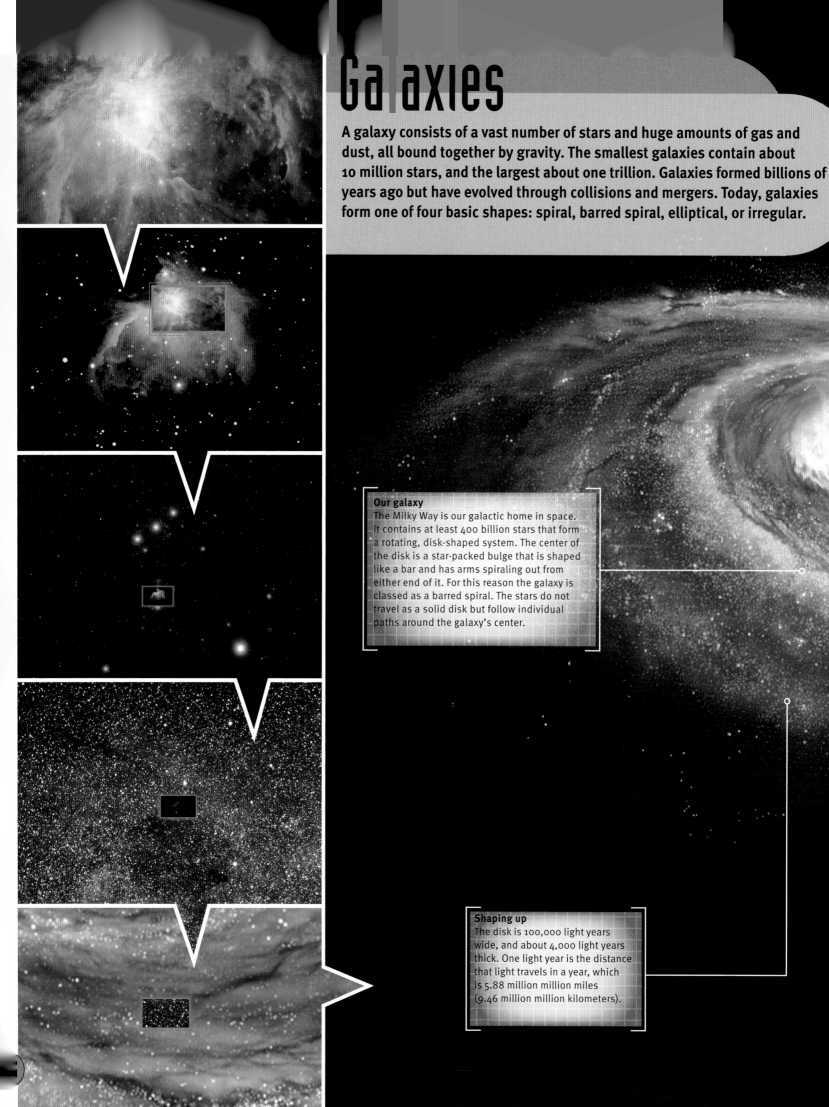

Galaxies

A galaxy consists of a vast number of stars and huge amounts of gas and dust, all bound together by gravity. The smallest galaxies contain about 10 million stars, and the largest about one trillion. Galaxies formed billions of years ago but have evolved through collisions and mergers. Today, galaxies form one of four basic shapes: spiral, barred spiral, elliptical, or irregular.

Our galaxy
The Milky Way is our galactic home in space. It contains at least 400 billion stars that form a rotating, disk-shaped system. The center of the disk is a star-packed bulge that is shaped like a bar and has arms spiraling out from either end of it. For this reason the galaxy is classed as a barred spiral. The stars do not travel as a solid disk but follow individual paths around the galaxy's center.

Shaping up
The disk is 100,000 light years wide, and about 4,000 light years thick. One light year is the distance that light travels in a year, which is 5.88 million million miles (9.46 million million kilometers).

Central bulge

The stars in the center are old red and yellow stars, giving the central bulge a yellow tinge. Also in the galaxy's heart is a supermassive black hole called Sagittarius A*, three million times more massive than our Sun. A black hole is a region of space where gravity is so strong that not even light can escape. Material far enough away not to be sucked into the black hole is kept in orbit by its massive gravitational pull.

One of the crowd

The Sun is a middle-aged star, 27,000 light years from the galaxy's center. It is located within the Orion Arm, one of the galaxy's partial arms. The Sun travels around the center once every 220 million years.

Spiral arm

Both young and more mature stars exist within the spiral arms. They are also found between the arms, but because those in the arms are particularly young and bright, the arms appear more brilliant.

Milky light

All the stars seen in the night sky surrounding Earth belong to the Milky Way Galaxy. One part of the sky is packed with stars that form a milky path of light that can be seen on dark nights. This path was named the Milky Way by the ancient Greeks who believed it to be a milky river created by the goddess Hera. It is our view along the plane of the galaxy's disk.

Spiral galaxy

Bode's Galaxy, also known as M81, is a spiral galaxy. This type of galaxy is similar to a barred spiral but its central star-packed hub is round rather than bar-shaped. This colorful infrared view of M81 highlights clumpy knots in the galaxy's spiral arms where massive stars are being born.

Elliptical galaxy

Compared to other galaxies, elliptical galaxies are smooth, almost featureless, structures. The galaxy shown here is M49, which is shaped like a flattened ball, but other ellipticals are round like a ball, or oval like a football. Small ones called dwarf ellipticals are the most common type of galaxy.

Irregular galaxy

Galaxies with no regular shape, such as the Large Magellanic Cloud (LMC), are classed as irregulars. Irregulars are relatively small and have high proportions of young and newly forming stars. Once spiral-shaped, a close encounter with another galaxy changed their shape and triggered star formation.

Colliding galaxies

The two galaxies shown here in false color are on a collision course that will shape them into a single massive galaxy. The two galactic cores look like blue eyes peering through a mask. Clusters of new stars, which form the apparent mask, were produced when the galaxies met about 40 million years ago.

Universe

The Universe consists of everything: everything we know about and everything yet to be discovered. It came into being 13.7 billion years ago in an event called the Big Bang, which created all the material and energy in today's Universe, as well as time and space. Just 4.6 percent of the Universe is made of ordinary material like planets, stars, and galaxies. The rest is dark matter and dark energy.

Today's Universe
There are at least 125 billion galaxies in the Universe. They are all around us, in every direction we look. This view, taken by the Hubble Space Telescope of a tiny patch of sky, is our deepest look into the Universe and shows thousands of galaxies of different ages, shapes, and sizes. The image was created from 800 exposures of about 20 minutes each; a total of 11 days and 7 hours.

Changing shape
Some of the galaxies are so close together that they interact with each other. The gravity of each tugs on the other and their shapes become distorted. These two will eventually combine into one galaxy.

Back in time

The galaxies in this image are so distant that it takes billions of years for their light to reach Earth. When we look at them we look back in time, seeing the galaxies as they were when the light left them billions of years ago. The small red galaxies are the most distant. They appear 800 million years old, but their light has taken 13 billion years to reach us. These galaxies look red because they are speeding away from us.

Milky Way star

Not quite everything in this image is a galaxy; this star is part of our own galaxy, the Milky Way. It appears much larger than the more distant galaxies because it is in the foreground.

Clustering together

Galaxies are not scattered randomly across the Universe—they exist in clusters. The smallest, called groups, contain fewer than about 50 galaxies. The Milky Way belongs to the Local Group, a cluster of more than 40 galaxies. The nearest large cluster is the Virgo Cluster, partly shown here. It consists of about 160 large elliptical and spiral galaxies, and about 2,000 small galaxies all spread through a 15-million-light-year volume of space.

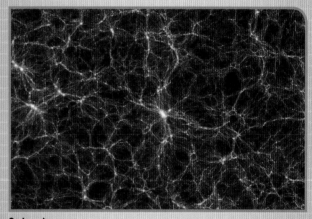

Going large

The largest structures in the Universe are superclusters. These are huge sheet- and chain-like structures made up of clusters of galaxies. This computer simulation shows how they form a web-like network across a one-billion-light-year region of the Universe. The crisscrossing chains and sheets of galaxy clusters are separated from each other by huge voids of apparently empty space.

Unknown Universe

The majority of the Universe is undetected, but we know about 23 percent of it is made up of dark matter, and 72 percent is a mysterious energy called dark energy. Dark matter is an unknown material that doesn't emit any energy and that cannot be detected directly. But we know it exists in galaxy clusters such as this one because it affects the light of more distant galaxies. Pale blue indicates the dark matter's location in this cluster.

GLOSSARY

ALGAE (singular: alga)
Simple, plantlike organisms that are usually found in water, and make their own food by photosynthesis.

ALLOY
A metal made from two or more metals, or of a metal and a non-metal.

ALTITUDE
Height above sea level or Earth's surface.

AMPHIBIAN
A vertebrate that lives partly on land and partly in water.

ARTERY
A blood vessel carrying high-pressure blood away from the heart.

ASTEROID
A lump of rock or metal in space, varying in size from a few feet to more than 600 miles (900 km) across.

ATOM
The smallest part of an element that has the chemical properties of the element. Made up of a nucleus consisting of protons and neutrons, surrounded by orbiting electrons.

BACTERIA (singular: bacterium)
Single-celled microorganisms that reproduce by splitting into two.

BIG BANG
The theory that the Universe began with a massive explosion of matter. It is thought that everything in the Universe is still moving apart because of the explosion.

BIOME
Many similar ecosystems around the world grouped together, such as tropical forests or tundra.

BLACK HOLE
A region in space where gravity is so strong that not even light can escape. Often they are the remains of a star that has collapsed in on itself.

CAPILLARY
A microscopic blood vessel that carries blood to individual cells.

CARBOHYDRATE
An energy-giving compound made up of carbon, hydrogen, and oxygen, found in foods such as potatoes.

CARNIVORE
An animal that gets all of its energy from eating other animals.

CELL
One of trillions of microscopic living units that make up organisms.

CHROMOSOME
Threadlike packages of DNA found inside cells, containing genes.

COMPOUND
A substance formed when atoms from two or more elements join.

COSMOS
Another word for the Universe.

CRANIUM
The part of the skull that encloses the brain. The other part is the mandible, or jaw.

CRUSTACEAN
An invertebrate with a tough exoskeleton (shell) and jointed limbs that lives mainly in water.

DEMOCRACY
A form of government ruled by elected representatives of the people.

DETRITOVORE
An animal or other organism that feeds on detritus—the decaying fragments of dead organisms.

DIAPHRAGM
A sheet of muscle underneath the rib cage that is involved in breathing.

DNA (deoxyribonucleic acid)
Large molecules found inside cells, consisting of two intertwined strands that carry the genetic instructions needed to build and operate those cells.

DWARF PLANET
A body that orbits the Sun and is massive enough for its gravity to make it almost spherical. Unlike planets, their gravity is not strong enough to clear other objects from their orbits.

ECOSYSTEM
A community of organisms and their enviroment, ranging in size from a puddle to a desert.

EFFICIENCY
The relation between energy used and useful work carried out. An inefficient machine wastes a great deal of energy.

ELECTROMAGNETIC RADIATION
Waves of energy that can travel through space and matter at the speed of light. It ranges from gamma rays (with the shortest wavelength) to radio waves (with the longest wavelength).

ELECTRON
A negatively charged particle that orbits the nucleus of an atom.

ELEMENT
A substance that cannot be broken down into a simpler substance by chemical reactions.

EMBALMING
A chemical process used to preserve a dead body and stop it decaying.

EMBRYO
The name given to a developing human during the first eight weeks after fertilization occurs.

ENZYME
A protein that acts as a catalyst to speed up the rate of checmical reactions.

EVOLUTION
The gradual process by which species develop and change.

EXTINCTION
When all members of a species die out.

FAULT
A break in the Earth's crust.

FERTILIZATION
The joining together of male and female sex cells to create a new individual.

FETUS
The name given to a developing human from the ninth week after fertilization until birth.

FOOD CHAIN
A process whereby food passes along a chain of living things as each one is eaten by the next.

FORCE
A push or pull that changes the movement or shape of an object.

FRICTION
A force that slows or stops the movement of one surface against another.

FUNGI
A kingdom of organisms, distinct from plants and animals, that absorb nutrients from dead and living matter.

GENE
One of the 20,000–25,000 instructions contained within a cell that controls its construction and operation.

GLACIER
A large mass of ice slowly flowing over land, often down a mountainside.

GLUCOSE
A simple sugar that cells use as a form of energy. Glucose is one of the main products of photosynthesis.

GRAVITY
A force of attraction found throughout the Universe. The greater the mass of a body, the greater its gravitational pull.

HABITAT
The natural home of an organism.

HERBIVORE
An animal that gets its energy from eating plants and is adapted for that purpose.

IGNEOUS ROCK
Rock that forms when molten magma or lava cools and solidifies.

INVERTEBRATE
An animal without a backbone.

ION
An atom or group of atoms that has lost or gained one or more electrons to become electrically charged.

KERATIN
The protein that makes up hair, horns, hoofs, nails, and feathers.

KUIPER BELT
An area of the Solar System containing millions of icy, cometlike objects. It extends from the orbit of Neptune outward to the inner edge of the Oort Cloud.

LARVA (plural: larvae)
The immature stage in the life cycle of certain animals, such as insects and amphibians.

LASER
A device that emits an intense beam of light.

LAVA
Molten rock released from the interior of a planet, usually through a volcano.

LIGHT YEAR
The distance light travels in one year. One light year is 5.88 million million miles (9.46 million million km).

MAGMA
Liquid, molten rock in Earth's mantle and crust. Once above ground it is called lava.

MAMMAL
A vertebrate animal that feeds its young on milk and has a covering of hair.

MANTLE
1. A thick, dense layer of rock under the crust of Earth and the other rocky planets.
2. In mollusks, an outer layer of tissue.

MANTRA
A sound, word, or group of words that is repeated many times as a devotional chant particularly associated with the rituals of Hinduism and Buddhism.

MARIA (singular: mare)
The large, dark areas on the Moon, originally thought to be lunar seas but now known to be huge depressions formed by ancient volcanic eruptions.

MASS
The amount of matter something contains.

MATTER
Everything that has mass and occupies space is matter.

MEIOSIS
A type of cell division that occurs in the ovaries and testes to produce sex cells.

METAMORPHIC ROCK
Rock that has been changed by great heat and pressure underground.

METAMORPHOSIS
A major change in an animal's body shape during its life cycle.

METEOR
A short-lived streak of light produced by an object entering Earth's upper atmosphere.

MICROBE
The general name for microscopic organisms that cause disease.

MINERAL
A naturally occurring substance that is not formed from plant or animal material.

MITOSIS
A type of cell division used for growth and repair that produces two identical cells from each "parent" cell.

MOLECULE
Two or more atoms joined together to form the smallest unit of an element or compound.

MOON
A rock or rock-and-ice body that orbits a planet or an asteroid.

NEBULA
A cloud of gas and dust in space.

NEUTRON
A particle in the nucleus of an atom, which has no electic charge.

NEUTRON STAR
A dense, compact star formed from the core of an exploding star. About the size of a city but with the same mass as the Sun.

NUCLEAR FUSION
A reaction in which the nucleus of an atom, such as hydrogen, splits into two smaller nuclei, releasing energy.

NUCLEUS (plural: nuclei)
1. The central part of an atom, made up of protons and neutrons.
2. The part of a living cell that contains the genetic material of the cell.

NUTRIENT
Any material taken in by a living thing to sustain life.

OMNIVORE
An animal that gets its energy from eating both plant and animal matter.

OORT CLOUD
A sphere of more than a trillion comets that surrounds the planetary part of the Solar System.

ORBIT
The path that a natural or artificial body makes around another more massive body.

ORGANISM
A living thing consisting of one or more cells.

OVUM (plural: ova)
A female sex cell, also called an egg. Ova are produced by, and released from, a woman's ovaries.

PERISTALSIS
A wave of muscular contraction through a hollow organ that, for example, pushes food through the esophagus and stomach, or urine down a ureter.

PHILOSOPHY
A group of ideas or a way of thinking about the world, its people, and the Universe.

PHOTOSYNTHESIS
The method by which plants make food from water and carbon dioxide using energy from the Sun.

PLACENTA
The organ that develops in the uterus during pregnancy to supply the fetus with blood, food, and oxygen from the mother.

PLANET
A body that orbits the Sun, that is massive enough for its gravity to make it almost spherical, and that has cleared its orbit of any other comparatively sized bodies.

PLANETARY NEBULA
The expanding shell of gas ejected by a dying red giant star.

PLANKTON
Tiny plants and animals that drift around near the surface of bodies of water.

PLASMA
1. The liquid part of blood.
2. A hot, electrically charged gas, in which the electrons are free from their atoms. One of the four states of matter.

POLLEN
Microscopic grains produced by the anthers of flowers and containing male sex cells.

PREDATOR
An animal that hunts, kills, and eats other animals.

PRIMATE
A mammal with flexible fingers and toes and forward-pointing eyes. Humans are primates.

PROPAGANDA
Organized spreading of information— true or false—to promote a specific cause.

PROTEIN
One of a group of organic compounds, made up of carbon, hydrogen, oxygen, nitrogen, and sulphur, that perform many different roles inside the body, including making enzymes.

PROTON
A particle in the nucleus of an atom that has a positive electrical charge.

PUPA (plural: pupae)
The resting, non-feeding stage in the life cycle of certain insects when they turn from larvae into adults.

RENAISSANCE
A period in 15th- and 16th-century Europe that saw a new interest in Greek and Roman ideas.

REPTILE
A cold-blooded vertebrate animal that is covered with hard, dry scales, and lays shelled eggs.

RIFT
A place where Earth's crust is being pulled apart.

SATELLITE
An object that orbits a planet that may be naturally occuring, such as a moon or an asteroid, or it may be artificial, such as a craft used to transmit radio signals.

SEDIMENTARY ROCK
Rock formed when fragments of material settle in layers on the floor of a sea or lake and are fused together over time.

SPERM
Male sex cells, which are contained in, and released from, a man's testes.

SPORE
A single-celled reproductive unit of some plants, fungi, and bacteria.

STARCH
A complex carbohydrate formed in plants that is used as a store of energy.

SUBDUCTION
When one edge of a tectonic plate is forced downward beneath another plate as they push together.

SUPERNOVA
When a massive star explodes and becomes extremely luminous. This happens when a supergiant star runs out of fuel, or when a white dwarf star explodes.

SYMBIOSIS
A close relationship between members of two different species that may be mutually beneficial or one-sided.

TAIGA
A type of forest characterized by evergreen coniferous trees.

TECTONIC PLATES
The slabs of solid rock that make up the Earth's crust.

TSUNAMI
A huge, destructive wave that is often caused by an earthquake on the seabed.

TUNDRA
The cold, treeless, largely barren land that fringes the polar regions.

VALVE
A structure in a hollow passage, such as the heart, that controls the flow of fluid.

VEIN
A blood vessel that carries low-pressure blood toward the heart.

VERTEBRATE
An animal with a backbone.

VIRUS
An infectious, non-living agent, much smaller than bacteria, that invades cells and causes disease. Viruses include the common cold and measles.

WHITE DWARF
The collapsed core of a Sun-like star that has stopped generating energy.

INDEX

INDEX

CREDITS

DK would like to thank:
Carron Brown, Shaila Brown, Niki Foreman, and Victoria Heyworth-Dunne for additional editing; Ralph Pitchford for additional design; Charlotte Webb for proofreading; Jackie Brind for preparing the index; Anne Millard for advising on the Ancient Egypt spread; JB Illustrations for commissioned artwork; Amber at MOT Models for modelling; Philippa Wulwik for make-up.

Picture credits
The publisher would like to thank the following for their kind permission to reproduce their photographs:

(Key: a-above; b-below/bottom; c-center; l-left; r-right; t-top)

8 akg-images: 144crb, 178cla; **Alamy Images:** 24BY36 81br, 80eight Photography & Design 211cb, Ace Stock Limited 176bc, allOver photography 143br, Amazing Images 222-223c, AR Archive 177bl, armphotos 128cla, John Arnaud 144-145bc (pavement), Art Directors & TRIP 171cl, The Art Gallery Collection 166cla, 178tl, Jeffrey Blackler 210-211c (background), Michele Burgess 122cla, Scott Camazine 96cla, Christine Osborne Pictures 134cla, David Cole 109cra, Judith Collins 211bl, Roger Cracknell 16 121crb, Dinodia Photos 189br, Reinhard Dirscheri 10cb, Rebacca Erol 152bl, Eye Ubiquitous 210bl, fashionpix 159tr, Gabbro 96tl, David D. Green 211cla, David J. Green 210crb, david hancock 147tr, Hemis 138-139c, John Henshall 172bc, Peter Horree 166bl, D. Hurst 114bc, Ian Trower Photography 190bl, imagebroker 123ca (Rollercoaster), 143crb, 192cl, adam james 186bl, Marcin Jamkowski / Adventure Pictures 187clb, John Joannides 210cl, JTB Photo Communications, Inc. 186cra, kolvenbach 169tl, John Lee / Aurora Photos 133bc, Liquid Light 185tr, Dennis MacDonald 150cl, Mary Evans Picture Library 190cla, mediablitzimages 221clb (USB memory stick), Michael DeFreitas Caribbean 122tl, Mim Friday 158br (toy car), ian nolan 176-177c (background), North Wind Picture Archive 164cb, 174cla, PCL 186-187 (postcard stand), Pete Marshall People and Places 121tr, Photo Network 145cr, Photos 12 149br, Pictorial Press Ltd 187bl, Picture Contact BV 117cra, The Print Collector 180bc, Prisma Bildagentur 158bl (telephone), Realimage 211tc, Red Clover 158ca (clock), Red Cover 158-159cb (table), Right Perspective Images 166clb, Robert Harding Picture Library 147crb, Robert Harding Picture Library Ltd 81cra, 109tr, Pep Roig 131bl, Kevin Schafer 98-99c (Mosasaur fossil), sciencephotos 96clb, Alex Segre 144-145c (man and wall), Neil Setchfield 191br (leech bottle), Stocktrek Images 75tr, Travelshots.com 192cla, Mireille Vautier 171tr, World Pictures Phototshot 121cra, World Religions Photo Library 189tr; **The Art Archive:** 182clb, British Museum 166-167c (Standard of Ur), Granger Collection 169cr, National Anthropological Museum Mexico / Gianni Dagli Orti 168cr; **The Bridgeman Art Library:** Archives Charmet / Private Collection 178-179c (Louis XVI execution), 182-183c (image on book), Musee de la Tapisserie, Bayeux 166cra, Boltin Picture Library / Private Colletion 177c, National Gallery, London 139tr, Museo Archeologico Nazionale, Naples 176c, 176cr, Bibliotheque Nationale, Paris 190tl, Peterhof Palace, Petrodvorets, St. Petersburg, Russia 181cra, The Royal Collection © 2011 Her Majesty Queen Elizabeth 182bl; **Bryan & Cherry Alexander / ArcticPhoto:** T Jacobsen 82-83c (background); **Collection Of The National Palace Museum, Taiwan, Republic Of China:** 172-173c; **Corbis:** 3d4Medical.com 45br, 191clb (petri dish), 234-235c, Noah Addis 116-117c, Lucas Allen 174-175c (wallet), Paul Almasy 150tl, James L. Amos 19crb, Colin Anderson / Blend Images 170-171 (background), Arctic Images 91cra, The Art Archive 177cr, 184-185c, Atlantide Phototravel 141crb, Alistair Baker 214-215 (background), Kapoor Baldev / Sygma 134bl, David Ball 188-189c, Tom Bean 18ca (Bromeliad), Manuel Bellver 214-215c (posters), Zohra Bensemra / Reuters 133tr, Tobias Bernhard 28bl, Poppy Berry 24ca (garden and chair), Bettmann 155cra, 164bl, 170crb, 174tl, 179tr, 182tl, 183tl, 233tr, 233crb, Stefano Bianchetti 186cb, Philippe Body / Hemis 185crb, Christophe Boisvieux 122crb, 123ca, Mark Bolton 31cr, John-Francis Bourke 62tl (skeleton), Gary Braasch 19tc (tree trunk), 19bc (tree roots), 20-21c (background), Brisbane Airport Corporation / Reuters 198bl, Andrew Brookes 61cr, Ben Burgeson / NewSport 157br, Oliver Burston 130-131c (balloons), Jan Butchofsky 202tl, Car Culture 182-183 (chairs and audience), Stephane Cardinale / People Avenue 160tl, Giuseppe Castiglione 173br, David Cheshire / LOOP Images 181br, Ralph A. Clevenger 16-17cb (ocean floor), Construction Photography 214c (excavator), 215bl (skip), Jim Craigmyle 220c (woman on screen), Sherwin Crasto / Reuters 147br, Scot D.Smith / Retna / Retna Ltd 152-153c, Cameron Davidson 77crb, Tim Davis 31cra, Dennis Kunkel Microscopy, Inc / Visuals Unlimited 31cb, Destinations 73tr, 94bc, 117br, 200cl, Mick Eason / Newsports 156-157c, Oswald Eckstein 32cb, Juergen Effner / dpa 32bl, Terry W. Eggers 88bl, Emely 178-179b (background), Cecilia Enholm / Etsa 206-207c (view through window), Alejandro Ernesto / epa 126bl, Macdudd Everton 171bl, Fadil 197cra, 235br, Shannon Fagan 197br, Wolf Fahrenbach / Visuals Unlimited 51crb, Eliseo Fernandez / Reuters 128bl, Fly Fernandez 65tr (background through window), Michael & Patricia Fogden 21cra, 21crb, 41bc, Dan Forer / Beateworks 158-159c (background room), Andrew Fox 221br, Owen Franken 89br, Free Agents Limited 160cla, Stephen Frink 13bl, The Gallery Collection 164-165c, 165bl, 178clb, Colin Garratt / Milepost 92 1 / 2 215br, Chris Gascoigne / View 166-167c (background), Gaurier / photocuisine 206-207bc (creme fraiche), National Geographic Society 182cla, Gianni Dagli 174clb, 186clb, Tim Graham 88br, Sonja Grunbauer 119br, Klaus Hackenberg 13tr, Michael Haegele 209br, Halfdark / fstop 182-183c (book), George Hall 48cl, Tony Hallas / Science Faction 243cra, John Harper 192bl, Blaine Harrington III 111br, Lindsay Hebberd 189cra, Hemis 113cra, Heritage Images 177br, Carlos Hernandex / Westend61 146-147c (main image), 147c (dancer purple bandana), Richard Hewitt Stewart / National Geographic 170bl, Frithjof Hirdes 118c (factory interior background), Hoberman Collection 176bl, 192tl, Fritz Hoffmann / In Pictures 125tr, Hola Images 170cr, Jack Hollingsworth 170bc, Jim Hollnder / epa 166-167c (men carrying), Peter Hudek / epa 118cb, Hulton-Deutsch Collection 175cla, Image Source 51br, Gallo Images 41cb (chameleon's tongue), Imaginechina 213tr, 233cra, Alexander Joe / Pool / epa 142bl (Mandela image on book), Mark A. Johnson 16cra (top of wave), 17tc (tropical island), Peter Johnson 34ca (African buffalo), Wolfgang Kaehler 145br, Karen Kasmauski / Science Faction 117tr, Yevgeny Khaldei 165br, Rehan Khan / epa 120bc, Knaup / photocuisine 26bl, Tamas Kovacs / epa 48tl, Frank Krahmer 34cb, Bob Krist 70-71c, 106-107c, 109crb, Kulka 213c (speakers), Matthias Kulka 44-45c, 215cra, Dai Kurokawa / epa 141br, Robet Landau 149c (film crew on booms), Jacques Langevin / Sygma 111crb, Ian Langston / epa 117crb, Frans Lanting 19tr, 25br, 73cr, 73br, 75crb, 87tr, 94bl, 192-193tc (fire), Last Refuge / Robert Harding World Imagery 162-165c, Ben LÍ 203cb (jet plane body), Floris Leeuwenberg 120-121c, Charles & Josette Lenars 93crb, 192-193ca (Roman soldiers), George D. Lepp 13crb, Peter Lillie 31tr, W. Wayne Lockwood 84clb, Ren Long / Xinhua Press 157crb, Araldo de Luca 177cl, John Lund 202cla, Johannes Mann 173bl, Steve Maslowski 28cb, Rob Matheson 230-231c (background), 232-233c (background), 234-235c (background), Andrew McConnell / Robert Harding World Imagery 186crb, Brendan McDermid / Reuters 174-175c (woman and wall), Joe McDonald 34crb (Zebra mouse), 35bl, Jose Mendez / epa 168-169c (girl at screen), Gerold & Cynthia Merker / Visuals Unlimited 21tr, Benjamin J. Meyers 133cra, Diane Miller / Monsoon / Photolibrary 24ca (window frame), Marli Miller 96bl, Daniel Mirer 58-59 (background), Momatiuk-Eastcott 130-131c (background sky), Buero Monaco 208-209 (winter scene), moodboard 190-191c (background), Arthur Morris 205cra, David Muench 20bc (Amaryllis blooms), Mushtaq Muhammed / Reuters 125br, Louis Murray / Visuals Unlimited 191bc, NASA 72-73c, 93br, Clive Nichols 143bl (bluebell woods image on book), F. Nicol / photocuisine 64cl, Kazuyoshi Nomachi 97br, David Northcott 41bl, Richard T. Nowitz 136-137c, Dale O'Dell 77cra, Charles O'Rear 126clb, Ocean 191cl (calendar dates), Kalervo Ojutkangas / Nordicphotos 199br, 206cla, Christine Osborne 126tl, 139br, Nigel Pavitt 87cra, Photo Quest / Science Photo Library 53bl, Photosindia 122cra, Christopher Pillitz / In Pictures 119bl, Dick Poe / Visuals Unlimited 27cr (growth on mushroom), Mike Powell 198bc, Louie Psihoyos 149bl, Radius Images 168bl, Redcover / Arcaid 158-159tc (light), Trinette Reed 62-63 (background), Seth Resnick / Science Faction 83crb (iceberg & reflection), Roger Ressmeyer 91crb, 226bl, Reuters 131br, Jim Richardson 226-227c, Lynda Richardson 19cra, Christian Richters / View 175cr (walkway), Martin Rietze / Westend61 79br, Patrick Roberts 133crb, Michael Rosenfeld / Science Faction 221crb, Jonathan Ross / Spaces Images 142-143c (background), Jeffrey L. Rotman 12bl, 12-13c (background), Gus Ruelas / Reuters 155crb, Koichi Saito / amana images 114-115bc (glasses), Nick Saraco 118c (fork lift truck), Kevin Schafer 18tl (Bromeliad Bloom), 20-21c (Red-eyed tree frogs), 92-93c, David Scharf / Science Faction 54cla, Alan Schein 133br, Schlegemmilch 213cra, Schultheiss Productions 187cr (postcards), Gregor Schuster 63bc (book), Robert Sciarrino / Star Ledger 215crb, Sea World of California 35cb, Shepard Sherbell / SABA 214cb (poster paper), Tom Sibley 126-127 (background), Radu Sigheti / Reuters 34-35c (zebra), Hens Sinith / epa 128tl, Ariel Skelley / Blend Images 127c (women at till), FrÈdÈric Soltan 171br, Paul Souders 18cb (large leaf), 28bc, 213crb, Specialist Stock 11tc, Soeren Stache / dpa 139cra, Gabriela Staebler 122br, Ruet Stephane / Sygma 160clb, Stocktrek 197crb, STR / epa 91tr, Hans Strand 75cra, Keren Su 113crb, 172bl, 186cla, Jane Sweeney / Robert Harding World Imagery 113br, Ramin Talaie 182-183tc (auction room), Con Tanasiuk / Design Pics 181bl, Steve Terrill 150cr, Bernd Thissen / dpa 182-183bc (hands on book), Transtock 198-199c, 205crb, Chris Trotman / Duomo 157cra, Henrik Trygg 77tr, Masaru Tsuda / amanaimages 141tr, Peter Turnley 187br, US Air Force - digital version / Science Faction 151cl, Sandro Vannini 145cb, 185cra, Bill Varie 8-9c, Steven Vidler 205tr, Steven Vidler / Eurasia Press 87crb, 123cla (Eiffel Tower magnet), Visuals Unlimited 40bc, 82clb, Robert Wallis / SIPA 178bl, Karl Weatherly 202-203 (sky and rainbow), Robert Weight / Ecoscene 113cb, Stuart Westmorland 39crb, 40bl, 105br, Josh Westrich 194-195, Robin Whalley / Loop Images 87br, Staffan Widstrand 169br, Uli Wiesmeier 208br (snowman), Tim Wimborne / Reuters 123br, Jeremy Woodhouse 152clb, John Woodworth / Loop Images 122-123bc (phone box magnet), Alison Wright 118c (cardboard box), Norbert Wu / Science Faction 16tl, 219br, Michael S. Yamashita 90-91c, Robert Yin 12-13c, Han Yuqing / Xinhua Press 157tr; **Dorling Kindersley:** British Museum 171crb, Jon Hughes 169tr, Colin Keates 98bl, Jamie Marshall 11crb, Arlette Mellaart 166tl, Museum of the Moving Image, London 148c (light), Lindsey Stock 221ca, Michael Zabe 171tl, 171clb (golden eagle head); **exchange3d.com:** Behr Bros / Arran Lewis 48-49c; **FLPA:** Fred Bavendam / Minden Pictures 13cb (snail), Nigel Cattlin 23cra, 23br, 26-27cb (fungus), Paul Hobson 23tr, Derek Middleton 37cra, Konrad Wothe / Minden Pictures 37tr; **Fotolia:** 11tr, andreapetrlik 143cl (artwork on book cover), DavidMSchrader 142cr (background on book cover), kameramann 25tc, Andres Rodriguez 220tr (web-cam), Richard Seeney 221bl, Speedfighter 142cr (artwork on book cover); **Galaxy Picture Library:** Yoji Hirose 244tl, Robin Scagell 242-243c, STScl 248-249c; **Gensler:** 109bc; **Getty Images:** AFP 111tr, 111cra, 122clb, 125cr, 126cla, 128clb, 134clb, 144cra, 148cl (man holding boom), The Agency Collection 47tr, altrendo images 217bl, amana images 114cl (globe base), Dan Biglow 202-203bc (jet engine), Bloomberg 210tr, Paul Bradbury 212-213c, Brand X Pictures 59cla (stand), Bridgeman Art Library 123cr, 143cra, Buena Vista Images 140cra, Robert Cadloff 217tr, Kathy Collins 206clb, Jeffrey Coolidge 56-57c (computer screen), Jan Hakan Dahlstrom 211tr, DAJ 161tr, Peter Dazeley 47cr, DEA / G. Dagli Orti 143tr, Danita Dellmont 176cl, Erik Dreyer 200-201 (window), Nicholas Eveleigh 59tl (blood bag), Grant Faint 46tr, Denis Felix 204-205c, David Fischer 148-149b (background), Jakob Fridholm 209bc (grill), Getty Images 189crb, Gavin Hellier / Robert Harding World Imagery 187cla, David Humphreys / Foodpix 126-127cb (shopping trolley), Image Source 95bl, Imagemore Co, Ltd 154bc (camera), Dr. Kessel & Dr. Kardon / Tissues & Organs 59tr, Heath Korvola 192-193c (cinema), Claire Leimbach / Robert Harding 152tl, David Liittschwager / National Geographic 14-15c (background), M. Llorden 147cra, O. Louis Mazzatenta 150bl, Medioimages / Photodisc 130bc, Ricky John Molloy 200-201c (girl), Dana Neely 130bl, 134tl, Paul Nicklen / National Geographic 15bl, NY Daily News 151crb, Willoughby Owen 77br, photosindia 154-155c, Martin Pickard 219tr, PM Images 146-147cb (boom box), Popperfoto 174tr, 174c, 175bl, purpleflames 206tl, Andreas Rentz 46-47c (runners), David Scharf 54clb, Science Photo Library 58c (doctor), Gregg Segal 149c (director), Mark Segal 118clb (magazines on fork lift), Juan Silva 206-207c, SSPL 180bl, 180-181c, 190cb, 221cra, Luke Stettner 46tr (man), Harold Sund 118bl, Thinkstock 220-221c (laptop on train), Michele Westmorland 15clb, Norbert Wu 11br; **Kenneth A. Goldberg:** 202bl; **Google Earth:** MapLink / Tele Atlas 114-115c (image on pc); **Brian Guzzetti/Far Corners Photography:** 91br; **Innovation First:** 218-219c; **The Kobal Collection:** Chaplin / United Artists 148bl, Dreamworks / LLC 144-145cb, Paramount / Marks, Elliot 145tr, Warner Bros / DC Comics 148bc; **Lebrecht Music and Arts:** Matti Kolho 160bl; **Legoland California:** 124-125c; **MVRDV:** 109br; **NASA:** 54428 227bl, 227bc, 228-229c, 230-231c (ISS), 231cr, 231cb, 231br, 232-233c (space walk), 229tr, 229cra, 229crb, 229br, 233br, 235cra, 235crb, 236tl, 236cla, 236-237c, 237tr, 237cb, 238tl, 238-239, 239cr, 239br, 240cl, 240-241c, 241tr (Jupiter), 241cr, 243tr, 244-245c, 245cr, 245br, 247tr, 249br, ESA / J.Hester(ASU) 155br, Goddard Space Flight Center 112-113c, Planetary Photojournal 196-197c, 224-225c; **NHPA / Photoshot:** Ernie Janes 13cra, David Maitland 38bl, Ann and Steve Toon 36-37cb (wound on buffalo); **OLPC:** 132-133c; **The Opte project:** 115br; **Ordnance Survey © Crown Copyright:** Bournemouth Borough Council 115cr; **Photolibrary:** Kelvin Aitken / Age fotostock 80-81tc (waves), Alaska Stock Images 16bl, Steve Allen / Imagestate 34tc (tree), Walter Allgˆwer / Imagebroker.net 100clb, Stephen Barnett 119c (newspaper plant), Bianchetti Bianchetti / RESO 215tr, Jonathan Bird / Peter Arnold Images 37crb, Russ Bishop 96-97c, James Braund 198-199 (background), Denis Bringard / Bios 22bc (white stamen), Doug Cheeseman / Peter Arnold Images 83cl (orca surfacing), Creativ Studio Heinemann / Imagebroker.net 216bl, Paulo Curto / Tips Italia 104-105c, Dominic Dibbs / Fresh Food Images 159cr, Paddy Eckersley 219crb, Mark Edwards / Still Pictures 100bl, Chad Ehlers 100cla, Eye Ubiquitous 215bc (wheelbarrow), Michael Fogden / OSF 39br, Foodfolio / Photocuisine 216cra (mint sprig), Patrick Frischknecht / Still Pictures 98-99c (rock face), Michael P Gadomski / Superstock 26-27c, Marc Gerritsen / Sheltered Images 158cl (entertainment centre), Steve Gschmeissner 42-43c, GTW / Imagebroker.net 25tr, Fraser Hall / Robert Harding Travel 94-95c (background), Howard Hall / OSF 10bl, Kevin & Suzette Hanley / Animals Animals 39cra, John Hartman 134-135, Martin Harvey / Peter Arnold Images 32-33c, Barbara Heller 171cra, Thorsten Henn / Nordic Photos 105crb, Gerald Hinde / ABPL / Animals Animals 35cla (kudus), Georgie Holland / age fotostock 12tl, Alex Howe 216c, HSchweiger / Wildlife 82tl, John Hyde / Alaskastock 82cla, Imagebroker 34cl, Dennis Inc / Phototake Science 60-61c, The Irish Image Collection 103br, Karlheinz Irlmeier 155tr, John Warburton-Lee Photography 98bc, JTB Photo / Japan Travel Bureau 216-217 (background), Juniors Bildarchiv 35cr (two zebra), 80-81c, Satoshi Kuribayashi / OSF 29br, Last Refuge / Robert Harding Travel 103cr, Alvaro Leiva 122-123cb, Zigmund Leszcznski / Animals Animals 25cr, Peter Lewis 103tr, Alan Majchrowicz / Peter Arnold 84-85c, Marevision / age fotostock 11bl, R Matina / Age fotostock 100-101c, Chris Mattison / age fotostock 21br, Grahame McConnell / Ticket 105cra, Tony McConnell 209cra, John Miller 104-105c (view outside cave), Juan Carlos Munoz 99br, Darlyne A Murawski / Peter Arnold Images 37br, Darlyne Murawski / Peter Arnold Images 55br, Eric Nathan / Britain on View 148cla (clapperboard), David B. Fleetham / OSF 12-13c (octopus), OSF 81crb, OTHK / Asia Images RM 108-109c, Alfred Pasieka 51cra, Douglas Peebles 74-75c, Peter Arnold Images 99bl, Sergio Pitamitz / Robert Harding Travel 34-35c (background), Planet Observer 76-77c, Fritz Poelking / age fotostock 30-31c, Keith Porter / OSF 24cb (butterfly), The Print Collector 185br, Quadriga Images / LOOK-foto 158crb (red chair), R H Productions / Robert Harding Travel 215tc, Radius Images 88-89c, Gustavo A Rojas / age fotostock 16-17c (fish), Antonio Lopez Roman / age fotostock 22-23c, Jaques RosÈs / Bios 25cl (Green shied bug), Cyril Ruoso / Bios 84bl, Kevin Schafer / Peter Arnold Images 40-41c, Ted Schiffmann / Peter Arnold Images 28-29c (background), Malcolm Schuyl / Still Pictures 36-37c, AndrÈ Skonieczny / Imagebroker.net 24cr (honey bee), Witold Skrypczak / Superstock 94-95 (foreground cactus), Gerard Soury / OSF 31br, Stoelwinder / Bios 24bl (grasshopper), Egmont Strigl / Imagebroker.net 100tl, Jochen Tack / Imagebroker.net 205br, Nicolas Thibaut / Photononstop 128-129c, Guy Thouvenin 102-103, Travel Pix / Robert Harding Travel 143bc (Statue of Liberty image on book cover), Steve Vidler 140-141c, James Watt / Pacific Stock 39tr, James Watt / Index Stock Imagery 16cla, John Wilson / Robert Harding Travel 152cla, Gordon Wiltsie / Peter Arnold Images 84cla, Heinz Wohner 121br, Alison Wright / Robert Harding Travel 84tl, Sven Zacek / OSF 82-83clb (ice flow), Ariadne Van Zandbergen 122bl, Gunter Ziesler / Peter Arnold Images 34bl; **Planetary Visions Limited:** 79bc, 110cla, 110clb, 110bl; **Primal Pictures Ltd:** © Primal Pictures with courtesy 45tr; **Ron Arad Associates:** ronarad.com 159cla; **The Ronald Grant Archive:** 145ca, Goskino 144-145c; **Science Photo Library:** 3D4Medical.com 68bl, Mary Beth Angelo 11bc, P.Plailly / AT. Daynes / Eurelios 168-169tc, John Bavosi 69tr, British Antarctic SUrvey 82bl, BSIP, Chassenet 52bl (contracted pupil), 52bl (dilated pupil), Dr Jeremy Burgess 191clb (penicillin culture), CDC 54bl, Celestial Image Co. 245tr, Peter Chadwick 41cra, Julius T Csotonyi 69br, 168tr, Dennis Kunkel Microscopy, Inc / Visuals Unlimited 19br, 29bl, Georgette Douwma 41tr, David Ducros 236clb, Kenneth Eward / Biografx 57bl, Eye of Science 26cla, 37cb, 56-57c (Fertilisation SEM), 61br, 64tl, 67cr, 68-69c, Astrid & Hanns-Frieder Michler 26clb, Bob Gibbons 95br, Steve Gschmeissner 51tr, 63cr, Steve Horrell 89bl, Innerspace Imaging 58c, Jacopin 44tl, James King-Holmes 48bl, Mehau Kulyk 199bl, Jerry Lodriguss 244cl, Barney Magrath 246clb, Dr Ken McDonald 81tr, Joe McDonald, Visuals Unlimited 41crb, Tom McHugh 168crb, Will & Deni McIntyre 53br, 223crb, Medi-Mation 62-63c, Medical Images, Universal Images Group 63br, 67br, National Museum of Health and Medicine 174bl, 190clb, Mark Miller 63tr, Hank Morgan 197tr, Allan Morton 247bc, Dr. G. Moscoso 57br, P. Motta / Dept. of Anatomy / University "La Sapienza", Rome 61tr, 67tr, NASA 88crb, 236bl, 241tr (Neptune), 247crb, NASA / JPL / MSSS 234bl, NASA / JPL / STScl / VASSAR 247br, NASA Earth Observatory 78-79c, Dr Yorgos Nikas 57cr (four-cell embryo), 57cr (two-cell embryo), 57fcr, NOAO / AURA / NSF 247cra, David Nunuk 226cb, OAR / National Undersea Research Program 75br, Power and Syred 54tl, Profs. Motta, Andrews, Porter & Vial 68cb, 69bl, Royal Observatory, Edinburg / AATB 249tr, Royal Observatory, Edinburgh 246cla, John Sanford 229ca, Friedrich Saurer 241tr (Venus), Victor de Schwanberg 211crb, Science Source 52cb, SOHO / ESA / NASA 238cla, Volker Springel / Max Planck Institute for Astrophysics 249cr, TEK Image 211br, Sheila Terry 223tr, Javier Trueba / MSF 105tr, US Department of Defense 211cra, 213br, Walter Myers 241tr (Uranus), Charles D. Winters 217br, Paul Wootton 238br; **SeaPics.com:** Phillip Colla 16clb, Doc White 33bl; **Igor Siwanowicz:** 33cb, 38-39c (Mantis); **The Art Agency:** Stuart Jackson-Carter 246-247; **TopFoto.co.uk:** Granger Collection 155bc, Japan Information & Cultural 160-161c; **Wellcome Images:** 190tc; **Wikimedia Commons:** Androstachys 38-39bc (grasshopper); **wildnatureimages.com:** Ron Niebrugge 86-87c; **Peter Wilson:** CONACULTA-INAH-MEX 171clb (reclining figure)

Jacket images: *Front:* **Corbis:** Image Source cb; Hans Georg Roth br. **Getty Images:** Flickr / by Philippe Reichert cr; Photographer's Choice / Michael Dunning b; Stone / Sylvain Grandadam bl. *Back:* **Alamy Images:** Martin Strmiska tc. **FLPA:** Fred Bavendam / Minden Pictures tr, ftr. **NASA:** U.S. Geological Survey ftl. **Science Photo Library:** PlanetObserver tl.

For further information see: www.dkimages.com